EMPIRE OF BORDERS

EMPIRE OF BORDERS

The Expansion of the US Border
around the World

Todd Miller

VERSO
London · New York

First published by Verso 2019
© Todd Miller 2019

All rights reserved

The moral rights of the author have been asserted

1 3 5 7 9 10 8 6 4 2

Verso
UK: 6 Meard Street, London W1F 0EG
US: 20 Jay Street, Suite 1010, Brooklyn, NY 11201
versobooks.com

Verso is the imprint of New Left Books

ISBN-13: 978-1-78478-511-6
ISBN-13: 978-1-78478-513-0 (UK EBK)
ISBN-13: 978-1-78478-514-7 (US EBK)

British Library Cataloguing in Publication Data
A catalogue record for this book is available from the British Library

Library of Congress Cataloging-in-Publication Data
A catalog record for this book is available from the Library of Congress

Typeset in Minion Pro by MJ & N Gavan, Truro, Cornwall
Printed and bound by CPI Group (UK) Ltd, Croydon, CR0 4YY

For Sofia, Memito, and Lauren.

"Names are only the guests of reality," the Chinese sage Hsu Yu noted in 2300 BCE, suggesting that borders are little more than collective myths—fictions that a certain number of people, for a certain period of time, believe are fact.

—Kate Harris

Contents

Introduction:

"Massive Paradigm Change"

We arrived at the Guatemalan military base in Zacapa on a hot morning in early June. In the front there was a closed gate guarded by soldiers in green jungle camouflage and floppy hats, cradling automatic weapons. Zacapa, one of 22 department capitals in the country, sits in the eastern borderlands with Honduras. Its name comes from Nahuatl; it means "river of grass." From Zacapa, if you wanted to go to Brownsville, Texas—the closest point in the United States—you'd travel almost 1,440 miles overland, mostly up Mexico's Gulf Coast highway. But if you wanted to see the U.S. border, you wouldn't need to travel at all; it has already come to this small city in Guatemala. That's why I was there.

I had come with fellow researcher and photojournalist Jeff Abbott to meet with the Chorti task force, Guatemala's new border patrol, but I wasn't at all sure they would let us in. We were two hours late. Luckily, the soldiers—who looked as if they were in their late teens—heard me out. I explained the 200-mile journey we'd taken to get to Zacapa from San Pedro Sula, where we'd been the day before. I told them that the buses in Honduras didn't run at night and the bus driver this morning decided to have a 45-minute breakfast (I was wary about adding this last detail because, really, how could I blame him? But I had to build my case). I told them about the delay at the international border. They nodded because they knew. They knew what it was to travel, to move, to migrate, especially across international borders—so fraught with difficulties, including an endless string of checkpoints. At the Zacapa base, I wondered if any of the soldiers who stood before me, someone perhaps from one of Guatemala's many poor communities, would be permitted entry into the United States. I wondered how many had tried.

Indeed, the vast majority of humans on the planet are prohibited from crossing international boundaries. Most people, including in the United States, do not have passports. If you do have one and you are from the United States, United Kingdom, France, or Germany—among several other countries—you can freely travel to approximately 160 countries without a visa. However, if you don't have a visa and are from Iraq or Afghanistan, doors will be slammed shut in all but approximately thirty.[1] As a U.S. citizen, I did not need a visa to enter Guatemala, but Guatemalans—including the soldiers before me—would need one to get into the United States. And most people in the world's Global South—from places like the Americas, Asia, and Africa—do not meet the requirements to get a visa in the first place. For example, to acquire a visitor visa to the United States if you are from most places (excluding Europe, Canada, and some wealthier Asian nations), you have to pay exorbitant application fees, wait in long lines, even travel to distant cities to complete the process. Then you have to convince a consular officer that you have no plans to stay in the United States, that you have a stable job or profitable business, that you have money in a bank account, that you own a home or property. "Many people who would like to visit don't bother applying, since they expect to be rejected,"[2] write immigration experts Jane Guskin and David L. Wilson.

Although a bustling international airport might seem to tell another story, according to the educated guess of a former director of the Safety, Air Transport Association, only six percent of the world's population boards an airplane in any given year.[3] Much as there is a yawning global gap in wealth, there is also an enormous chasm between those who have freedom of movement and those who do not. "For most of the world's population," writes historian Aviva Chomsky, the "freedom to travel is a distant dream."[4]

We live in a world of the included and the excluded, of those who can vacation (and do business) where they please and those who are walled in by borders and armed guards. And many of those armed guards, as was clearly the case with the soldiers at the Zacapa base, would themselves be prevented from crossing a good percentage of the globe's political borders.

In Zacapa, we waited while one of the soldiers made phone calls. We tried to find shade under the corrugated metal roof overhanging the front gate. From where we stood there was a view of a parched mountain, with "Segunda Brigada de Infanteria C.G.R.C." (Second Infantry Brigade) inscribed on the ground on the side of the mountain, in large white letters amid bushes and small, shrubby trees under what looked like a cell tower. The military base was in the Central American dry corridor—a long swath of territory that extended into Honduras, El Salvador, Nicaragua, and as far as Panama—and at this very moment, in June 2015, they were experiencing a historic drought. For small farmers in the region, the drought was going to eat away harvests, leaving hunger in a place that climate scientist Chris Castro called "ground zero" for climate change in the Americas.[5] These droughts have persisted now for years (in 2009, Guatemalan president Alvaro Colom declared a "state of calamity," or a famine), and according to Castro, if climate-changing trends continue, it will get worse.[6] Not only has the planet's earth-altering era of climate change, which some call the Anthropocene, been a gut punch to a place like Guatemala, it's gone hand in hand with an unprecedented thrust in border militarization across the globe. Long-term forecasts have predicted that ecological upheavals are going to drive unparalleled levels of human migration. I had plenty of time to think about all this while we waited for permission.

Finally the soldier making the calls returned. "Are you with BORTAC?"

I was stunned. Had I heard him correctly?

There was only one possible way that the soldier could have known about BORTAC—the U.S. Border Patrol special forces and tactical unit. Agents of BORTAC must have stood at this gate before. Even in the United States, very few people knew about BORTAC's SWAT-style operations in the U.S. borderlands, or about its "global response capacity." Fewer still were aware that BORTAC had conducted "training and operations both in the United States and in other countries in furtherance of the U.S. Border Patrol's mission."[7]

"No," I said, looking down at my wrinkled, half-tucked shirt. BORTAC agents were the U.S. Border Patrol's robocops. They had to do rigorous physical testing involving sit-ups, push-ups, pull-ups; 1.5-mile runs; and pistol qualification. The training was designed to "mirror aspects of the U.S. Special Operation Forces' selection courses."

BORTAC has played a big part in pushing out the U.S. borders abroad. It supported U.S. military actions such as Operation Enduring Freedom in Afghanistan and Operation Iraqi Freedom. BORTAC agents trained the Iraqi border police and its tactical team from 2006 to 2011, serving as advisors and working alongside Iraqi border patrol in the field. "Clearly, this was a critical mission," said the magazine *Tactical Life*, "because the Iraqi Border Police are responsible for preventing smugglers, insurgents, weapons, or the money needed to fund terrorist organizations from entering their country."[8]

In Iraq, U.S. boundary-building efforts began even before BORTAC's arrival, in 2004, with an operation labeled "Phantom Linebacker" in which 15,000 Iraqi border guards were trained to patrol in—as the name of the operation indicates—the spirit of American football.[9] BORTAC's operations were hardly limited to Iraq: They had extended around the globe to places like Jordan, Afghanistan, Colombia, Haiti, Peru, Panama, Belize, Mexico, Kenya, Costa Rica, Ukraine, Kosovo, Argentina, Honduras, Ecuador, Armenia, Tajikistan, and, of course, Guatemala.

During international training operations, BORTAC (often as part of a larger Customs and Border Protection team) was doctor, diagnosis, and prescription. As one CBP trainer told me later, they would "travel and see the border operations in various countries and make an assessment of their border security, and make recommendations on what could be done to improve their security." The CBP team would then present the plan to either the U.S. DHS or State Department and make recommendations for changes and funding for training, assistance, or equipment. In most cases, the countries would agree to what CBP prescribed.

"It's a rewarding job," said the trainer, who wished to remain anonymous.

In the twenty-first century, hardened borders are proliferating throughout the globe, with much-touted proclamations that they are meant to protect the individual countries' sovereignty. Often, however, the lines of division are established at the behest and insistence of the United States (or the European Union or Australia) with much more lofty goals in mind, associated with global power dynamics. Consider the words of George Kennan, the first director of policy planning at the U.S. State Department. He caught the dynamics of who and what would be protected perfectly in 1948: "We have to accept a certain unchallengeable antagonism between 'him that has' and 'him that has not' in this world."[10] While at the time hardened borders were almost unknown in the United States and the rest of the world, Kennan set the conceptual stage for what was to come in terms of a U.S. structure of power and domination in the postwar world.

Indeed, almost 75 years later, the evidence of U.S. international border expansion is everywhere. A major general I spoke to in Amman, Jordan, mentioned Highway 90, a locally known route between Tucson, Arizona and the Fort Huachuca military base. How did one of Jordan's top border experts know about that? Well maybe because Fort Huachuca was a launching place for Customs and Border Protection's Predator B drones, which conducted surveillance on the U.S.'s southern border. In the Philippines, a coast guard commander told me, as we stood next to a command watch center constructed by Raytheon Corporation with U.S. funds, that he had attended a big homeland security conference in Scottsdale, Arizona. The architect of the West Bank wall in Israel-Palestine, Israeli Colonel Danny Tirza, recalled talking borders with sheriffs in Texas. "I have very good connection with the sheriff's union in the United States," Tirza told my colleague and author Gabriel Schivone in an interview. "If the sheriffs in the United States have one thing in common with the Israelis, they are not polite. They are straight talkers ..." And there was the police commandant in Nairobi who maybe met those very straight-talking sheriffs in Texas during his training in the United States. He told me that he had worked on all of Kenya's borders, and he had been trained by both the United States and Israel.

There is possible evidence of U.S. border expansion in the rolling coils of razor wire now on the international boundary line of Hungary, a country that has "graduated" from the United States Export Control and Related Border Security Program (EXBS), run by the U.S. State Department, and in the Zeppelin drones on the Turkish frontiers, a country currently in the same program. As we shall see, EXBS is just one of multiple programs and fronts of the U.S. border extension juggernaut.

Before going into this project I knew the U.S. was expanding its external borders. I did not know how gargantuan these efforts were, nor how significant to U.S. strategy. Close your eyes and point to any landmass on a world map, and your finger will probably find a country that is building up its borders in some way with Washington's assistance.

It was Alan Bersin, former U.S. CBP commissioner, DHS assistant secretary, and border czar during the Clinton administration, who pinpointed when the shift toward U.S. international border policing happened and put words to the scope of the change at hand. Since 9/11, Bersin writes, there has been a shift "in our perception of borders not only as lines, but also as movements—flows of people and goods on a global scale both legally and illegally." There were international border programs before 9/11, but nothing comparable in size, scope, and impact to what was put in place afterward. Bersin doesn't mince words. He calls it a "massive paradigm change."[11]

Indeed, the justification for this U.S. global border building can be found in two sentences of the 1,000-page 9/11 Commission Report, published in 2003:

> 9/11 has taught us that terrorism against Americans "over there" should be regarded just as we regard terrorism against Americans "over here." In this same sense the American homeland is the planet.[12]

In Guatemala, on one of my earlier research trips, I was just starting to glimpse the real extent and reach of U.S. border expansion and its human impact. The new border patrols, ironically, had been given indigenous names—the Tecun Uman force, named for a great leader of the K'iche Maya, patrolled the Mexican border; the Xinca task force on the Guatemalan-Salvadoran divide. The Chorti, a Mayan people, had no involvement in drawing the border with Honduras (Spain first demarcated it in 1785, though the two countries didn't become independent until 1821), but here in Zacapa, the Chorti border force was now policing it.

And as I stared up at the parched mountain, I realized that the base was also just as much a part of the U.S. border as the wall in Nogales, Arizona, behind where mounted cameras perpetually stare into Mexico. What was happening on this Guatemalan military base, and on other bases around the world, was just as important to U.S. border strategy as the Prevention Through Deterrence policy initiated in the early 1990s, which radically altered Washington's tactics (particularly in the Caribbean and along the Mexico land divide) and completely remade the U.S. border policing apparatus. An upsurge in agents, technologies, and walls blockaded people from crossing in urban areas and funneled them into potentially deadly rural locations like the Sonoran desert. With a variety of operations and recalibrations since then, there has been a breathless expansion of the U.S. border enforcement apparatus in terms of budgets, personnel, and— of course—geography. For example, in 1978 the yearly budget of the immigration and enforcement apparatus was $287 million (this was the Immigration and Naturalization Service budget that year).[13] In 2018, if you combine Customs and Border Protection with Immigration and Customs Enforcement, the total is $23 billion.[14] Never, since the inception of the Border Patrol in 1924, has there been such growth. U.S. border zones, like Nogales, are filled with buzzing helicopters and green striped vehicles, thousands of implanted motion sensors, and the most extensive concentration of surveillance technology found anywhere in the world. However, as former DHS secretary and commander of Southern Command, General John Kelly, put it, "border security cannot be attempted as an endless series of 'goal line stands' on the one-foot line at the ports of entry or along the thousands of miles of border between this country and Mexico … I believe the defense of the Southwest border starts 1,500 miles to the south, with Peru."[15] In other words, the border fortifications around Zacapa were just as important to U.S. aims as the Integrated

Fixed Towers, high-tech cameras, ground-sweeping radar, implanted motion sensors, checkpoints, and drones policing U.S. borderlands. It was fundamental to the paradigm change.

Michael Flynn, founder of the Global Detention Project (not the retired Army Lieutenant and former National Security Advisor for Donald Trump), in his seminal 2003 article "Dónde Está La Frontera? / Where's the Border?" was one of the first researchers to examine the post-9/11 planetary expansion of U.S. border enforcement. He described the U.S. border externalization (in the context of the global war on terror) as essentially a new way of defining and consolidating U.S. empire in the twenty-first century. "U.S. border control efforts," he argued, "have undergone a dramatic metamorphosis in recent years as the United States has attempted to implement practices aimed at stopping migrants long before they reach U.S. shores."[16]

In this way, borders were, in a sense, being fortified against the poor, and made porous or simply erased for the wealthy and powerful. What might be called our global borders now extend not only to places like Guatemala and Mexico, but also across continents to the edges of the vast U.S. military-surveillance grid, into cyberspace, and via spinning satellites and other spying systems into space itself. As criminologist Nancy Wonders writes, "if it is more accurate to focus on the process of bordering than on borders, then the struggle is over the *process* of creating and proliferating borders, rather than at the site of border control."[17]

I began writing this book during a 2012 trip to Puerto Rico. On the beautiful *isla*—officially a U.S. territory or, more accurately, semi-colony—I interviewed a man named Wilfredo Ramírez who represented law enforcement for Puerto Rico's Department of Natural and Environmental Resources, equivalent to the U.S. National Parks Service. Ramírez met me near the U.S. Border Patrol station, where I saw the same green striped vehicles that police the Arizona-Mexico divide patrolling Puerto Rico's west coast. It was eye-opening to witness the Border Patrol scouring this Caribbean coastline, presumably in search of undocumented people arriving in rickety boats. Ramírez worked on Mona Island, the third largest island in the Puerto Rican archipelago. Often called the Galapagos of the Caribbean, it lies

32 miles off the coast of the Dominican Republic, and Ramírez told me he was deputized to police immigration, and that agents of the U.S. Border Patrol regularly came to arrest stranded, detained, and undocumented people.

That's when it dawned on me: The U.S. border was much bigger, and capable of much more, than I'd thought. This was not only in terms of power and influence, but also in actual physical presence. Here in the Caribbean it "legally" reached almost to the shores of the island of Hispaniola, 1,000 miles away from the U.S. mainland.

And that was only one small example. Leaving Puerto Rico I crossed the Mona Strait to the Dominican Republic, where I learned (just as I would in Guatemala) that the United States was sending resources and providing training for a new D.R. border guard unit, known as CESFRONT (Specialized Border Security Corps), whose agents were already patrolling the Dominican-Haitian divide. The more I looked, the more I saw how much the U.S. border indeed was expanding and extending. Geographer Nancy Hiemstra has written extensively on U.S. Coast Guard operations just outside Ecuador's coastal waters in the eastern Pacific, where it has interdicted and sunk Ecuadorian boats. This activity was particularly intense between 2002 and 2006. "Coast Guard operations in the eastern Pacific served to "push out" U.S. borders," Hiemstra wrote, "by setting a precedent for international boundary policing activities."[18] Journalist Seth Freed Wessler writing for *New York Times Magazine*, described Coast Guard ships in international waters as "floating Guantánamos" in which suspected smugglers are shackled for weeks or months before facing a judge in U.S. courts.[19]

The same international cooperation is at work along the U.S.-Canadian divide. In 2011, the United States and Canada announced their "Beyond the Border Declaration: A Shared Vision for Perimeter Security and Economic Competitiveness," a multifaceted agreement intended to address threats "early" through "information sharing," such as the biographic and biometric information of visa applicants. The agreement also facilitated trade and integrated cross-border law enforcement into programs like Shiprider and the Integrated Border Enforcement Team, in which U.S. Border Patrol and the Canadian

Royal Mounted Police do joint patrolling operations along the shared border. And inevitably it has led to much harsher application of the law. In February 2017, a Reuters photographer documented a U.S. Border Patrol agent trying to stop eight people from Sudan, including four children, from crossing into Canada through a bitterly cold snowscape, hoping to ask for asylum in the supposedly friendlier nation. "Nobody cares about us," one of the men in the group told the reporter.[20] In May of the same year, a 57-year-old woman from Ghana died attempting to cross the Minnesota-Manitoba border, en route to Toronto to visit her five-week-old grandchild.[21] The agreement between the United States and Canada was that a person had to have a visa from the country where they arrived first, in order to enter the other—even to win asylum cases—cases where the person could not safely return to his or her home country.

And although even by the time I visited Zacapa I could still be surprised that a soldier in a Guatemalan outpost had heard of BORTAC, no one working with U.S. Homeland Security would have been shocked. Over and over again, officials—like Bersin—have repeated the importance of externalization to U.S. border strategy. The Homeland Security Act of 2002 states that DHS must promote "information and education exchange with nations friendly to the United States in order to promote sharing of best practices and technologies relating to homeland security."[22] CBP commissioner Robert Bonner in 2004 explained it as "extending our zone of security where we can do so, beyond our physical borders—so that American borders are the last line of defense, not the first line of defense."[23]

The 2007 National Strategy for Homeland Security noted that "security at home ultimately is related to security abroad: as partners protect and defend their homelands, the security of our own Homeland increases."[24]

Also in 2007, DHS Secretary Michael Chertoff stood in front of students at Johns Hopkins University School of Advanced International Studies and told them:

The fact is that homeland security does not simply begin at the water line. That is the last place you want to stop problems, not the first place.

Much of what we do in homeland security begins even before a person sets foot on an airplane in Europe or a container is loaded on a cargo ship in Asia. We work internationally to identify potential threats well before they reach our shores, strengthen our perimeter defenses, and then partner with the international community to build resiliency into our shared systems of commerce and travel so that we can have these systems secure without undermining the fundamental fluidity which is the basis of the twenty-first-century global system.[25]

Notably, Chertoff, like many top brass, after his stint at DHS started a private company, called the Chertoff Group, that sells its homeland-security consultations worldwide. As part of the research for this book I went to the Chertoff Groups' Washington, DC office to interview its principal and head of security services, Jayson Ahern, former acting head of Customs and Border Protection. As we sat in his ninth-story office in May 2017, looking out on a sweeping view of the city, Ahern gave me the history of U.S. border externalization from the 1980s to the present, throughout his thirty-three years in law enforcement. "The border mission certainly is about protecting the homeland first and foremost, keeping bad things and bad people out of the country," he said, "but also at the same time it is to ensure economic prosperity."

And that same year at a panel at the Border Security Expo in San Antonio, Texas, when I asked about the United States pushing the border out, Jim McLaughlin of CBP's National Targeting Center—one of the epicenter points of the U.S. international border program, described in Chapter Eight—stressed that the 2014 United Nations Security Council resolution 2178 was fundamental. According to McLaughlin, the resolution calls on member states to put border security systems in place "similar to that of the United States" for counterterrorism purposes.

The U.S. border model has been paramount to the scaffolding of the current order of the globe, managing the antagonisms, as Kennan noted more than seventy years ago, between the haves and have nots.

The Global North—a political if not a geographical north, a network of countries including the United States, the European Union, Australia, and Israel—controls four-fifths of all income amassed anywhere in the world. Border externalization, or linked border-enforcement regimes, ripples from these places of financial and political power into the world at large. This book examines the dividing lines this creates between the world's included and excluded. The wars waged along them are far away from the public eye, near train tracks in Southern Mexico, in Arizona's oven-hot summer desertscapes, grouped off the side of the two-lane road near Spanish Ceuta's militarized border with Morocco, or along the route Somalis travel south in Kenya from the Dadaab refugee camp without movement passes, avoiding checkpoints on the way. These wars are resisted by the thousands of Syrians unable to cross into Jordan and caught at the "Berm," a makeshift refugee camp that grew by the thousands, even tens of thousands, in 2016. They are resisted by the West Bank Palestinians anxiously awaiting the correct moment at dawn to climb over the towering cement wall that surrounds and encloses Palestine. And by filmmaker Khaled Jarrar, who documented their attempt in *The Infiltrators*, and who took a sledgehammer and chisel to that wall. As humanitarian Paul Currion has said, the border has become the new "antiballistic missile system": a weapon of the powerful deployed against the displaced and the dispossessed, the most important and most hidden battlefield of the twenty-first century.

The global border system is too vast to be encompassed in the pages of this book, and so I have limited my investigation to the United States and its policies and practices. Its ever evolving and growing program has largely escaped scrutiny, as media discussions around borders in the United States at least since 2016 have focused on the extravagant campaign promises of President Donald Trump, including the 50 foot, two thousand mile, concrete wall. However, the "new" U.S.-Mexico border exists not only along the southern border but around the world. In examining this massive security apparatus, I hope to clarify what and who, indeed, it really protects, and is meant to protect; who profits by it, what it means for the geopolitics of a twenty-first century mired not only in endemic inequality but also in persistent ecological disaster; and, finally, who is challenging and organizing against it, and trying to tear it down.

The investigation begins in Central America and Israel-Palestine, with the U.S. training and arming of other nations' border forces, and the burgeoning global homeland security market and industry. It moves to the Maasai Mara in Kenya, the west coast of Puerto Rico, and the harbors of Manila Bay in the Philippines, all examples of the racialized, colonial history of political borders and how they are embedded into the concept of private property.

From there, it travels to a CBP preclearance site in Vancouver, then to a homeland security convention in Paris where I heard a future of sophisticated new techniques projected to forward the goal of open borders for privileged individuals and powerful corporations and closed ones for the poor and oppressed.

That trip to the future was no detour: It is important to emphasize that this is an evolving subject, in constant dynamic change. My research produced many surprises, which I try to capture in these pages. In Ramtha, Jordan, on the Syrian border, an enforcement project infused with hundreds of millions of U.S. dollars and led by Raytheon Corp. seemed to foreshadow that shoot-anything-that-moves border of the future, necessary to maintain the status quo of a segregated, unsustainable world. Yet I also found the greater region around Ramtha to be home to some of the fiercest resistance to borders, ranging from insurrections to artistic rebellion to the subtle subversion of hospitality.

Finally, I describe the borderscapes of the African continent, from Ceuta on the Northern coast of Morocco to Kenya and its fringes, one of the most vulnerable places in the world to climate disruption, and discuss why climate change offers the most complete and coherent argument for dissolving our world's hardened militarized borders and to imagine something new.

Back in Guatemala, the soldiers finally let us pass. Col. Obed Lopez, the military commander of the Chorti, had agreed to speak with us. They escorted us to a shelter opposite a thin airstrip that also served as Zacapa's airport. While we waited we watched soldiers march in perfect lockstep, backdropped by that same mountain that spoke to a world on the brink of severe environmental shifts. Col. Lopez arrived, out of uniform, wearing a white T-shirt drenched with sweat, and earmuffs—he'd come directly from the shooting range. He had already been to Guatemala City and back that day, departing at 3 a.m. to run in an early morning race. Despite this, his energy was high and exuberant. He led us to his office, where he began to talk quickly and excitedly about the history of the extension of the U.S. border into Guatemala. Nothing could be greater or more positive.

It was a "massive paradigm change," but here in Guatemala there was nothing new about the United States, behind the scenes, directing the show. The U.S. border was much bigger than a border wall. The American homeland, after all, was the planet.

Part One
New World Border

Those who build walls will become prisoners of the walls they put up.
                                                          Pope Francis

1.

Twenty-First Century Battlefields

Although Arriaga, Chiapas, a town of 25,000 people, was 150 miles away from the Guatemalan border, it had the feeling of a border town. Up until the summer of 2014, it thrummed with Central Americans, many of whom would congregate in the train yard that divided Arriaga in two. But in July, it changed dramatically, as if a switch had been flipped. The U.S. border extension had clicked on. As I sat with Carlos Bartolo Solis in his dark office in the town's only migrant shelter, he told me that authorities wouldn't let people board the train, and crowds of people—primarily Central Americans from Guatemala, Honduras, and El Salvador—had just vanished from the train yards. When the train blasted its baritone horn and began to chug north, immigration agents in sleek vans, accompanied by the Mexican federal police and sometimes the army, rode along in search of unauthorized people. At night, Solis said, they used blinding spotlights.

Things had changed quickly and suddenly on the Mexico-Guatemala frontier. It was perhaps one of the best places to see the anatomy of U.S. border externalization, how swiftly it could strike, with the force of a superstorm, impacting any human being unfortunate enough to be in its path. The border battle we were seeing played out in Arriaga was what anthropologist Jeff Halper has called a "securocratic war." In his book *War Against the People*, he explains its origins: Inequality between countries has skyrocketed in a short period of time. The ratio of per capita GDP between the richest and poorest nations went from a ratio of 22:1 at the beginning of the twentieth century to 267:1 by the year 2000. In this situation, "the experience of the vast majority of people worldwide becomes one of impoverishment, marginality, exploitation, dislocation and violence."[1] European-style conventional warfare between nation-states amassing gargantuan armies has become a thing of the past, kept alive only in the imagination of Hollywood. In its place, securocratic wars, waged to protect and secure not individual nations but the international class of wealthy nations, insert themselves into the yawning gaps of global inequalities. Wars on drugs, on terror, on immigrants have created never-ending battlescapes, often along borders. In the summer of 2014, Arriaga had become such a battle zone.

After talking with Solis, I went to the train yard with Jeff Abbott who was lugging his camera. It was a broiling day—a contrast to the cool air of San Cristóbal de las Casas in the high mountains, where we had been the previous day. At a small wooden stand near the train tracks, a teenager selling sodas and snacks told me, when I asked about the border crossers, "They are down there, way down there." She pointed down at tracks that stretched to the horizon. Central Americans, as she put it, had been her primary clients. What made Arriaga a "border town" was that it was the departure point for one of the most dangerous trains in the world: the notorious La Bestia, "The Beast," described in brutal detail by Salvadoran journalist Oscar Martínez in his book of the same name. The Beast was a freight train that many undocumented people boarded with hopes of going north, often to the United States. So many terrible things had happened on La Bestia that in Mexico it was known as *el tren de la muerte*, "the death train," or *el tren de los desaparecidos*, "the train of the disappeared."

Abbott and I walked past the cemetery on the outskirts of town, where the rust-colored rails entered the woods. Once in a while a cool breeze cut through the thick humidity, carrying a faint smell of the nearby Pacific Ocean. We started to see men sitting on the rails, shirts covering their heads to protect them from the sun, their feet in the overgrown grass.

Approximately one month before, in July 2014, the U.S. media rediscovered the U.S. southern border. In one memorable segment, Sean Hannity of Fox News interviewed Texas governor Rick Perry about border dangers on the Rio Grande, which at that point meant an influx of "unaccompanied minors," mainly from Central America.[2] Hannity and Perry were dressed in combat helmets and flak jackets, with bullet belts strapped over their chests. To maintain the "war zone" appeal, Hannity's camera crew, like those of other armed and ready U.S. media delegations, most likely had to avoid filming the screaming, dancing merriment on the party boats from Reynosa in the background.[3] It was difficult, indeed, to capture a security war on film.

On July 7, during the U.S. media firestorm, Mexican President Enrique Peña Nieto announced his "Programa Frontera Sur," a border operation Mexico had been building for years, with massive U.S. support and encouragement. With great fanfare and assiduous media coverage inside Mexico, the U.S. southern neighbor enacted "enforcement belts," extending from its Guatemala border hundreds of miles into the Mexican interior, following the model of the U.S.'s "multilayered" border policing strategy. The government ordered 2000 soldiers and 400 police officers to the border zone, reinforcing its gauntlet of military, police, and especially immigration agents— stopping buses, vans, cars, and trucks at numerous checkpoints along the 150-mile route from Tapachula to Arriaga, among other places.

"Subordination is part of the relationship Mexico has with the United States," Miguel Ángel Paz from the Mexican immigration rights organization Voces Mesoamericanas told me, explaining how Mexico, whose citizens were policed with considerable rigor in the United States, could agree to build up its border enforcement apparatus with assistance from their neighbor to the north. Yet this securocratic war, blockading "terrorists" and "drug runners" and "smugglers"—which Perry, Hannity, and others have claimed is essential—was in the end a war against the poor.

Toward the outskirts of Arriaga, Abbott and I began seeing the encampments. They reminded me of camps I'd seen in the U.S. desert borderlands—except in Arizona, the people were usually absent, fled, their existence only visible in the remnants left behind: cardboard mattresses, black plastic water jugs, electrolyte bottles, clothes, back-packs. Once I found a child's backpack, small and pink, with an image of a smiling Goofy. In Arriaga, the people were still there. Maybe it was because the operations of Programa Frontera Sur were so recent.

They sat in groups near the train tracks, and were obviously unsure what to make of Abbott and me. Similar changes had followed the dramatic strategy shifts in U.S.- Mexico border operations in the 1990s. When Operation Blockade began in El Paso in September 1992, for example, the transformation came overnight. Suddenly, U.S. Border Patrol agents were stationed side by side by side directly on the borderline, reinforced by buzzing helicopters, stopping all movement from Ciudad Juarez. It didn't take people long—people, often undocumented, who had been working in El Paso for years in a number of vocations—to learn to circumvent the apparatus by going to the deserts on the outskirts of town and creating new routes into the United States. Operation Blockade turned to Hold-the-Line. Operations Gatekeeper, Safeguard, and Rio Grande Valley spread along the 2,000 mile border, sealing off traditional crossing places, urban zones such as San Diego, El Centro, Yuma, Nogales, Douglas, El Paso, Laredo, and Brownsville, the foundational strategy of today's U.S. border-policing apparatus. This period also saw the first major U.S. border wall construction project, which came long before Donald Trump figured in the political scene. In 1999, I witnessed the U.S. Army Corps of Engineers constructing a wall of rusty landing mats (from the Vietnam and Persian Gulf Wars) between Douglas and Agua Prieta. The border crossers were not there; they had moved to the fringes, the deserts, far away from the surveillance gaze, in areas that were more isolated, desolate, and dangerous.

Similarly, the impact of the sudden policy shift of 2014 would not be found on the Rio Grande where Hannity and Perry "patrolled" in an armored boat, but rather in the hidden fringes of the Mexico-Guatemala border, in a place like Arriaga, 1,000 miles to the south. Arriaga's outskirts, where Abbott and I walked that day, would not make it onto the cable news cycle, would not be broadcast into a million homes, would in many ways simply not exist, not merit a thought, not affect perception, not become a political issue, not impact the known status quo. While Hannity and Perry fought their cinematic battle, the real border war was elsewhere. They were reporting from the wrong place.

Beside the train tracks a rotund man wearing a white T-shirt and jeans was waiting for the train. Gerardo was with a group of approximately ten other men and boys who looked as if they'd been sitting on their flattened squares of cardboard for a couple of days, in the shade of the green, shrubby trees. They were from El Salvador, Honduras, and Guatemala, the very countries from which more than 60,000 kids had arrived that year in the United States. The younger ones in the group wore expressions of bewilderment that seemed to ask: How on earth did we arrive at this place, so far from home, yet so far from our destination? Father Alejandro Solalinde, a priest who ran a migrant shelter in nearby Ixtepec, Oaxaca, calls this obscure Mexican borderlands region a "cemetery for the nameless."

Gerardo—from Chimaltenango, Guatemala, where he worked as a butcher—was anxious to talk. He told me he was going to Miami to see his two kids. He had been trying to get through the 150-mile gauntlet from the Guatemalan border to Arriaga since early July, and had already been deported from Mexico three times in one month. "This is my fourth attempt," he said. His eyes followed the rails, as if trying to deduce his future. The tracks seemed to go off endlessly in the coastal shrubbery. How could a trip to Miami, which for many in the United States would be as easy as hopping on a plane, be so difficult for Gerardo? I could still smell the sea in the air, but even the ocean seemed far away. The rest of the group listened as he spoke.

These men were a part of a record number of people in the world displaced and on the move and living outside their country of origin. The 244 million recorded by the United Nations in 2015 was up from 232 million in 2013, 173 million in 2000, and 152 million in 1990.[4] In the past 15 years, according to these totals, the number of people traveling across borders without papers has increased by 41 percent. And since many cross-border migrants are undocumented and unauthorized, and thus difficult to count, these totals are certainly low. If you couple the counts of international migrants with the internally displaced, about 763 million, then there are close to a billion people on the move worldwide.[5] One in seven people.

In 2016 the United Nations recorded its highest number ever for people forcibly displaced from their homes: 65.6 million. "This equates to one person becoming displaced every three seconds—less than the time it takes to read this sentence," the United Nations High Commission on Refugees wrote.[6] According to geographer Joseph Nevins, even these figures are conservative:

> The UNHCR's notion of "forcibly" is limited by the international refugee regime, one that defines a refugee as someone fleeing political persecution or physical violence. Per this logic, those fleeing deprivation, insecurity, and poverty of the everyday, "normal" sort—normal in terms of reigning political-economic conditions within their home country—are mere migrants.[7]

Their true numbers, Nevins concluded, are "considerably higher than the UN agency estimates." Gerardo seemed to fit this category.

Another potential "black swan,"[8] to use the U.S. Department of Homeland Security's own term, is the impact of environmental breakdown in the world. The numbers put out by agencies and organizations regarding the future displacement of people caused by climate change are in live debate and range between 150 million and 1 billion by 2050.[9] According to one report, these displacements will be "staggering," without an antecedent in human history.[10] Already disasters are displacing "three to ten times more people than conflict and war worldwide," according to the Norwegian Refugee Council.[11]

The other rising number—a reality assuredly known to Gerardo's group—is of deaths and disappearances of people on the move. In 2016, according to the International Organization on Migration's official count, 7,763 people were killed crossing borders, a 47 percent increase from 2015. And since 1996, the IOM estimates, more than 60,000 people have died or gone missing while crossing borders.[12] It must be stressed that, again because of the clandestine nature of this travel, the statistics can at best be estimations, as the IOM makes quite clear. In Mexico, the migrant dead aren't even counted by the government. The Mesoamerican Migrant Movement, an activist group led by family members of people who disappeared migrating, estimates that more than 70,000 people have gone missing in Mexico en route to the United States.[13] The organization calls what is going on a "migrant holocaust."[14]

This reality is what Gerardo and the others faced that day. To get through southern Mexico, some walked around the checkpoints. Others took public transportation, but would get off right before the border, detouring through gorgeous green mountains, sometimes crested with low clouds, always accompanied by an intense, well-justified fear of being targeted by robbers or police. If immigration agents caught a person like Gerardo, they'd whisk him off to the gigantic deportation center in Tapachula, where he'd be detained and, if he were a "person of interest," possibly questioned by a U.S. CBP agent stationed right there on the sweltering Mexico-Guatemala divide.[15] In 2015, for the first time, Mexico would deport more Central Americans than the United States.

Gerardo and his group were sitting right on the ever-changing front lines of the twenty-first century securocratic battlefield—a battlefield rarely discussed in martial terms, but at the same time highly weaponized and extremely violent. You could practically smell the fear in the humid air. Here, the idea that immigration should be treated as "an act of warfare," as *The American Conservative* columnist William S. Lind proposed, was neither paleoconservative nor strictly Trumpian. "In Fourth Generation war," Lind wrote, "invasion by immigration can be at least as dangerous as invasion by a state army."[16] "Fourth Generation war," in Lind's mind, implies a blurring between the civilian and the combatant. The plethora of militarized borders across the world, from Chiapas to the U.S.-Mexico borderlands, the Indo-Bangladeshi steel wall, and the Turkey-Syria divide, showed how countries had already adopted Lind's assertion: They were treating the unauthorized breaching of a border as an act of war.

But "border security," a phrase repeated with mind-numbing frequency by politicians and the media, is an inaccurate and unclear description of what is really happening. Both ubiquitous and untouchable, the term "security" has become so accepted that it's simultaneously invisible and fetishized. Who, asks legal and political scholar George Rigakos, can argue against security? Yet, he continues, "social problems have become security problems." This was a "war without end." When security "worked," you sought more. When it didn't "work," you needed more.[17]

Rigakos suggests that the term "security" has become analytically useless and should be shifted to "pacification." Pacification, he writes, "can excite our critical imaginations in new ways. Pacification captures the mobilization of policing in a manner that sheds light on the objects, history and politics of such interventions. Thus, rather than obscuring global capitalist relations, pacification unpacks these connections."[18]

Such a shift in framing, when considering borders, reveals a type of enforcement that is less about "protecting" national sovereignties and much more about policing the global fault lines, the jagged borders between the "north" and the "south," a division that can exist between regions or countries, or even within cities. As geographer Stephen Graham writes in his book *Cities Under Siege*, borders are now a "'multiplicity of control points' that become distributed along key lines of circulation and key geographies of wealth and power, crossing territorial lines between states as well as those within and beyond these boundaries."[19] It is no longer entirely accurate to think of borders as lines of dispute between states; instead, they are places where states work together to pacify nonstate entities using special zones of exception.

In broiling Arriaga in the Mexico-Guatemala border zone, Gerardo's group had no idea when that train would come. Nobody knew. Nobody had any money. In Gerardo's wallet, which had no cash, was a tattered picture that he pulled out to show us. It was a photo he must have gazed at a thousand times: His 10-year-old son, staring back. The picture was from 2006. His son was 18 now, Gerardo told me. Gerardo had a long way to go to see him. He hadn't even gotten on La Bestia yet. And there were more checkpoints up ahead, they said. There were more *migra* (immigration authorities) and police and possibly gangs and robbers.

BROKEN WINDOWS BORDERS

Three days after I met Gerardo's group, I went to the U.S. Embassy in Mexico City. Again, I almost didn't arrive in time. My bus had made an all-night haul through the border zone—which extended hundreds of miles in Mexico—constantly stopping at checkpoints while officials boarded with flashlights, walking slowly down the aisle, profiling everybody. One person was pulled off the bus by an agent, never to return. Only once did an official ask to see my passport.

On Paseo de la Reforma—the broad main avenue in Mexico City—it felt like I was in a completely different reality. Armed guards stood behind the iron gates of the U.S. Embassy. Thanks to centuries of U.S. invasions and meddling in Mexican affairs, protests have occurred there so frequently that the park area in front had been made impassable, thickly barricaded with metal fencing. Since it was "casual Friday," the man assigned to greet me at the door wore a polka-dot bow tie. Despite his friendly attire, I felt the rich symbolism of some serious bars between us. One of the embassy officials checked my almost-ten-year-old, slightly warped and frayed passport. Because I was carrying electronics, I had to leave my backpack. Then I walked through the security apparatus. All the while my embassy escort beamed down upon me.

He guided me to a well-lit room, where an official from the office of the attaché of the U.S. Department of Homeland Security and Customs and Border Protection told me he could "sense" who the smugglers, gang members, and other bad guys were because they "speak English." "And the tattoos," he said, as if he were pointing out the obvious. In that ultra-clean room, I felt millions of miles away from Gerardo on the tracks in Arriaga. I still couldn't get the picture of Gerardo's child out of my mind, his purple striped shirt, the blue background, and the way Gerardo showed it to us. I wondered if the group was now on the train.

This CBP attaché office in Mexico was among the first created, in 2003, along with offices in Belgium and Canada. Attachés were a part of the "massive paradigm change" that extended the "zone of security." Attachés were, as a CBP representative in Washington, DC, explained to me, "in-house specialists" who worked under the ambassador. Now there are 21 CBP attaché offices around the world. (Immigration and Customs Enforcement, known more for its internal immigration policing and operation of the U.S. detention-deportation regime, also has a considerable international presence with forty-eight offices worldwide.) CBP's offices support and oversee all homeland security operations that push out the border, including the "Container Security Initiative," the "Immigration Advisory Program," the "Customs-Trade Partnership Against Terrorism," and "robust" training and capacity-building programs. Each of these programs extends the U.S. border in a different way—as I will discuss in depth—whether by scrutinizing U.S.-bound people and shipments before they board or are loaded on planes or ships, or by using the war on terror as a justification to protect private companies' "supply chains." Armoring capitalism is part of the deal.

In order to execute their international programs, DHS and CBP have to navigate limits put upon them by the 1961 U.S. Foreign Assistance Act, which requires that all assistance go through the Department of State and Department of Defense. DHS, for the most part, cannot directly donate equipment or start an advisory program abroad. The budgets for DHS border-building programs, therefore, come from many tributary sources. They come from the State Department's Export Control and Border Security Related (EXBS) Program, or from the Bureau of International Narcotics and Law Enforcement Affairs (INL), or from various defense programs. When I met with Adam Isacson of the Washington Office on Latin America, in DC, he told me he had identified a baffling 107 active U.S. government programs to give foreign assistance. "Seventy-five can be used in Latin America," he said, "eighty-seven are Department of Defense programs. And fourteen State programs. And two joint DOD-State." He also told me how the Department of Homeland Security funded its programs: "They are always using somebody else's money, with tiny, tiny exceptions." CBP had essentially become a "contractor," as they put it in Washington, for "capacity building"—doing trainings, donating equipment, sending advisors. It was, as officials put it, "a whole of government" approach.

The CBP international program is divided into regions: North America, Latin America, the Caribbean, Europe, Africa, Asia, and the Middle East. In this sense, the U.S. border and enforcement missions are everywhere. Each region works to support and facilitate the work of the attachés. Even in a country or region where CBP had no official presence, it could still claim representation through Immigration and Customs Enforcement. Additionally, the U.S. Border Patrol has offices in Vancouver, Winnipeg, and Toronto, and two in Ottawa, sometimes stationed together with the Royal Canadian Mounted Police. It is also in Hermosillo and Monterrey, Mexico.

When I asked one of the CBP international affairs representatives to describe how much the international programs had grown after 9/11, he answered that if he could say it with only one word, it would be *exponentially*.

My meeting in 2014 with the CBP attaché in Mexico City was one of the first of many that I would have with U.S. and foreign officials as I researched that exponential expansion for this book. Security was a "thorny" subject, and just as in Mexico City, many officials interviewed wished to remain anonymous. During one meeting in Nairobi, I thought the commander of a police unit might have me arrested for simply asking about "security." My fixer in Jordan had no trouble setting up interviews until I mentioned that I wanted to visit the Syrian border. He wrote to me, "as you clearly know, security is always a very sensitive subject everywhere, and here in Jordan it could be more sensitive than other places." It was, and it wasn't. Security was sensitive everywhere, period. Try taking a picture of the U.S. Embassy in Manila, and the security guards will confiscate your camera. "Security, security," a taxi driver once told me outside the Tel Aviv airport, "There's always security. Security for you," he said, after I complained of problems in the airport, "security for me. Security for everybody."

In Mexico City, the U.S. official fixed me with slightly reddened brown eyes—I wondered if he'd stayed out a little too late the night before—and quickly homed in on the subject of Arriaga. Like an Army general fleshing out the purpose of border enforcement strategy, he talked about "infrastructure."

"Infrastructure?" I asked.

Like the hotels, he said. Then he paused, staring up at the ceiling. But not hotels like you know them, like the Hilton or Sheraton, he clarified.

Actually, they were "not really hotels" at all. Yet, he was indeed referring to small hotels that huddled along the rails in that small

Chiapan town where so many Central Americans arrived before the July 2014 crackdown. "These hotels," the official said, sometimes have more than fifty people packed into a single room, and he insinuated that because of this, the proprietor must be part of a criminal ring. The official paused to allow the gravity of the situation sink in. But Mexico was patrolling "broken-windows" style, he said, with "preemptive" stop-and-frisk-style policing, going into places where migrants gather and where "gangs victimize the migrants, steal their money, assault them, or even rape them."

As he talked, the impression he gave was that DHS, far away and paternalistic, was patting Mexico on its head for its good work. And in fact, a cable from the U.S. Embassy just a month before our meeting, on July 8, had done just this, applauding Mexico's "strategy for its southern border."[20]

Under the multibillion-dollar military aid program known as the Merida Initiative, the cable reiterated, U.S. programs existed to support and enhance the Mexican government's strategy, especially in enforcement and in Mexico's biometric and other information systems.

"Who doesn't have the necessary documents to enter into our country and enter the United States, we can't allow them into our territory," said Mexico's interior minister Miguel Angel Osorio Chong in July 2014, explaining that Mexico would be targeting places like Arriaga.[21] Osorio Chong's admission was intensely forthright: Mexico had in a serious way been "hired" by the United States to "protect" the U.S. border from 1,000 miles away.

Isabel was one of the hotel proprietors along the train tracks in Arriaga that led out to the *monte* where groups of Central Americans now hid from the forces of the state. From the small, yellow hotel she and her son ran, you could hear the loud, long moan of The Beast before it chugged north, up the tracks. When I entered this twenty-first-century battle space, lines of drying clothes crisscrossed the patio. She and other proprietors had been floored by the *operativos*, or border operations—one had happened precisely where we were standing. When Isabel saw me, and saw that I was a foreign journalist, her first words were, "Migrants are human beings." She said it with attitude, as if she were talking beyond me, to this huge, swelling global border enforcement apparatus that had arrived in her town, criminalized her, and pretty much shut down her hotel. Her thirty-something son spoke of Ferguson, Missouri, and the killing of Michael Brown (which had happened just a few weeks before) and the militarized police forces with racist tactics in the United States as if they explained the operations of Mexican immigration forces in the Programa Frontera Sur. In fact Isabel and her son, like almost everyone I talked to throughout southern Mexico that August, were convinced that the United States was behind it all. Police and military officers and agents had raided not only their hotel but several other properties as well, including food stands. They also were closing down roads. Isabel shook her head, and then along with her son described a scene in which seventy Guatemalan migrants had knelt in prayer before boarding the train, "in this patio," they said, pointing to the cement floor over which the clothes hung.

I couldn't help thinking of Gerardo, and the picture of his son staring out at us across eight long years. That small group of Central Americans heading north hadn't had to reach Brownsville, McAllen, Laredo, or Nogales to find the U.S.-Mexico border. It had come to them. Regardless, when Gerardo had tenderly held the creased, shabby picture of his child with his index fingers for us to see against the sturdy backdrop of his brown wallet—held it up for an extraordinarily long time—he'd said, "I'm going to Miami," as if nothing, absolutely nothing, could stop him.

2.

The U.S. "Border Set" on the
Guatemala-Honduras Divide

In January 2017, I returned to the Zacapa military base in Guatemala. This time, there was no trouble getting in to see one of the world's newest border patrols. In fact, at first I was treated as if I might have some sort of key advice to give to the new Chorti Task Force, Guatemala's border guard. "This threat that exists on borders is always impacting our country," said a government official from Guatemala's Ministerio de Gobernación (Ministry of the Interior). He pointed at U.S. Major Miguel Angel Juarez, who was sitting in full uniform—a green camouflage outfit—with the contingent of Guatemalan military, police, and government officials. I was truly surprised to see a U.S. soldier; I'd expected any U.S. presence to be hidden. The United States, the official explained, looking at Major Juarez, has "given us much support in training, equipment, and some orientations that we have received."

The official then looked at me, and said, "We are trying to figure out how to better control our borders. I don't know if you'd be able to share your experience with us?"

This question came during a thorough briefing the Chorti was giving me: details about its three-year history, details about the resources it had received—really the nuts and bolts of how a new border patrol was created in this century with U.S. support. I looked at Major Juarez and the other ten to fifteen uniformed men, all awaiting my answer. The silence was awkward. They expected me to speak of my findings on the border zones I had visited, from the Moroccan-European divide (where fortified border walls enclose Spanish enclaves) to the Syria-Jordan frontier. Maybe my knowledge would be applicable here in the drought-stricken mountainous borderlands around Zacapa. I was startled by the request. Didn't they know that as a journalist, I was examining the global border system through a critical lens?

Their very different assumption, however, was fascinating—that naturally I would want to help them improve their operation. And in hindsight I realize it made sense. Why wouldn't they think that? All of their other U.S. visitors had given them training sessions, consultations, more armored jeeps and guns. The United States had been "assisting" Guatemala for more than a century, and now it was assisting this new Guatemalan border force improve its "border security." Nothing could be more uncontroversial.

Major Juarez sat there as if his presence among these Guatemalan soldiers and police were banal and commonplace, and maybe it was, considering the massive U.S. military presence of nearly 800 bases in seventy territories and countries worldwide. Indeed, while active U.S. participation in the construction of foreign border regimes was new, this military aspect of the U.S. empire was so normal, it was practically boring. No other country's military footprint comes close. Britain, France, and Russia combined have just thirty foreign bases.[1]

Author and activist Arundhati Roy wrote "There isn't a country on God's earth that is not caught in the crosshairs of the U.S. cruise missile and the IMF checkbook."[2]

And in his book *Harvest of Empire* journalist Juan Gonzalez writes, "Most of us are uncomfortable thinking of our nation as an empire, even if Wall Street speculators and investment banks have repeatedly shown their ability to wreck entire economies halfway across the globe in a matter of hours."[3] But empire, Gonzalez stresses, is visible through the lens of migration. Empires are created through an unfettered and often violent extraction of wealth from vulnerable regions like Latin America and the transfer of that wealth—what CBP now often refers to as "supply chain security"—to powerful ones such as the United States or Europe. The logical result is that people, including the people of the despoiled countries, gravitate towards the imperial metropolises where wealth has become concentrated.

Stephen Peter Rosen, professor of National Security and Military Affairs at Harvard, describes empire as "a political unit that has overwhelming superiority of military power" and uses it to "influence the behavior of other states." Rosen also describes the underlying premise of a securocratic war: "Our goal is not combating a rival but maintaining our imperial position and maintaining imperial order."[4]

Scholar-activist Harsha Walia coined the term "border imperialism" to describe the border controls "most severely deployed by those Western regimes that create mass displacement." Border controls, she notes, are for "those whose very recourse to migration results from the ravages of capital and military occupations," that is, from the very foundations of Rosen's empire.[5] And in these militarized border zones, "practices of arrest without charge, expulsion, indefinite detention, torture, and killings have become the unexceptional norm."

Central America is a particularly strong example not only of the U.S. creation of border patrols, but also of border imperialism. Since the beginnings of the Monroe Doctrine in the early nineteenth century, the U.S. political lexicon has demeaned Latin America as "America's Backyard." Thanks to that policy and perception, much of Guatemala's twentieth-century history was dominated by a series of U.S.-backed military dictatorships and repressive economic oligarchies that resulted in mass displacements and migrations. Twentieth-century ideas about counterinsurgency, especially regarding control of potentially incompliant civilian populations, are basic to the twenty-first-century idea of homeland security.

It is important to underscore that this is not just true of Guatemala, or even of Latin America. The United States has become a global border-building machine. CBP has trained new patrol and homeland security units for Kenyan, Tanzanian, and Ugandan borders. U.S. Border Patrol and Drug Enforcement Administration officials trained the Ukrainian "Sokil" rapid-reaction unit.[6] U.S. homeland security trainers can be found in the Philippines, or across the Mona Strait in the Dominican Republic where bored soldiers in Dajabon sit on their Xs with long assault rifles. Much like U.S. Border Patrol agents, they stay in one position, guarding one section of border, except in the Dominican case they stand instead of sit in an idling vehicle. From their stations, sweating, they deter Haitians from crossing the Massacre River. The United States has helped form, train, and sometimes reinforce all of these border patrol units. The Indian Border Security Force, with similar assistance, deploys 245,000 agents on the Pakistani and Bangladeshi borders; CBP has an attaché office in New Delhi. There is the Frontier Corps in Pakistan and the Border Gendarmerie in Turkey. There is the Vietnam Border Defense Force. And there is Frontex in the European Union. The United States sent the Shadow Wolves, a border-patrolling unit of Native Americans that covered the U.S.-Mexico border on the Tohono O'odham Nation in Southern Arizona, to Poland to train patrols there in tracking human beings, or what the Border Patrol refers to as "cutting sign." As Shadow Wolf Kevin Carlos explained, "It was very rewarding to work with our Polish law enforcement partners. We provided them training and daily practical tracking exercises, and they performed exceptionally well."[7]

U.S.-trained patrols are being established worldwide. In 2014, the U.S. State Department facilitated a border trip for a news team from Kyrgyzstan, because "strengthening capacity of border guards and improving infrastructure at border posts has been one of the priorities of the U.S. Embassy in Bishkek," according to an email I received about the endeavor. The hope was that Kyrgyzstan's television viewers would "understand the importance of having well-guarded borders" and "be mobilized to influence the government to pay more attention to the borders and be more proactive in negotiating demarcation with neighboring countries." It is hard to believe that 100 years ago, the passport barely existed. Today, the shift toward border enforcement is global. As border scholar Elisabeth Vallet has meticulously reported, the number of border walls is on the rise—there are seventy-seven around the world, a significant increase since the fall of the Berlin Wall in 1989, when there were fifteen. Two-thirds of them were constructed in the post 9/11 era.[8]

I told the Chorti officials that I couldn't help them with any suggestions on border enforcement, reminded them that I was a journalist, and said that I hadn't yet drawn any conclusions from my research. Fernando Archila Gozalvo, one of the officials from Guatemala's Ministerio de Gobernación, asked if I had ever seen anything like this new Chorti homeland security force, combining two institutions, the military and police. Gozalvo was one of our chief guides; he'd come with us from Guatemala City. He had the aspect of a fatherly figure with a full head of brown hair and graying sideburns. He had been in the military for 33 years (beginning in 1979) and had been retired five years before taking this stint with the border task forces. It was clear he thought that the Chorti was onto something innovative, new.

But it wasn't new. Global examples of this fusion have grown increasingly prevalent post 9/11. As anthropologist Jeff Halper said, "You can't look at homeland security as policing or military; it is a whole integration." These forces now control conflicts that seem to never end, that challenge the status quo—conflicts over globalization, politics, climate change. Guatemala was simply one of the newest countries to get in line.

BORDER SETS

Major Juarez emphasized that he did not represent the views of the U.S. government. But he had seen what Gozalvo was describing, a new security force combining military and police in the United States: Joint Task Force Six—now known as Joint Task Force North—which ran U.S. military operations with the U.S. Border Patrol. One of two colleagues accompanying me that day, Justin Campbell, a former U.S. soldier and now a history PhD student at the University of Arizona, concurred. He had run Joint Task Force missions as a soldier, planting motion sensors along the U.S.-Mexico border in 2004 under the command of a U.S. Border Patrol agent.

In the military and as a contractor, Campbell had worked on several other border operations. He had a ton of stories; he'd lugged a 50-pound rucksack stuffed with motion sensors along the 38th parallel, the line separating North and South Korea. And after he left the military, he worked on the oven-hot Iraq-Iran divide, doing retina scans and fingerprinting and inserting names and faces into a huge data base for the company CGI. In many ways, he embodied the new empire of borders, as an expert not only in practice but also in theory. Very few in the world knew more about how borders worked than

Campbell. When I met him, he had already undergone several personal transformations that made him seriously question the border work he had done while in the military. This had led him to doctoral work focused on U.S. border extension into Latin America, developing a concept he called "border sets."

According to Campbell, a border set is "a collection of multiple borders" that share similar characteristics, relate to one another, and as a more holistic system can help us understand a border enforcement apparatus much more completely than if we examined each border individually. He explained to me that the U.S.-Mexico, Mexico-Guatemala, and Guatemala-Honduras divides were part of a border set "where all borders face south—for the most part—and tried to prevent the same things from going north." In other words, thinking of the U.S. southern border as simply its divide with Mexico drastically reduced its immense geographic scope and masked its true nature as an instrument for domination. U.S. programs to fortify border patrols in other countries have become an intricate part of these border sets, and part of the U.S.'s "comprehensive, multi-layered approach" to border policing, according to CBP's Vision and Strategy plan for 2020.[9]

Major Juarez, who spoke Spanglish with us, offered an interesting—if not complex—and highly personal analysis of the border. He had grown up in Brownsville, Texas, right on the U.S.-Mexico divide, and in his forward, friendly, and earnest way told us that everything had changed after the "amnesty" of 1986. The air quotes were his. Before the Reagan administration law known as the Immigration Reform and Control Act of 1986, you could cross the border without problems. As sociologist Timothy Dunn wrote in *The Militarization of the U.S.-Mexico Border: The Low Intensity Conflict Doctrine Comes Home*, the 1986 law was meant to "reduce drastically undocumented immigration into the United States." It used a "carrot-and-stick" approach. The "carrot" was an extensive legalization program for undocumented people already in the U.S., and the "stick" was a vast expansion of border enforcement to keep new undocumented migrants out.

"First there was a toll," Major Juarez recalled, "then they wanted papers." His family had to choose one side of the border: Mexico or the United States. They chose the United States. The 30-year-career soldier knew from that experience the essential similarity of borders everywhere: they divided peoples, communities, families. He understood the border set. That included here, near the Guatemalan-Honduran borderlands.

"And the Guatemalan government says, yes, I know that you are brothers—but if you're on this side you are Guatemalan; if you are on that side, Honduran," Major Juarez continued. "But how can it be this way? This is my brother, we were born in the same country." Juarez knew that the Mayan world stretched from Mexico to Guatemala, El Salvador, Honduras. And yet, caught in the ultimate dilemma he was now tasked with bolstering the very boundaries that had cracked this indigenous world, on behalf of the United States.

Although Juarez spoke broadly about his role "advising the task force," by the nature of his unit it was clear that he provided training on the equipment that the Chorti received from the United States. He also made it clear that he left the in-depth border training to the "professionals," the INL, meaning the U.S. State Department's Bureau of International Narcotics and Law Enforcement Affairs, an agency that my other colleague and fellow researcher Miriel Manning and I had attempted to contact multiple times at the U.S. Embassy in Guatemala City. (A counternarcotics officer, Douglas Johnson, had given us the run-around for weeks and finally stopped answering emails, after recommending that we contact the ICE Homeland Security Investigations office.) Major Juarez also mentioned the Border Patrol by name. Almost all the funding of U.S. CBP and ICE training operations in Central America came through the INL.

The INL states that its goals include reducing the entrance of illicit narcotics and crime into the United States. Managing yearly budgets that hover at about one billion dollars[10]—nearly five times more than its 1997 budget, for example, that was $200 million[11]—it is the perfect agency for twenty-first-century securocratic warfare. One of its color-coded maps shows its vast reach into huge swaths of Africa—including Libya, Egypt, Kenya, and South Africa—and Asia, and its concentration in Mexico, Central America, Colombia, and Peru, ninety countries in total.

The INL is behind some of the most rapidly fortifying U.S. international border fronts and is fundamental in border guard construction. It worked with CBP, for example, "to place nine CBP Advisors throughout Central America" for "capacity building and technical assistance" and to "more effectively address migration issues in-country," according to testimony from Ronald Vitiello, acting chief of the U.S. Border Patrol, in 2016.[12] (Vitiello was responding to the question "Does the administration have a plan to stop the border surge and adequately monitor the children?") Just for the Western Hemisphere in 2019, approximately $380 million will be allotted to the INL "to disrupt the activities of transnational criminal organizations, improve citizen security, and reduce drug production and the flow of illicit narcotics, migrants, and cash to the United States."[13]

Later that day, after we returned to Guatemala City from Zacapa, I would find out that the INL did not like a journalist being at the military base one bit.

FROM COUNTERINSURGENCY TO THE BORDER

How did the training program to form Guatemala's Chorti border patrol evolve? During my first trip to the Zacapa military base in June 2015, Colonel Obed Lopez—the sweating Chorti commander who came straight from the rifle range—had told me that the initial training sessions were three months long and carried out "by the United States." BORTAC, the National Guard, special forces units, and "police that they used in the cities" had all arrived, each providing different instruction, in "weapons, tactics, ground movements and agility training, first aid," he said.

In this country where 80 percent of the indigenous population lived in poverty, many in extreme poverty, millions of dollars were going into a new border force. Since 2008, the U.S. program known as the Central American Regional Security Initiative (CARSI) has funded countries such as Guatemala, Honduras, and El Salvador with nearly $1 billion, and one of its priorities is to remedy "border security deficiencies."[14] During this period the Pentagon has provided another

$357.2 million on top of the CARSI funding for similar purposes including border enforcement, according to numbers compiled by the Washington Office on Latin America (WOLA). These figures surged after 2014, the same year that Mexico announced its Programa Frontera Sur and amid Washington's "concern" about the unaccompanied minors from Guatemala, Honduras, and El Salvador arriving at the U.S.'s southern border. In 2016, Central American military and police forces received more U.S. assistance "than they have in over a decade," Adam Isacson and Sarah Kinosian wrote in a report for WOLA.[15]

As for the Chorti, U.S. Southern Command had provided $13.4 million for its initial development in 2015.[16] John Kelly, who would become chief of staff and the first secretary of DHS for the Trump administration, was then the top commander of Southcom. "It was a complete training," Lopez said of the formation of the Chorti in 2015. It was so intensive that U.S. security forces weren't allowed to leave the base, except on Sundays.

Back at the briefing where I met U.S. Major Juarez in January 2017, the police commander of the Chorti, Nicolas Eliseo Garcia Cholotio, gave a presentation on the state of this new border force. He stood behind a podium, his PowerPoint presentation projected on a wall behind him, otherwise barren except for one red fire extinguisher by the door. One of his slides showed the precise trainings that they had received in 2015 and 2016, mostly from the United States, including one session on "counter-transnational threats." One of the training programs caught my eye because it had taken place in Fort Benning, Georgia, at the U.S. Army School of the Americas (SOA). The SOA—after 2001 operating under the name Western Hemisphere Institute for Security Cooperation, or WHINSEC—has been training Latin American military officers in counterinsurgency, particularly anti-communist insurgency, tactics since 1946. Of the seventeen training courses the Chorti completed in 2015, eleven were carried out by U.S. forces. Subjects included communications, night vision navigation, counter narcotic operations, human intelligence, psychological operations, firearms training, and intelligence. The Chorti also went to Colombia, where they took courses in gathering intelligence and one course titled simply "Jungla"—"Jungle." The training continued in

2016, still mainly led by U.S. forces, covering command and control, police intelligence, transnational threats, human intelligence, and car mechanics and maintenance.

CBP officials told me when I visited them in the Washington International Affairs office in May 2017 that one of the biggest challenges they faced with their international training courses was that sometimes other countries forming border patrols or immigration forces were "constrained." What did they mean by constrained? Sometimes the foreign border guards didn't "have the ability to arrest at all." Or they were "only clerical." They didn't have the ability to search, so "they have to seek help" from the police. "Or they can't search without a court order."

This was different from CBP, which was "able to do searches, seizures, audits, detentions without anything, without any sort of prior warrant." One of the officials put it to me bluntly: "We're exempted from the Fourth Amendment; the Supreme Court ruled that many decades ago." The Fourth Amendment to the U.S. Constitution protects people from unwarranted searches or seizures. The official was telling me that the ability to break through the constraints of civil liberties was fundamental to U.S. border expansion. Like the U.S.'s CBP, foreign homeland security forces needed "extra-constitutional" powers.

One U.S. institution that has long been connected to human rights violations throughout Latin America and the Caribbean is the U.S. Army School of the Americas, dubbed the School of the Assassins by activists. Anthropologist Lesley Gill has described the SOA as "a central tool in the construction of U.S. hemispheric dominance." It has created an "elite transnational military culture" characterized by "enmity toward popular forces and unscrupulousness in the use of violence to maintain the status quo."[17]

Since 1946, the SOA/WHINSEC has trained over 64,000 Latin American soldiers in military intelligence, commando and psychological warfare, and counterinsurgency techniques. As the organization SOA Watch has documented, "countries with the worst human rights records have consistently sent the most soldiers to be trained at the SOA."[18] Historic examples abound: Bolivia under the bloody regime of General Hugo Banzer, the long-standing Somoza family dicta-torship in Nicaragua, and the perpetrators of the violent repression during the 1970s and 80s in El Salvador, to name a few.

Gill also emphasizes that in our post-9/11 era, as U.S. elites pursue a more imperial agenda "that provokes unpredictable responses," the "School—or surrogate institutions—will remain a vital instrument of U.S. policy." In this comes the shift to heavy border policing.

I came to understand this when I visited Professor Celina Realuyo at her office at the Washington, DC–based William J. Perry Center for Hemispheric Defense Studies, part of the National Defense Insti-tute, in May 2017. Behind the professor's desk was a framed picture of her with the late Arizona Senator John McCain. Realuyo mentioned that she had just met with then–U.S. secretary of state Rex Tillerson. "Say what you will about Trump," she said, "he's surrounded himself with business people." When Tillerson made an investment, Realuyo asserted, he wanted to see a result.

I was there not only because she had expertise from a governmental perspective of the expansion of the U.S. security apparatus into Latin America, but also because, like SOA-WHINSEC, she gave classes to senior civilian and military leaders throughout the Americas "to build strong, sustainable networks of security and defense leaders and insti-tutions." And Realuyo was all about borders. It didn't take her long to cut to the chase and describe the U.S. border enforcement apparatus with dreadful accuracy: as a "cyber-physical wall"—a term that fully expressed the system's extension, intense biometric capabilities, and data bases.

"I'm trying to push General Kelly to use the word 'cyber-physical wall,' as opposed to "build the wall," which is Trump's thing," she said in a joking tone. "It's so old school. He's seventy, what are you going to do?"

As she talked it was evident that she really liked then-Secretary of the Department of Homeland Security John Kelly, whom she described as "a great man," and well worth following on Twitter.

"Cyber-physical," she explained, "means drones, satellites, surveil-lance, cameras, you know, the sensors and things, we're already doing it, so his staffers are like, 'That's kind of interesting.'"

Realuyo was one of the very few who knew exactly what we were talking about when we mentioned the Chorti border patrol. She had been to Guatemala, but the U.S. Embassy wouldn't permit her to go to the Zacapa military base, she said, rolling her eyes. Her focus was Latin America, but her scope was international, and her specialty was "foreign fighters," about which she had many stories. One that she mentioned on several occasions exemplified what she saw as the "deficiencies" of the hemispheric border set. A Somali man had landed in Brazil and then, incredibly, made it to Panama before the cyber-physical wall trapped him, she said. "That's a long way to go," she said, laughing, "over land, right? So that's the bigger thing, we're doing tons of biometric stuff. Panama's a good example." What was his name? Realuyo didn't know, much less anything else about him, only that he was on the "terror-watch list" and a "special interest alien" from a "special interest country." Special interest alien was a specific category assigned to anyone from Afghanistan, Iraq, Iran, Pakistan, Syria, or Somalia—all nationalities that the Trump administration had targeted for "extreme vetting." She also had a story about "three Syrians in Honduras with Brazilian passports. They landed, and it looked like they went through Brazil too. So we're on Brazil's case for all these special interest aliens." Listening to Realuyo, I realized that thinking of the border as a single line was ludicrous.

I found out later that the William Perry Center was under fire following an allegation that a senior staff member (Lt. Col. Craig Deare) had conspired to cover up the center's support of the 2009 military coup in Honduras. Whistleblower Martin Edwin Andersen, a former assistant professor at the Perry Center, claimed in February 2017 that Deare had a "checkered record of support for and involvement with some of the Western Hemisphere's most notorious human-rights abusers." The Senate Armed Services committee was concerned that the center carried the "vestiges of the old School of the Americas, the U.S. program that trained Latin America military officers, many of whom then went on to be brutal dictators in their home countries."[19] And the Center for Public Integrity found in 2015 that the "flagship military university [the NDU and Perry Center] hired foreign officers linked to human rights abuses in Latin America."[20]

Yet here they were, central to the "paradigm change" of U.S. border extension. "I'm still mad at the Panamanians," Realuyo said. "You had the Somali in your midst, we could have at least observed him. Because someone's feeding him and caring for him on their way up. I am really interested in the support networks. Because they are obviously trying to go someplace. But in the meantime, how are they supporting themselves?" She claimed there were refugee camps in Costa Rica: There's Haitians and there's Cubans, she said, and this is where you have this "hodgepodge." There's Bangladeshis, Congolese, "it's literally the United Nations down there."

"And then there's these little ghettos of Africans who are starting to get into criminal activity," she said, without further explanation.

What are the new threats to the United States? I asked her. "So we did this projection of 2030," Realuyo replied, "you know—what will the world look like? Central America has everything going against it. Because of extreme weather. It has those terrible droughts." And the droughts were like "scorched earth"—coincidentally the same term used by late Guatemala dictator Rios Montt to describe the bloody counterinsurgency campaign under his rule that in 1982–83 killed tens of thousands of primarily indigenous people.

Toward the end of the interview Realuyo stressed that remittances should be an "investment, not a subsidy." Guatemala was "like the deadbeat uncle in the hammock waiting to get his next Corona... If you are just getting stuff that's handed to you, you're never going to be invested in your community." The answer was a world where the private sector became "the engine of growth," as opposed to "handouts from different countries, which every government should be happy about, right? Including ours, since it's our tax dollars there." The example she focused on was Walmart. I looked at her to make sure she was serious. Yes, she said, "evil Walmart." She talked about their "farm-to-table programs" and how they were investing in and vetting producers. She talked about how Walmart was investing in the children of employees, putting them in vocational schools, "because they are going to need people to do accounting, people to manage the store."

"They are training people who are going to be in the future workforce," Realuyo said, "but they know they have to have a workforce they can protect." She finished by saying that you couldn't have "prosperity without security."

Or as criminologist Nancy Wonders puts it, "borders are not simply a consequence of neoliberalism; they are also productive of it."[21]

The SOA changed its name in 2001 chiefly in response to immense pressures from social movements demanding its closure. The more sanitized Western Hemisphere Institute for Security Cooperation (WHINSEC) at first sounded like gibberish, but now—in the innocuous language of homeland security—it sounded like an apt description of the U.S. international border operation.

The rapid border response demonstration started with the police commander Cholotio, still behind the podium, speaking with a military commander named Moran, who wore a maroon beret with a yellow patch that identified him as a Kaibil, a special forces unit of the Guatemalan military. They were pretending to talk on the phone about a dire hypothetical situation in which some "bad guy" had breeched the border. It almost seemed like a *Saturday Night Live* skit, their quick and overly dramatized commands lost in the echoing room. All of us were watching intently, including the U.S. army major Juarez. I wondered if he was going to join the drama.

Right before this, after showing us the slide listing all the training courses, Cholotio, showed us maps of the illicit smuggling done through Central America. With my eyes, I followed a series of dotted lines that seemed to enter Guatemala from every conceivable direction. Many crossed the more than sixty "weak" points along the Honduran divide. Clearly in the skit we were dealing with one of those points. The Central American Northern Triangle country, considered a gateway into Mexico and possibly the United States, was quickly becoming a militarized gatekeeper, another layer of the U.S. border. Cholotio showed us the routes through Guatemala's jungle, northern and southern highlands, and Pacific coast. He talked about the 300 soldiers and police fused together in the Chorti border patrol, and about the border operations deployed in 2016 in different Guatemalan departments: Operation Quetzal, Operation Frontera Sur, Operation Frontera Norte, Operation Machaca, Operation Jaguar. Most of them involved roadside checkpoints. Another, Plan Cobra, had just gone into effect for the new year and would be operational until December 2017. He showed us the operations along the Honduran border, often carried out in conjunction with the Honduran border patrol, known as the Maya Chorti. He showed us pictures of their drug busts and their checkpoint operations, patrols, and reconnaissance.

All these efforts had increased over the last three years, he said. He spoke as if border enforcement were a factory with ambitious production quotas, and by god they were hitting them: The category of "identified people," or documents checked, had almost tripled from 2015 to 2016, from 11,000 to approximately 32,000. The same for "vehicles identified"; they'd increased from about 9,000 to 23,000. The checkpoints and patrolling operations were, in other words, more extensive, more thorough. Indeed, there was an almost sevenfold increase in deployed checkpoints from when the Chorti started in 2014, from 200 to 1500. And patrols had almost quintupled, from 152 to 731. Guatemala, like so many other countries around the world, had increased its border-patrolling apparatus and capabilities and had the numbers to prove it.

As they continued with the skit, my eyes fixed onto Moran's Kaibil patch. After Guatemala's 36-year armed conflict ended, in 1996, the report by the United Nations Truth and Reconciliation Committee placed special emphasis on the Kaibiles, whose soldiers, it said, were trained to be "killing machines."[22] The mustached Moran was in full camo uniform. He was the top tier of the command structure of the new border force. Over the decades many Kaibil commanders had trained at the U.S. School of the Americas. It is also worth mentioning, as documented by sociologist Stuart Schrader, during the Cold War it was common practice for Washington to send former U.S. Border Patrol agents to places like Guatemala to train foreign police in CIA-linked "public safety" programs, due to their alleged Spanish language ability.[23] Now in the eastern borderlands, Guatemala's past met its future in a very tangible way.

The skit was the first part of the operation, the phone conversation vivid proof that the police and military were working together nicely. The next thing we knew, in a burst, everyone was running at a full sprint outside into the overcast January day. All the military and police commanders, the rank-and-file agents and soldiers, a blur of green and blue. They were mobilizing as if a real border incident were happening. The feeling was, indeed, that of a war. The border was not a passive line, but potentially aggressive. The "enemy's" arrival was clearly imminent. As we ran outside, Gozalvo looked at us and said, "I'm going to let you do something that I never ever let anyone do." He paused. Partly, he said, because it's "illegal." I looked at him, wondering what on earth this could be. "You can get on the back of the truck." It was as if we were kids. And I had a feeling that they had done things in this place more "illegal" than that. In the back of the truck we rode with the Kaibil commander Moran, he of the maroon beret, who didn't seem to care that we were doing something illegal. He told us as we rode that "the olive green was respected in Guatemala." He said, "I know this because I am a student of history."

The Kaibiles were trained by U.S. Green Berets in the 1960s, just ten years after the United States, in a Central Intelligence Agency–engineered coup, removed the democratically elected President Jacobo Arbenz from office. Arbenz had threatened a fraction of the Boston-based United Fruit Company's fallow land holdings in Guatemala, claiming that he was going to redistribute it to the landless. What followed was called by many the Mayan Holocaust: more than 200 massacres that killed more than 200,000 people in Guatemala and displaced tens of thousands more.

Seeing the Kaibil was like witnessing a history that was still live, a violence still fresh in this country. I recalled December 4, 1982, when fifty-eight Kaibiles arrived in the small, indigenous community of Dos Erres in northern Guatemala at 2:30 a.m. Massacres are often carried out on people just roused from sleep, at their most disoriented. After forcing residents from their homes, the Kaibiles separated the adults, whom they accused of being guerrilla sympathizers and communists, corralling the men in the schoolhouse and the women into two churches. By early afternoon, the Kaibiles had begun killing the children. They bashed the smallest children's heads against the walls and trees. They killed the older kids with hammer blows to the skull. They interrogated the men and women one by one. They raped the women. They pulled the fetuses from pregnant women's bodies. They killed everyone, with hammers, dumping the corpses into a well. By the end, 226 people were dead. "The massacres, scorched-earth operations, forced disappearances, and executions of Mayan authorities, leaders, and spiritual guides," according to the Truth and Reconciliation Commission report, "were not only an attempt to destroy the social base of the guerrillas, but above all to destroy the cultural values that ensured cohesion and collective action in Mayan communities."[24]

Not long after the Dos Erres massacre, one of the Kaibiles who'd been in command, Pedro Pimentel Rios, became an instructor at the School of the Americas. In 2012, Rios was extradited from the United States to Guatemala, where he was sentenced to 6,060 years of prison for his involvement at Dos Erres. Other high-profile Guatemalans who were implicated in the genocidal bloodshed and also graduated from the SOA were the late dictator Efrain Rios Montt, deposed president Otto Perez Molina, and Byron Disrael Lima Estrada, the alleged mastermind behind the murder of the human rights–defending Bishop Juan Jose Gerardi. During Montt's rule, from 1982 to 1983, he ordered the killings of 1,771 Ixil Maya indigenous people. According to the United Nations Truth Commission Clarification, Guatemala's military and state forces were responsible for 93 percent of the violence, mostly high-profile killings and massacres, during Guatemala's 36-year armed conflict.[25]

Kaibiles are systematically desensitized. Their training is infamous for its harsh hazing. In one exercise, they are allowed to raise and bond with a small puppy, then forced to kill it, eat it raw, and drink its blood. They must bite the heads off chickens. They learn to eat "anything that moves," and must demonstrate that they can patrol "thorn-filled" brush in nothing but their underwear, and roll around in the thorns.[26]

Speaking in 2015, a Kaibil colonel said about the Kaibiles' continued relationship with U.S. special forces:

> With the training and support we receive from the U.S. Soldiers, we continue to hone our techniques to counter narcotics trafficking. As Soldiers, we need to be united against those who threaten our livelihoods,

and only by being united can we overcome the enemy and defend innocent lives so they may prosper.[27]

We rumbled on the truck to a building where the stash of all their guns and assault rifles were located, including 173 Beretta and eight Glock handguns. The Glock was a constant at borders and homeland security trade shows worldwide, and presumably a gun of choice for the world's forming border patrols. The Chorti patrol had seven Jericho semi-automatic pistols developed by Israel Weapon Industries, nineteen UZIs—the Israeli open-bolt, blowback-operated submachine guns first developed by Major Uziel Gal in the late 1940s, from the beginning days of the Israeli state and the Palestinian *Nakba* (the catastrophe). This gun was in use in more than ninety different countries. It had been instrumental in the 1967 Israeli Six-Day War, and the principal weapon of the Israeli Defense Forces until the 1990s, when it was replaced by the Tavor assault rifle. On par with the IDF, the Chorti had two of those as well, and 100 Galil 5.56-caliber assault rifles, also produced by Israeli Weapon Industries, and thirty other machine guns. They were ready for war, a border war. The Chorti were as much members of the U.S. border guard as the Border Patrol agents patrolling the deserts of Texas and Arizona.

"Seven minutes," Gozalvo told me tapping his watch, "This is important." That was the time it took the force in hard helmets and full uniform to get the guns, attach them to the armored jeeps.

Before in the barracks, Cholotio had also laid out all of the equipment the Chorti received from the United States, including the jeeps that skidded off in front of me and the satisfied Gozalvo on the dirt road through a forest of trees all painted white on the bottom of their trunks. Also, in 2016, the United States transferred thirty GPS maps of Central America, fifty tactical backpacks, 188 bulletproof vests. There were fifteen cameras, twenty-nine pairs of night-vision goggles, and six pairs of night-vision binoculars. There were 135 bulletproof helmets, forty rifles, 230 rifle cleaning kits, forty-two machine gun–cleaning kits, and forty complete first aid kits. There were seven heavy-duty Ford F450 trucks, two trucks from the Colombian company Hino, and twenty-five Toyota Hilux pickups. There were forty-two armored J8

Jeeps. And Jeep, according to its advertising, "didn't design the J8 for armchair warriors. They designed it for the extraordinary men and women in uniform facing real threats and transport challenges in the world's toughest environments ..." Jeep had a special "BPV," or "Border Patrol Vehicle," that was "ideal for command and control missions."

In each of the armored vehicles a soldier sat on top behind the machine gun, his face hidden by a mask, a spooky sight I had seen hundreds of times throughout the region. The six vehicles came back up the road, turned the corner, stopped, and constructed a blockade with orange cones. They were setting up a border where a border hadn't existed before. While the soldiers did perimeter surveillance, the police worked the checkpoint.

The scenario ended predictably. A white truck pulled up packed with "the bad guys." After a rather quick interrogation, the police forced everyone out of the truck. They threw them to the ground and handcuffed them. They then lay them prostrate on the dirt on the side of the road, where they were backed by the armored jeeps and soldiers doing perimeter surveillance behind the large machine guns. The scenario, although simplistic and not resembling real life, was still a momentary journey into how the twenty-first century was being imagined, reimagined, and produced, straight from the Cold War counterinsurgency manuals.

Back at headquarters after the simulation, I was able to talk to the police and soldiers. Some of them mentioned that they were capturing "Africans." They said they could distinguish them easily; they knew they were not from here. I could not help thinking of Realuyo's story of the Somali, or the "African village" she mentioned in the refugee camps of Costa Rica. During the interview, the police stood before me in four rows, three officers per row, at attention on the checkered floor, arms at their sides, helmets on their heads, bulletproof vests beneath their navy blue uniforms, black boots on their feet. Their commander, standing at the front, answered most of the questions. The soldiers stood in the same formation, and though they nodded occasionally, not one of them said a word.

I asked if all of them had to go to the border. Several police said,

"All of us, *todos*." I asked if they went in those armored Jeeps and they said yes. I asked if they then patrolled the border, and one answered, "Patrols and checkpoints." Sometimes, they said, they had to go to other places in northern Guatemala, like the Petén or Izabal. They did patrols and went to the different indicated points to do "controls." The shifts "in the field" were about seven hours.

The police commander said that if they arrested a person without papers, "there is a process that happens with the immigration office. The immigration office then will do a formal deportation to the country where they come from." They checked people at all the control points and then used the Interpol database to make sure "this person hasn't been a criminal in their own country." (Interpol, the international police, are charged with facilitating police coordination between countries.)

Do you have families? I asked. Every single person nodded. All of them had children. And none of their families lived in Zacapa, but sometimes they went back to visit them, taking a bus. One police agent said his family—he was married with a two-year-old child—lived 400 kilometers away, and others, according to the commander, were even farther. The agent was rather short, and his commander quipped that his kid by now must be taller than he was. Every two weeks the agents were given seven days' leave to see their children. When I asked if they missed their families, everyone replied "Sí" in unison, with a tinge of underlying sadness. The soldiers served for two years, but "*un servicio*" as the commander put it, for the police was twenty years. This lot's been here for three years, the commander said jocularly: seventeen more to go. There was no doubt that the toughest part of it was being divided from your family. But I already knew that from speaking with Gerardo.

I had a feeling as I talked with this group that I would have heard different stories if they had been able to talk without supervision: stories of needing employment, maybe even stories of northward migration, commonplace stories throughout Guatemala, where nearly 60 percent of the population lives in conditions of poverty or extreme poverty. For the Guatemalan National Police, salaries hovered around $500 USD a month, higher than the dismal minimum wage, but still just enough to scrape by.[28] It was a salary that would disqualify them from obtaining a visa to the United States. If individuals in this new world border patrol themselves moved across a border, they would be arrested, detained, and deported. The border patrol agents themselves came from a group of potential migrants. The watchers and the watched were the same.

WEIRD QUESTIONS

Campbell, Manning and I returned to Guatemala City. On the drive back, we passed people walking and biking; I noticed one person lugging a bag twice the size of the bike he rode. In the town of Jutiapa, a procession of people walked slowly up a curving hill with tall trees hanging over its shoulder. Two people in the middle tenderly carried a small, white coffin.

Inside the car there was only stupefied silence. The day had been long. Bougainvillea spilled over walls outside, an explosion of color that almost stretched onto the road itself, and when we crested a mountain before descending into Guatemala City, the conical silhouettes of the volcanoes that surround Antigua were visible against the embers of the setting sun. Strange, triangular clouds hung above. It might have been partly because I was tired, but the beauty drove me to tears. Our driver, an anti-narcotics agent who carried a bulging pistol under his shirt, brought us down to the hotel.

We had just sat down in the lobby when the receptionist came over and asked me my room number. He had a phone in his hand, and when I realized it was the Guatemalan government on the line, I knew I had made a mistake in telling him. The call was from the 5th Viceministerio de Gobernación. The only reason that office would be calling was that someone was suddenly suspicious about our visit with the Chorti.

The woman on the phone wanted to know how Vice Minister Oscar Miguel Davila could contact me. I'd met him the day before at the Ministry of the Interior, where he'd sat with five other men, all in suits and ties, including Gozalvo, who had accompanied us that day.

It had been my official briefing about the new Guatemalan border patrol, before I headed to Zacapa.

Davila had slicked-back hair, and one of his eyes looked slightly discolored. He told us about a visit he'd made to McAllen, Texas, bringing along one of the border patrol (task force) agents to be trained to set up "*bloqueos*," or checkpoints, in the border zone, much as I'd seen the Chorti do it that day in Zacapa. Agents also trained at the wall in various exercises, such as *rastreo*, or what the U.S. Border Patrol calls "cutting sign," in which they clear dirt roads—often with tires dragged from vehicles—to be able to see fresh tracks of people crossing the border. Davila called these exercises their annual "*dosis*"— doses—of U.S. border training. The same word they'd use for medicine —or a drug.

In the discussion, Davila specifically mentioned terrorism and the Special Force of Counter Terror and Counter Terror Interdiction. Another mouthful. Now, when Miriel Manning asked Davila about terrorists in Guatemala, the vice minister said there had been no incidents. A special force, but no incidents. Then he corrected himself. Once there'd been a truck that was heading north through Guatemala packed with weapons. Their special force captured it as it passed through the jungles of the Petén, on its way to Honduras; the drivers were going to assassinate the president of that country, according to the vice minister. He shrugged his shoulders. "I don't know," he said. Maybe they had saved the Honduran president's life? But besides that, there had been no acts of terrorism.

"But if there were a terrorist act we would be prepared for it," added Gozalvo, leaning forward.

When, later, I related this anecdote to José Santos Sapon, an indigenous leader from the Quiché department, he immediately said that it sounded like a prison.

What sounded like a prison? I asked.

The patrols, he said.

I had been talking to Sapon about the extractive industries in Guatemala, the mining companies that were taking over whole communities, digging into the earth, exploiting the minerals, poisoning the water.

What if the patrols, he asked, were meant to keep me in?

I confessed I hadn't thought about that.

Because, he asked, "what if I needed to flee?" What if as an "indigenous defender of land and resources" they came after me and I needed to run? And there were patrols keeping me in?

Indeed, I thought, what if these borders were intended not only to keep people from entering, but also to stop people from leaving? Sapon's point was that the anti-terrorism laws in Guatemala made it easy to label someone like him a "terrorist." He was part of an indigenous population that had been discriminated against and targeted for 500 years. For Sapon, the idea of running was not a new one. The lived experience of people from Quiché—Sapon, his family, his neighbors, his friends, his community—was that when attacked by the marauding U.S.-backed army, they had to run. They ran to other parts of Guatemala, to Mexico, and to the United States, where they lived as refugees, in exile, for countless years.

Although the vice minister had been friendly, he'd also given the impression that we'd better not give him reason to be anything else. Back once more in the hotel lobby, I got another phone call. This time, it was U.S. Army Major Juarez, who promptly introduced himself again, in spite of our earlier meeting that day. His tone had changed; it had a frantic ring to it. He had talked to the INL's man at the U.S. Embassy in Guatemala City, he said, and the man had come down on him hard. He had asked questions about me, including some "weird questions."

As soon as I'd hung up, the phone behind the front desk rang again. The receptionist rolled his eyes, signaled that it was for me, and reminded me that "this is a hotel." It was the 5th vice minister's office again. A woman on the other end asked me what institution I represented. I paused, then gave her my publisher's name, Verso Books.

Where were Verso's offices, and when would the book be published? What was the nature of my journalism, and was it for commercial use?

These were invasive questions. I answered because I didn't know what else to do, and I wondered whether the U.S. Embassy, and particularly the INL, had called the Guatemalan government. In fact, I felt pretty sure they had. After all, I knew about the historic

U.S.-Guatemala relationship. Finally, the woman said that she hoped my answers would satisfy the vice minister, and we hung up. Suddenly, I did not feel safe in Guatemala. I wondered if they would try to confiscate the recordings of my interviews and my photos. Perhaps that was the point of a world where counterinsurgency meets border security, it is a psychological operation, it gets into your head.

Part Two

The Global Pacification Industry on the Palestine-Mexico Border

Sadness is but a wall between two gardens.

Khalil Gibran

3.

"Selling a Security State"

With gushing enthusiasm, the man in shades and white button-down shirt announced the entrance of the DOGO, a small, square, black robot made by General Robotics. A loosely assembled crowd, mostly men, milled around the DOGO and the announcer, under the blue Mediterranean sky. It was still early on this September day in 2016, and the burning sun was low; in the distance you could see the white, multistoried condominium complexes side by side by side on the outskirts of Tel Aviv.

The Orbiter 3, known as the suicide drone, still flew overhead ("quieter than a bird"), on display for the people gathered at this unmanned-systems exhibition and conference put on by Israeli Homeland Security (IHLS). This company prides itself on being a "security accelerator." It connects industries and investors through the multiple conferences it puts on each year. And the Orbiter 3? "You can gather intelligence for 2.5 hours," Adi Cohen of Israeli Aeronautics later told an audience, "and then it can become a missile."

Geographer Ian G.R. Shaw writes in his book *Predator Empire*, "State power in the twenty-first century is incredibly atmospheric." But it is more than that; it is part of something bigger. Shaw argues, "The infrastructures we build here on earth directly condition the spaces of everyday life, from the conduct of state violence down to our psychological dispositions." He is speaking of drones, but the same can be said of the globe's border barriers, whether they're high-tech or concrete, whether they protect gated communities or guard settlements, whether you are employed by the vast, growing industry that creates them or, because of it, forcibly separated from your family.

The Orbiter was an original innovation of the company Aeronautics, but the true drone masterpiece was Israel Aerospace Industries The Heron, on display in the adjacent Rishon LeZion LAGO conference center. Gathered around the massive drone, a group of high school students listened attentively to a company representative's explanation that this unmanned plane could haul 5 tons and fly at 60,000 feet. Men stood gazing at the blue plastic skin of this specimen —whose wings extended across the showroom—as if to touch it would make them shiver with pleasure. From front to back, this showroom was packed with people and robots of all shapes and sizes. Later, Lt. Col. Momi Aikobi of the Israeli Defense Forces (IDF) would say, using the Heron as his prime example, "Israel is a technological superpower in this field," adding that this expertise came "from needs on the ground."

Indeed, watching the DOGO crawl around I felt as if I were standing in a laboratory where the world's future tech battlefields were being hashed out. The robot's presenter, still laying out the quality bullet points of the product, noted that it could fit into a briefcase. The DOGO was almost cute, like a cross between R2D2 and a compact black poodle. It buzzed around with a sort of endearing innocence, making little forays into that loose semicircle of international spectators. The announcer spoke in perfect American English with the fervor of a sportscaster, or a preacher. He said this cute robo-box could be armed with a 9mm Glock pistol. With that, he cued another man, in a purple shirt and blue jeans, who had been controlling the robot with a tablet like a teenager playing a video game. This man pulled out a pistol and inserted it into the DOGO with an audible click. Was it loaded? The presenter didn't say. The robot started buzzing around the clearing again. I could see the gleam of the metallic pistol barrel through one of its round eyes. The announcer told us, "Simply touch a screen and the DOGO knows your target. The shot is made. And then the target will be neutralized." A soldier, he said, could be trained to deploy a DOGO in "seven minutes." It could execute a number of missions, including "remote reconnaissance." When the DOGO approached the big photographer who was kneeling for a close-up, the announcer cracked, "Don't neutralize the cameraman." The audience chuckled as the DOGO spun away and buzzed up to the announcer himself. "Or the announcer."

I was not in Israel-Palestine to cover the direct IDF military operations associated with the occupation, or their aftermath, such as Operation Protective Edge (2014) or Operation Pillar of Defense (2012). Rather, I was here to research the day-to-day grind of "homeland security" in ordinary life, its products, and how Israel had come to be a dominating force in the border enforcement global industry. Indeed, this convention was similar to others I had visited throughout the globe—in Paris, Mexico City, San Antonio—and exemplified how Israel had become what the University of Ben Gurion's Neve Gordon calls, a "Homeland Security/Surveillance capital."[1]

The conference was buzzing with what seemed—at first—to be innocuous tales. Inside, the flamboyant Prof. Dror Artzi gave a presentation on the "art" of drone development. UAV (unmanned aerial vehicle) systems, he explained, were a complex mixture of engineering and art, "connecting the square with the round." His slides were filled with pictures of his tech students preparing the drones for competitions, underscoring the vast world of student and even youth programs behind today's global homeland security systems. He gushed about being the "supportive professor" who would always encourage students' "crazy" ideas, such as the Nose Camera Turret Design, a camera made to fit in the nose of the drone. (He left it a mystery whether this idea had taken hold or no.)

No idea was too bizarre.

Noam Brook, of the Israeli company Rafael, talked about the Protector and other unmanned boats. Unmanned systems were no longer just in the sky. They were also deployed at sea and on the ground. And they were deployed along borders. Israel Aerospace Industries representative Ohad Dvir spoke at length about RoBattle, the hulking, armored unmanned ground vehicle, surrounded by a half-dozen flowing Israeli flags, that had greeted everyone at the door of the convention center. It had the height and weight of a Humvee and carried a three-ton payload. A similar unmanned ground vehicle, called the Border Protector[2]—a Ford 350 equipped with an Elbit surveillance system—was already rumbling down the roads along the Gaza annexation wall, where mounted machine guns pointed into the place that Noam Chomsky called an "open-air prison."

The Border Protector was the ultimate U.S.-Israeli hybrid, enshrining not only the "special relationship" between the two countries, but also the synergy of their private industries. Such transnational synergy has not only created the drone-patrolled barriers and border zones in Israel and the United States but is also, in powerful ways, what is behind the most massive proliferation of border zones that the world has experienced.

While certainly companies of many other countries have been involved, Israel has long been the leader of an industry that former dissident soldiers of Unit 8200 (the Israeli intelligence outfit often compared to the U.S. National Security Agency) described as being for "the continued control over millions of people through thorough and intrusive supervision and invasion of most areas of life."[3] Although in terms of sheer numbers there were more surveillance companies from the United States, no other country even comes close to topping Israel in surveillance companies per capita: 0.33 companies per 100,000 people, compared with 0.04 in the United States or 0.16 in the United Kingdom.[4] And the list of companies compiled by Privacy International, as pointed out by journalist Alex Kane, doesn't even include companies such as Narus, founded by other Unit 8200 soldiers and bought up by the U.S. company Boeing. Kane called Unit 8200 "a feeder school to the private surveillance industry in Israel." [5]

Israeli innovation is also on the industry's cutting edge. As Lt. Col Leon Altarac said at the conference, "The IDF is the first army in the world to operationally deploy robots to secure the border, gather tactical intelligence, clear roads, and engage in urban warfare." It no longer seems impossible or even unlikely that the RoBattle will one day be commonplace on the world's borders or beyond. What would have been considered the stuff of dystopian science fiction novels 25 years ago—was now rumbling into the world under the banner of security.

After lunch, during which Leonard Cohen and the Beatles sang through the conference halls (which seemed surreal and out of context to me), Ehud Biederman, of the 12,000 employee–strong monolith

Elbit Systems—a military and surveillance company that operates not only in Israel but also in the United States, Western Europe, and Brazil—took the podium. In 2014, Elbit Systems received a prime contract from the U.S. CBP to build a series of surveillance towers along the U.S.-Mexico border.

"The world has changed," Biederman declared, wistfully.

"The challenge," he said, "is much wider."

"Homeland security takes a much bigger place. Today the world is much more gray," and "the shades are multiplying."

Ofer Sachs, CEO of the Israel Export & International Cooperation Institute, echoed Biederman's words when in June 2014 he told the trade magazine *Israel Defense*, "the world is switching from defense to HLS [homeland security]." It is "a growth engine for Israeli exports."[6] Indeed, in the 2020s the global industry is predicted to exceed more than $700 billion, doubling its revenue in 10 years.[7] As one researcher-activist told me in Tel Aviv, "Security has become god."

"THE LABORATORY OF THE EXTREME"

I had not come to Israel-Palestine to report on the occupation, but the occupation was the reason that Israel's homeland security industry was a global leader. The enactment of heavily patrolled lines of division has become a significant part of this occupation, especially since the construction of the West Bank border wall system began in the early 2000s. When I visited one small part of this border wall outside the community Beit Ijza on the West Bank, it was hard to imagine that only fifty years ago this land was Jordan. If you looked at the results of the 1995 Oslo II "peace" accords on a map, it was as if the land had been dropped from a height and its shards glued back together. The whole West Bank had been carved into zones—a world of borders.

All of these borders converged at the house of the Sabri Gharib family, a Palestinian family completely surrounded by the wall. I had come to interview them, but first I stood there, about 100 yards in front of the house, looking out over a two-lane road where a distant military vehicle was slowly descending the crest of a hill. Behind it were the rolling hills of the West Bank, formed by the fissure of the ancient Great Rift Valley, a 5,000-kilometer tectonic crack that I would also see outside Nairobi, Kenya. Jerusalem was only a thirty-minute drive from this place, but the snazzy malls and throngs of tourists there seemed a world away. I raised my camera, ready to shoot a picture.

The jeep slowed. I could clearly see the two soldiers in it, even their faces under their helmets. The soldiers were quite clearly looking up at me. I could see they had guns. I held their gaze for one mesmerizing second, then backed up slowly from where I had been peering down. In the carved-out spaces of the West Bank—there were 165 disconnected islands throughout the three areas designated to the Palestinian Authority, Area A was supposedly free of Israeli presence. The IDF actively policed Area B. In Area C, which represented 60 percent of the West Bank landmass, Israel controlled both security and civil affairs. Now, startled by the soldiers' interest in me, I wondered if I had accidentally stepped into the wrong area. Should I run? Get out of there? Or was I okay? Perhaps I was experiencing "constructive blurring," a term coined by former U.S. Secretary of State Henry Kissinger for a strategy that seeks to simultaneously "obfuscate and naturalize the facts of domination," in the words of forensic architect and human rights scholar and organizer Eyal Weizman.[8]

But there was nothing blurry about the signs all around me. A red one on a steel fence said in Hebrew, Arabic, and English that if I crossed, my life would be "in danger." To my left was a large cement structure with a yellow steel gate opening onto a narrow driveway. The wire mesh fencing over the gate was equipped with detection sensors. It looked like a combination border wall and checkpoint, and I expected soldiers to emerge from it as they do at any one of the hundreds of permanent and mobile checkpoints throughout the Palestinian occupied territory, to examine license plates and papers. I did not expect the gate to lead into the home of the Sabri Gharib family, who had been resisting the occupation for more than three decades.

Weizman writes that to understand the "linear border" here you must understand that the "nation state has splintered into a multitude of temporary, transportable, deployable and removable border-synonyms—'separation walls,' 'barriers,' 'blockades,' 'closures,' 'road blocks,' 'check points,' 'sterile areas,' 'special security zones,' 'closed military areas,' and 'killing zones' that shrink and expand the territory at will." In other words, where I stood looking down at the soldiers was emblematic of how confusingly this territory was divided. The Occupied Palestinian Territories are a "frontier zone," and such zones, Weizman says, are "deep, shifting, fragmented, and elastic territories."

This is also visible in other border zones around the world. The United States, for example, is encircled by a 100-mile border enforcement zone, where not only are constitutional protections waived in the name of national security, but residents' rights are routinely trampled. In 2012, a farmer, Stewart Loew, was out one night irrigating his land near Amado, Arizona. Homeland Security officials saw him and demanded his papers.[9] In Mexico, the frontier zone expands hundreds of miles to the north from the Guatemalan border, as far as Oaxaca and Veracruz, where immigration checkpoints have long been etched into the landscape. Border zones also zigzag through Zapatista territories and places of rich natural resources, ranging from hydroelectric dams to petroleum deposits. A Somali who travels to Nairobi without a movement pass will run into an elastic border that extends into the streets of the Kenyan capital, where cameras perched on metal arches, are constantly blinding drivers at night with their flash photography. Nevertheless, Israel has, as geographer Reece Jones observed in *Violent Borders: Refugees and the Right to Move*, the most complete system of barriers and surveillance in the world. And despite—or because of—the wall system's zigzagging fragmentation, the Israeli apparatus is notorious for its mastery of the strategies and infrastructure of exclusion.

I continued backing off the crest of the hill until I was no longer in the soldiers' line of sight. I didn't think they would shoot, but what did I know? I walked through the gate between the towering steel-mesh separation walls on either side, which created the illusion of a long driveway leading up to the one-story house where the Sabri Gharib family has lived for generations, and where the two children of the family—ages five and two—were playing outside. Atop the gate, a hanging camera transmitted their images and mine seven miles away to the Israeli border police.

This family has become one of the iconic stories of Palestinian resistance to the border wall, and an example of what Weizman characterized as a "laboratory of the extreme," where the borders "may even erupt into Palestinian living rooms, bursting in through the house walls."

The towering electronic barriers here were "sensitive," as Colonel Danny Tirza said in his interview with my fellow researcher Gabriel Schivone, in September 2016, because of the black cables weaving through its steel bars. Schivone and I traveled together to Palestine, Israel, and Jordan on this particular trip, and after much perseverance, he arranged an interview with the Israeli Colonel in a high-end West Jerusalem hotel a couple of days after I returned to the United States. Tirza designed the 420-mile wall that zigzags through the West Bank. If you touched, cut, or climbed on this barrier, or even came near it wearing or carrying any metal, the fence would give "a precise indication of what is going on there," Tirza told Schivone. In places the wall was protected by deep ditches, sniper posts, barbed wire, and minefields, but here at the Sabri Gharib house, such measures are impossible because of the settlement, Ha'hadasha ("Renewed Spirit" in Hebrew), that surrounds the house on all sides. The settlement's large homes with red tile roofs could easily be in suburban Phoenix. They press so close that I could hear the sizzle of a frying pan; the smell of the food wafted from the settlement to where we stood. A woman nonchalantly walked her dog down the lane that ran against the border wall. Author Ben Ehrenreich, describing the site in *The Way of Spring: Life and Death in Palestine*, said, "The house was entirely encaged."

We sat in that one-story stone house on flower-patterned couches. A soft afternoon light came through the open windows. Outside I could see the grapevines. There was almost a feeling of serenity, despite the turbulent history all around us. The power brokers assigned Beit Ijza primarily to Area C (complete Israeli control), with only 6 percent designated Area B. Over the years, Israel has confiscated thousands of dunams (quarter-acres) for various uses, including military bases, settlements, and the separation wall.[10] In 1980 the Giv'on Ha'hadasha settlement seized 159 dunams. Settlers took most of the surrounding land used by the Sabri Gharib and other Palestinian families for growing grapes, vegetables, and olives. During the first 15 years of the resistance, starting in 1979, Sabri Saádat Gharib told Ehrenreich, "there wasn't a year when one of us wasn't in prison." The family refused to move. The well that supplied their water was covered by a strip-mall style parking lot for the settlement. All that remained to them were 61 dunams, a swath that was kept under military lock and key. Like most of the Palestinians in the area, they had to get special permission to access their traditional lands. "They try to make the land unusable so they can take it over again," Sabri told me.

In 2003, to construct the segregating wall, the Israeli military confiscated 334 dunums in Beit Ijza and several other nearby communities, and then more in 2004 and 2005 for further wall construction and military purposes. Sabri Gharib's family stood their ground against the stones and verbal abuse hurled from the settlement. It was in 2006, Sabri said, when the soldiers came and built the gate and locked it shut. He and his family woke up at 6:30 a.m. to a border dweller's worst nightmare: No one could leave. They were locked out and locked in. At 4 p.m., the soldiers came and opened the gate. They said the family could not enter or exit without coordinating with the border police. Imagine having to coordinate with the military every time you needed to go to the grocery store, to drop your children off at school, to have a visit from your best friend. For three months, Ehrenreich writes, they waited for the border police on each occasion, sometimes five minutes, sometimes hours. And still the family stood their ground. Finally, a court decision forced the military to open the gate. But the "smart wall" that surrounded their house stayed.

How had this situation arisen in lockstep with the homeland security industry I had witnessed back in Tel Aviv?

A few days after the conference, Guy Keren, the CEO of Homeland Security Israel—the company that organized the unmanned-systems expo—explained that between 7,000 and 8,000 start-ups are constantly churning out proposals and products in Israel, literally the first station of the global-security assembly belt. How, I asked, did Israel, with a population of eight million, become second in the world for start-up companies, almost equal to the United States, and by far number one per capita?

"It's all about the Jewish mom," he said with a smile.

We were in the IHLS office, located in a Tel Aviv industrial park that on the outside reminded me of the *maquilas* located in clusters in Mexico near where I lived in the U.S. borderlands; it had the same faceless and barren concrete buildings. Inside, though, there were stark differences. The space felt like an oversized Starbucks, with long wooden tables and tasteful art on the walls. Twenty- and thirty-somethings in skinny jeans stared into their laptops, which flashed sketches of drones and camera systems. Dozens of others were stationed in cubicles and in small offices. The global homeland security regime was more than just uniformed guards with guns, more than just the architects, engineers, electricians, and plumbers who built and maintained border infrastructure. One of the world's fastest-growing industries also employed the world's nerds and hipsters.

It was casual Thursday, and Keren wore a black T-shirt. Earlier, he had explained that IHLS had only three full-time employees, but the building could fit 300 subcontractors, who all seemed to be present that day, if the collective buzz of voices was any indication. We were less than an hour as the crow flies from the Sabri Gharib household, but in a whole different reality.

"What's the difference between a Rottweiler and a Jewish mom?" Keren asked as we watched the corporate synergy play out behind him. He answered before I had a chance to reply, "The Rottweiler lets go sometimes." He was only half-joking. The mother pushed you, he said; however, it was the "crazy neighborhood" that put you on the edge. "Since you are thirteen years old you know that there's a chance if you get on a bus you won't get off." Risk was part of being Israeli, he told us. But at the same time, in Israel they were always able to "check their systems," their weapons systems, their surveillance systems. "It's because we are in a war situation all the time. If it doesn't happen right now, it will happen in a month." Stress, Keren said, was moving you forward all the time. "We build it [the surveillance system] in a live situation." This was not just a war; it was a laboratory.

Keren's premise was right in line with political scientist Neve Gordon's description: "Israel's homeland security industry sells its products and services by maintaining that Israel has experienced the horror—not virtually, but firsthand—and consequently both knows how to deal with such horror and has developed the appropriate instruments to do so."[11]

Keren said that in its accelerator IHLS at that moment had seven start-ups in a four-month incubation cycle. The idea was to create companies that could offer a viable product to "one of the fastest-growing markets today," homeland security. He said that most of the employees were engineers, for whom business language was like "Hebrush"—a proverbially unintelligible mixture of Hebrew, English, and Russian. That's where Keren and the IHLS came in. "I'm involved in each and every start-up," Keren said. "I am negotiating with each one. I am arranging meetings with the investors." The real job of IHLS was to use its connections and business know-how to connect these start-ups with the greater market, where borders were increasingly taking center stage.

Perhaps it was here where the Orbiter 3 suicide drone or the Glock-packing DOGO or the sensor systems in the West Bank "smart" wall that surrounded the Sabri-Gharib household had first been imagined. Now these engineers were inventing further technologies—new kinds of drones, robots, biometrics, and tracking. "We know how to help you reach the civilian market," the IHLS website explains, "and of course our unique capability and expertise is to connect you also to the security ecosystem."[12] That ecosystem includes IHLS accelerator sponsors such as Raytheon, Elbit Systems, and Verint, among others—companies that might even purchase the product. Getting the product deployed in the Palestinian occupied territories is a key step in the process. This makes it "combat ready." It makes it "battle proven."

In 2016, Israeli military exports, a good percentage of them attached to homeland security, would grow again by another $800 million to $6.5 billion,[13] and then to a record $9 billion in 2018.[14]

These exports included aircraft and aerial systems, observation and optronics, ammunition and weapons stations, radar and electronic warfare, information and intelligence, unmanned aerial vehicles, telecommunications, and maritime. The record number of sales, reported by Ora Coren and Gili Cohen in *Ha'aretz*, was fueled by "terrorism and Europe's refugee problem."[15]

What about "border security"? I asked Keren.

"Europe," said Keren, "was stupid enough to open their borders to refugees." Europe needed border security, airport security, infrastructure security, electricity security, he explained with irritation. They didn't realize "how deep people are in the inside." There were 1.5 million refugees residing in Germany, and if, as they say, 2 percent of them "are bad"—and here he paused to let us do the math, or maybe for dramatic effect. Well, that was a lot, and they would "rape you and discriminate against the gays."

Meanwhile, Europe was "trying to be politically correct." But thankfully, Keren said, IHLS was spreading its operations across the landscapes of the world. They were working with a Department of Defense/Department of Homeland Security foundation in the United States, Keren told us, though he couldn't disclose the details. An IHLS start-up was working on a border security pilot system in India, but again, that was all he could tell us. They were working with Global Tech Korea, a Korean government agency-foundation created specifically to promote research-and-development collaborations with Israel and share know-how regarding technologies. In fact, there was a large Korean delegation present at the LAGO convention center, and GT Korea had signed a formal agreement with IHLS in order to "promote joint activity in a variety of industries between the two countries."[16] And Keren could not stress often enough that Europe was tired of the whole situation. "The name Mohammed," he said, was becoming more and more common. The world was changing dramatically. "If you let them in, teach them about loving each other, not killing," he said.

At one point he paused, sweeping his hand to highlight the massive office space, this factory of ideas. He wanted to show us the difficulty of their work, how hard it was to get into this business, even if it was lucrative. "Nobody believes in you," he said. "You have to rent an apartment with six of your friends to make ends meet. Sometimes you work a day job and then come in at six at night, and work until the morning. You might have a family. You might have kids." Yet despite all this, "We are making more money than the rest of the world by far." It is a supporting system, he said, but a supporting Israeli system. "So it's kicking you, hitting you, killing you, then loving you." And the industry was driven by the inscripted draft. An Israeli 21-year-old, forced into the Army, Keren said, is older "than an American by a difference of at least ten years." Then, "I prefer that my son goes to the university, but we don't have the privilege to think otherwise."

"All I want to do," Keren said, "is to get home from work and kiss my wife."

Back at Beit Ijza at the Sabri-Gharib house surrounded by the "smart" wall, I asked how to get to the Ha'hadasha settlement, where we could still hear the food frying and smell its aroma. Sabri pointed vaguely toward the horizon, indicating that somewhere in the distance there was a road where only Israelis could drive. You would have to find Highway 436, and then in order to drive on it you would need the correct license plates to get past the military checkpoint. You would also need to show documents. Then there would be another checkpoint at the gate of the colony. Former U.S. President Jimmy Carter said in 2006, "When Israel ... connects the 200 or so settlements with each other, with a road, and then prohibits Palestinians from using that road, or in many cases even crossing that road, this perpetrates even worse instances of apartness, or apartheid, than we witnessed even in South Africa."[17] Former U.S. Secretary of State John Kerry agreed with Carter, saying in January 2017 that if Israel didn't make peace, it could become "an apartheid state." There are 1,661 kilometers of such segregated roads in the West Bank. Palestinian access to these roads was denied by permanent or "flying" (temporary) checkpoints, by military orders forbidding vehicles with Palestinian plates from being on the roads, and also by physical obstacles ranging from fences and gates to cement blocks, dirt mounds, earth walls, and trenches.

This was just a glimpse of what U.S. president Donald Trump called a model. A border wall can work, Trump told Sean Hannity seven days after his inauguration in 2017; "all you have to do is ask Israel."[18] In fact, former Secretary of State Hillary Clinton had already asked Israel, in 2008. Reporting on her trip to Israel and Jordan in 2005, she said:

> The top priority of any government is to ensure the safety and security of its citizens, and that is why I have been a strong supporter of Israel's right to build a security barrier to keep terrorists out. I have taken the International Court of Justice to task for questioning Israel's right to build the fence, and on this trip, I wanted to see the fence with my own eyes. I stood on a hilltop in Gilo and received a detailed briefing from Col. Danny Tirza, who oversees the Israeli government's strategy and construction of the security fence.[19]

Needless to say, Clinton didn't visit the Sabri Gharib household.

Col. Tirza explained the Israeli border system thoroughly to Schivone a few weeks after I went to the Sabri Gharib household when they met in a snazzy West Jerusalem hotel:

> The first thing you have to see is not that you want to build a barrier on the ground. The barrier is just part of the system. The main thing that you want to stop is people from illegal immigration, you want to stop smuggling, you want to stop guns, stop terror, so the first thing you have to define is all the problems that you have to deal with. OK? The second thing is to define the goal. What you want to achieve. In what you want to achieve there are different areas where people will cross only through checkpoints. So you have to pay a lot of attention to the checkpoints themselves, where the checkpoints will be, how the checkpoints will work, how much time people have to wait at the checkpoints, how can we give service to the people who are allowed to cross, and to close the way of the others who are not allowed to cross.

The wall was a part of something much bigger, he said: "It's not enough to construct a wall. You have to construct a whole system around it." He chopped his hand with a vigorous motion for emphasis.

There would be a dense and complex array of sensors and cameras, and there would be soldiers, "Eighteen- to twenty-year-old girls," he stressed, working in dispersed command and control rooms. "Boys cannot do it because boys have no patience." For these soldiers, it was a six-hour detail. Then twelve hours' rest. Another six hours. "The control rooms," Tirza said, "are a special system built here in Israel that we disseminate all over the world."

Contemplating these control centers as a camera hovered over me on the Sabri Gharib property, I thought of how the Israeli barrier and surveillance infrastructure functioned as a panopticon. Everywhere there were the smart walls with camera systems and motion sensors. If the wall was concrete, pillbox-shaped guard towers with window slits were built into the structure. Looking up, you couldn't tell if there was anyone in there or not. French historian and philosopher Michel Foucault wrote that the panopticon was a strategy used in prisons to induce "in the inmate as state of conscious and permanent visibility that assures the automatic functioning of power."[20] Here in Israel, you never knew for certain whether someone was watching from the other end of the camera, but just knowing that they might be was to feel their power—a power, as Foucault defined it, both "visible and unverifiable. Visible: the inmate will constantly have before his eyes the tall outline of the central power from which he is spied upon. Unverifiable: the inmate must never know whether he is being looked at any one moment."

The Sabri Gharib family, in their home where grapes hung from vines, was indeed front and center to the world's newest techno-battlefields of panopticons and surveillance. Inside the house, where interruptions from rambunctious two-and-a-half-year-old Ruba punctuated the interview, it seemed both ludicrous and tragic that this was so.

QALANDIYA

To find out more, I sought out Jeff Halper, Israeli activist and author of *War Against the People*, who argued that what was happening in

Israel-Palestine was a metaphor for the entire world under "the occupation of the ruling classes."

Getting to his house in West Jerusalem from Ramallah, where Schivone and I were staying, was fraught with obstacles. First there was the Qalandiya mega-checkpoint, located in what to an outsider's eye looked like a confusing mess of towering concrete walls and pillboxes; growling, idling cars and their fumes; and soldiers with long assault rifles. The highly surveilled chaotic collision of realities at Qalandiya reminded me in some ways of the international border between Ambos Nogales in the United States and Mexico.

In Qalandiya, people needed to go through five quite confusing stages, all involving turnstiles and soldiers. The first thing I saw was what looked like a cage built for humans. Between the bars, like bars in a jail, was a narrow passage where just one person, entering lengthwise, could fit. Schivone and I lined up like cattle in one of four such narrow passageways along with hundreds of Palestinians. (I assumed that for the most part, Israelis were prohibited from going through Qalandiya). It took me a while to notice the blank-faced soldier sitting behind a window, looking out at all of us from behind thick bulletproof glass that reflected the outside light and, as Weizman had pointed out, functioned in many ways as a "one-way mirror"—another panopticonal device used across the world for border policing. The soldier was in charge of buzzing people through the turnstile, in groups of two or three, and then abruptly locking it again. It took us about an hour and a half to get through, and felt like being strained through the metallic innards of the global classification system. After a while, once claustrophobia set in, I saw the process as a multifaceted and ritualistic act of submission before the soldiers and the cameras. Disembodied monosyllabic commands occasionally echoed throughout the building like incantations. The long, grinding trudge induced a meditation in which each person constantly reaffirmed, perhaps subconsciously, who was the master. This was not just a security measure to protect Israelis, but also an exercise in pacification for everyone else—especially Palestinians.

Qalandiya was the prime example of the twenty-first century breed of war, hidden behind the word "security." And Qalandiya's "upgrade," completed in 2006, was financed at least partially with funds from the United States originally meant for Palestinian reform projects.[21] Fifty million dollars went to twelve closure checkpoints, like Qalandiya, that were intended to serve as "international terminals" between the West Bank and Israel—since Israel brought in the Airport Authority to run them.

The journey from turnstile to turnstile was a micromanaged battlefield. You were the enemy until proven innocent. I wondered if, just as at the U.S. Mexico border, there was some sort of chip detection technology in the building that could sense your passport (or any card with a chip), allowing agents to preview your information in some back room packed with monitors. This by far was the most institutionalized checkpoint I had ever been through, and I had been through my share—including the conflict zones in Chiapas in the late 1990s, where soldiers, standing by a rudimentary bonfire with flames licking up towards the crystal-clear stars, would question you for hours about your intentions. Qalandiya took those interrogations to a new, surreal level. It was as if the National Security Agency had come out of its caves in Utah and you could actually see them—kind of—in front of you.

Once into Jerusalem, we arrived at Halper's apartment in a fraction of the time it took us to get through the checkpoint. We mentioned our experience at Qalandiya. He responded that we are in an age of endless, securocratic wars: border wars in which borders are everywhere that the ruling classes meet the people, the rich meet the poor, the powerful meet the dispossessed.

An example of this? Right where we were sitting in West Jerusalem. Halper pointed out how expensive the apartments above his very office had become. A British man had bought one such apartment, he noted, but was almost never there, coming from more than 3,000 miles away only for holidays and festivities. That didn't sit well with Halper, considering that many Palestinians, some of them fifteen minutes away, could never arrive to his office.

As we talked, Halper underscored everything we had been hearing. In *War Against the People* he had written, "For a small country, Israel has conceived, developed, and manufactured military projects greatly disproportionate to its size, including satellites, the Kfir fighter aircraft, UAVs, Merkava tank, Uzi submachine gun, Galil and Tavor assault rifles, missiles, and many more." The military provided "a fertile breeding ground for future generations of engineers and entrepreneurs." Further, "the ability to develop invasive (if concealed) systems gives Israeli companies like NICE, Verint, Check Point, Narus, Amdocs and hundreds of others that grew out of the IDF a distinct edge on the market, the acceptability of their products limited only by the laws of their clients' countries."[22] Halper's points were the same as Guy Keren's, but through a critical lens.

Qalandiyas were spreading around the world, in the securocratic war that was, he said, "globalizing Palestine." Israel was a "microcosm of the whole world," in terms of the Global North's domination over the Global South:

> You are living in a sense under an occupation. And you are under an occupation of the ruling classes. Then you get into this whole issue of capitalism in crisis. Neoliberalism, the whole system is unsustainable. The whole world is burning up. Income disparities are out of the sky. Even middle-class people are feeling the pressure—the Millennials and the Occupy movement, the *indignados* in Europe. There are many marginalized and impoverished by the system. The ruling classes have to have security states.

Halper told us wars weren't wars anymore: "They are operations." He said, "Israel is selling more than weapons. It is selling a security state."

4.

Securing Inequality on
the U.S.-Mexico Border

At a border technology conference in El Paso, Texas, in 2012, I asked a representative of the Israeli company RT Aerostat Systems whether the surveillance blimp hanging in the rafters of the expo hall could see the words I had scrawled in my notebook. Using the airborne cameras, the vendor zoomed in. Slowly but surely, my handwriting went from blurry to crystal clear on the large monitor for all to see. As in Tel Aviv, I was surrounded by vendors hawking everything from drones to desert-camouflaged armored vehicles, including one from Lockheed Martin that looked so dystopian I could barely take my eyes off it, a *Mad Max* scene, a future that nobody really wanted but everybody was being prepared for. Just five blocks away, the U.S. Border Patrol was policing one of the sharpest lines of division, in terms of inequality, on the face of the earth.

That same day, Israeli Brig. Gen. Roie Elkabetz stood in front of an audience of private-sector businesspeople, uniformed U.S. Border Patrol and other DHS officials, and border-patrol members from other countries, including a man from the Brazilian military dressed in full regalia. As Elkabetz lectured on how Israel did border enforcement, he clicked through a slide show of all of Israel's frontiers: with Egypt, Jordan, Lebanon, Syria, and, of course, the Palestinian occupied territories. Finally, a photo of the enclosure wall that isolated the Gaza Strip from Israel flashed onscreen.

"We have learned lots from Gaza," he said. "It's a great laboratory."

At the time I was shocked that the general had used the word *laboratory* so casually, pausing only briefly before continuing to the next point. Later, I would learn that *laboratory* was part of the common parlance. I had heard the term used to describe the U.S.-Mexico border as well, as if migrants in those borderlands and people in Palestine were not only threats but also specimens under a large security microscope. The idea of synergy between the two "laboratories" was not so farfetched, especially considering the long-standing "special" relationship between the two countries and the lavish funds that the United States has poured into Israel over the years. Stephen Graham, author of *Cities Under Siege: the New Urban Militarism*, has written that the security-industrial and military-industrial complexes of Israel and the United States were so "umbilically connected" that "it might now be reasonable to consider them as a single diversified, transnational entity."[1]

Indeed, one year after the creation of Israel in 1948, the new state received its first U.S. aid: a $100 million export-import loan. It would take another ten years for the United States to grant Israel its first large-scale military loan—$400,000 in 1958—but after that, the faucet stayed open. Only one year after former President Dwight D. Eisenhower's famous farewell speech in 1961 decrying the military-industrial complex, Israel purchased its first advanced-weapons systems from the United States, Hawk anti-aircraft missiles. In 1966 alone—the year before the Six-Day War, in which Israel would seize the West Bank from Jordan (including East Jerusalem), the Golan Heights from Syria, and the Gaza Strip from Egypt—U.S. assistance more than doubled, from $37 million to $90 million. Much of Israel's border building around and inside today's Palestinian occupied territories originated from this historic moment in 1967, and since then it has always been backed by incrementally growing U.S. military and economic aid. By the end of the 1980s, the United States was doling out almost $2 billion annually in military aid to Israel, and in 1999 began sending a series of ten-year military aid packages (at that time worth approximately $2.38 billion annually). Just a few weeks before I trudged through the Qalandiya checkpoint in September 2016, the Obama administration approved the third such ten-year agreement, amounting to $38 billion to be sent between 2016 and 2026, ensuring the small country would continue to be, by far, the largest recipient of U.S. military—and now, homeland security—aid. In total, since 1948, the United States has provided Israel $134 billion in bilateral assistance, out of which $95 billion has been military equipment and arms.[2]

Unlike other recipients of U.S. military largesse, Israel has been able to invest 25 percent of the money directly in its own private industry. (All other U.S. military aid packages require that countries use vouchers to buy their "assistance" from the United States and its industries.)

In January 2015, with a couple of other journalists, I climbed a steep hill on a dirt road in the Coronado National Forest, about ten miles to the north of Nogales, Arizona. From below I could see the scaffolding of a new surveillance tower the Haifa-based company Elbit Systems was building. As I walked, I could see a smattering of people above: a construction crew. When we reached the top of the hill, a burly man wearing a combat helmet and a T-shirt that said "International Towers" met us before we could proceed any farther. He had a gun strapped to his side; the border guard of the border infrastructure. It looked as if the long-term U.S. investment in the Israeli "laboratory" was bearing significant fruit. In 2014, Elbit Systems of America received the much-sought-after and potentially billion-dollar Integrated Fixed Tower contract.[3] Now here the firm was in southern Arizona, building 53 towers equipped with cutting-edge surveillance technology: highly sophisticated cameras that could see seven miles away, even at night, sensing the heat generated by living creatures; ground-sweeping radar systems that also fed into command and control rooms where bleary-eyed agents stared into monitors; thousands of implanted motion sensors that if "tripped" would beep in the same control rooms; and a GPS system able to home in on the exact coordinates of any border transgression. Jacob Stukenberg, a Border Patrol agent I talked to in a July 2018 interview, told me enthusiastically that the Integrated Fixed Tower was a "force multiplier" and that it could do the work of "100 agents." In the West Bank, Elbit had been one of the primary technology contractors for the "smart wall," which included sensors and cameras embedded into the wall itself, underground sensors, and drones patrolling the skies above. In its bid for the U.S. contract, Elbit touted its "ten-plus years' experience securing the world's most challenging border" as a selling point.[4] Much of Elbit's growing revenue—$3.4 billion reported in 2017, 3.6 percent higher than 2016—is a result of increased sales in the border surveillance–homeland security market.[5]

Particularly since 9/11, there has been considerable participation of Israeli companies in U.S. border enforcement. The first surveillance UAVs to do flyovers at the U.S. borderlands were Hermes drones made by Elbit Systems in 2004.[6] (The same drones have been extensively used in the occupied territories, especially Gaza.) And NICE Systems, a company founded by seven ex-IDF soldiers, got a contract from the infamous Joe Arpaio, then sheriff of Arizona's Maricopa County, to provide one of his prisons with closed-circuit television cameras.[7] The Golan Group, also made up of former IDF soldiers, trained U.S. Homeland Security officials in 2008 in Krav Maga, an Israeli martial art characterized by close-contact hand-to-hand combat. They taught Immigration and Customs Enforcement (ICE) agents the importance of seeing "the whites of the enemies' eyes."[8] This was during a time of massive expansion of the U.S. Homeland Security apparatus, particularly of its Border Patrol ranks. Between 2006 and 2008, the department hired 6,000 new agents. From 1994 to approximately 2014, the U.S. Border Patrol quintupled from 4,000 to almost 21,000 agents. Throughout this expansion, which included orienting police forces toward more securocratic combat, Israel has trained U.S. Customs and Border Protection, Homeland Security officials, and thousands of U.S. law enforcement officers in counterterrorism and border and perimeter security. One such program, the Law Enforcement Exchange Program (LEEP) claimed that more than 11,000 U.S. police agents have attended their training courses and conferences. One of those trainees was Gil Kerlikowske, before he became Customs and Border Protection commissioner during the last years of the Obama administration. When he went to Israel, he was chief of the Seattle Police Department. Referring to the importance of corporate participation in law enforcement, he told LEEP what he learned, "I think I need to do a much better job of embracing private industry and going after them, not waiting for them to knock on my door."[9]

The Israeli-U.S. border relationship has continued to be strong. On January 27, 2017, when the Trump administration doubled down on its campaign promise to build a border wall on the U.S. southern divide, Israel's Magal Security Systems, which claimed that it could build the exact wall desired, saw its stock jump 5.6 percent.[10] And in September 2017, DHS chose the Israeli firm Elta North America to build one of the border wall prototypes,[11] to name just a couple of examples.

As Jeff Halper argues, it is not just Israeli technology but also a "security state," an apparatus of practices and policies that is proliferating around the world. War has been reframed, the police have become more militarized; the military has been "policified." While law enforcement agents carry AR-15s and work in zones of exception, like border patrols, soldiers are taking on law enforcement duties; the National Guard polices the border. Halper calls this the MISSILE complex, an acronym for military, internal security, intelligence, and law enforcement. The divisions of the police and military of the nation-state are breaking down and reforming to create an even more powerful force: the crux of homeland security. Israel has modeled a system of control in a world characterized by increasing displacement and upheaval, the "Global Palestine."

To express this concept specifically for the U.S.-Mexico divide, journalist Jimmy Johnson coined the phrase "Palestine-Mexico border."[12]

Brig. Gen. Elkabetz is one of many people involved in the Israeli border and homeland security apparatus who have spoken to U.S. officials and the corporate nexus. In 2018, I saw an official from Elbit Systems—a former battalion and brigadier commander in the IDF—speak about Israel's border successes (the rules of the forum do not allow me to use his name). Comparing the U.S. and Israeli borders, he said, "We have a lot of similarities, but there are differences." As the former commander talked, he laid down the threats as one lays down bricks, building an edifice that stressed terrorism. When asked about the effectiveness of walls, he answered that it was important that walls work in tandem with technology and personnel. He explained just how effective the Israeli system was. He said that in 2014 Israel saw 40,000 immigrants from Sudan, mainly asylum-seekers, come over its Egyptian border. "This was huge for us," he said. In 2017, "we had fourteen." Claiming almost complete operational control of the border, the Elbit representative knew how to sell a product.

In 2012, Bruce Wright, CEO of the University of Arizona Tech Parks, told me his operation was trying to form the largest cluster of border-technology companies in North America right there in southern Arizona. When I asked him where the largest such cluster in the world was, Wright didn't hesitate: Israel.

Officials and practitioners were not bashful about talking about the umbilical connection between the two security leaders.

"If you go to Israel and you come to southern Arizona and close your eyes and spin yourself a few times," Tucson Mayor Jonathan Rothschild told Gabriel Schivone during an interview regarding prioritizing Israeli investment in the state, "you might not be able to tell the difference."

ISRAELI BUSINESS INITIATIVE

That's where inequality enters the story of how the US-Mexico border was manufactured, at least partially, by Israeli companies.

In June 2017, I interviewed a source, who wished to remain unnamed, with intimate knowledge of the work of Israeli companies in southern Arizona. Just the day before, Elta Systems Ltd.—a company that the Trump administration would give one of its wall prototype contracts in September 2017—had done a product demonstration on a ridge overlooking the U.S.-Mexico divide, on land belonging to the Tohono O'odham Nation, a Native American reservation that has a seventy-mile-long border with Mexico. It is common to hear people of the Tohono O'odham Nation, including members of the tribal council, to refer to the post 9/11 influx of U.S. Border Patrol agents as an "occupation." Tohono O'odham veteran activist and humanitarian Mike Wilson called it the model of a "border police state." It is also, apparently, a proving ground. My source said that the Border Patrol had gone looking for a radar system with a high-res camera and batteries that could be set up quickly and then see seven and a half miles.

Elta got one, and installed it in twenty minutes. "That's pretty damn good," he said.

"A wall is just a wall unless it can be smart," he told me. It means nothing unless when people are going around, under, or over it you can provide an immediate response. "We know in Israel," he said, "this is exactly the model they follow with border security." When I asked how long the response time was in Israel, he said, "Well, immediate." In a nutshell, this was what Israel was selling to the United States, not only technology, as Halper pointed out, but an entire strategy, an entire system. My source went on, "Gaza has got the best fencing and walls you can have, and the greatest deployment of technology that looks into Gaza is at the wall, and beyond, and the response there is immediate because the threat there requires it." One immediate response was seen when IDF snipers fired into Gaza in the spring of 2018, right after the U.S. Embassy opened its doors in Jerusalem, as unarmed Palestinian protesters approached the border wall.[13] They killed more than fifty people. The Egyptian-Israeli border, said the source, was different, more similar to what we have here in Arizona: "desert on desert." You don't need an immediate response time, but rather, in the Israeli model, five to ten minutes. This was the selling point. An aggressive, efficient border regime with quick response time, a border apparatus that could bring down an influx of refugees from 40,000 to 14 in just a few years.

In that 2012 interview with Bruce Wright, he said Tech Parks had identified more than fifty border companies already clustered in southern Arizona, and they wanted even more. He explained all the benefits of the park—how companies could test new equipment or methods with mock border crossings or checkpoints on any of the roadways in its 1,345 acres, and how the 18,000 linear feet of fencing surrounding its solar park could be a testing ground for sensor systems to be placed along a future border wall, among other things. Its other advantage was its location in the "field": Companies could test their technologies, much as Elta had that day, right in the border zone itself, maybe on real people.

Perhaps such testing and evaluating was what Wright and his colleagues at UA Tech Parks imagined when in 2012 they initiated

Global Advantage, in order to attract companies from all over the world to set up shop in southern Arizona, across a number of different market sectors that included border technology. One element of Global Advantage was the Israeli Business Initiative, which privileged Israel over all other countries. The intention? A fusion of U.S. academic and corporate knowhow, Mexican low-wage manufacturing, and Israel's border and homeland security companies. (An example of another sector Global Advantage works in is solar.) This fusion would ride the wave of growing demand for policing and surveillance. Global Advantage had originated as a business project based on a partnership between the Offshore Group, a business advisory and housing firm that offered "near-shore solutions for manufacturers of any size" just across the border in Mexico, and Tech Parks Arizona, whose lawyers, accountants, and scholars could help any foreign company set up shop in the United States. This included addressing legal issues, achieving regulatory compliance, and even finding qualified employees.

In the spirit of free trade that created the North American Free Trade Agreement, this corporate-academic border-fortification program is designed to eliminate borders for high-tech companies that want to be headquartered in the United States while manufacturing their products more cheaply in Mexico's *maquiladoras*. When Naomi Weiner, project coordinator for the Israeli Business Initiative, returned from a trip to Israel with University of Arizona researchers in tow, she couldn't have been more enthusiastic about the possibilities for collaboration. "We've chosen areas where Israel is very strong and southern Arizona is very strong," Weiner explained to Schivone by telephone, pointing out the surveillance-industry "synergy" between the two places. For example, one firm her team met with in Israel was Brightway Vision, a subsidiary of Elbit Systems. If Brightway decided to set up shop in Arizona (and up to this point it has not), it could then use Tech Parks' expertise to further develop and refine its thermal-imaging cameras and goggles, while exploring ways to repurpose those military products for border-surveillance applications. The Offshore Group would then manufacture the cameras and goggles in Mexico.

Arizona, Weiner said, possessed the "complete package" for such Israeli companies. "We're sitting right on the border, close to Fort Huachuca," a nearby military base where, among other things, technicians control the drones surveilling the border lands. And then the kicker: "We have the relationship with Customs and Border Protection, so there's a lot going on here."

So consider it anything but an irony that in this developing global set of boundary-busting partnerships, the factories that will produce the border fortresses designed by Tel Aviv start-ups at Guy Keren's IHLS and Elbit and other Israeli and U.S. high-tech firms could end up mainly located in Mexico. Ill-paid Mexican blue-collar workers will manufacture the components of a future surveillance regime, such as Brightway's night-vision goggles, the Glock-toting DOGO, the suicide drone Orbiter 3, all of which may well help locate, detain, arrest, incarcerate, expel, or even kill those same workers if they try to cross into the United States.

GLOBAL PALESTINE

Shortly after Marycruz Sandoval-Pérez and her family moved to Nogales, Sonora, in the winter of 1996, they and about a hundred other people organized a land invasion of an area of forested hills and canyons on the outskirts of town. They had come from the state of Sinaloa with little money, but hoped to find employment in one of the factories, the *maquilas*. Sandoval-Pérez recalls a fierce ice storm that roared through the tract of land where her family squatted; she put her three daughters to sleep under a table with a piece of plastic sheeting draped over it.

The squatters named the new *colonia* Flores Magon, after the brothers often credited with being the intellectual authors of the democratic movement that led to the early-twentieth-century Mexican Revolution. And the view from their new home was sweeping. At night there was the twinkling view of a city that in 1996 was exploding in population, thanks to NAFTA, implemented in 1994. During the day you could see the Santa Rita Mountains in Arizona, where jaguars have been spotted. The sunsets were gorgeous in this place of no electricity, where the squatters put together houses with discarded wood pallets from the factories, using cardboard as insulation. The rooftops were thin corrugated metal that, Sandoval-Pérez explained, barely kept the vicious winters at bay.

In Sonora's Nogales, tens of thousands of people depend on industrial employment in the *maquilas*. About 100 such assembly plants exist in the city; many arrived after 1994, though the Border Industrialization Project—luring companies with high tax breaks and promises of cheap labor—began in 1965. Most of the companies came from the United States: General Electric, Master Lock, Samsung, and Samsonite, to name a few. In many of the *maquilas*, workers drudged away making the electronic components for rocket ships, the aerospace industry, and even the vast global surveillance industry. It is possible that they made components for the towering "smart" walls of the border apparatus that prevented people from vast sectors of Nogales, and the rest of Mexico, from entering into the United States.

The high hill country of Flores Magon was an ideal place to organize —neighbors were situated so they needed only sticks and rocks to push back against any police who dared to come up to evict them. In Flores Magon, they had no electricity, no water, no garbage service. Everything was a struggle. The struggle to acquire each individual service carried its own intense story. When I first met Sandoval-Perez, in 2001, neighbors had developed an intricate system for getting pirated electricity to the homes in the *colonia*.

But the best story was about getting garbage service. Flores Magon was one of the places on the outskirts of town where people from Nogales came to dump garbage. The factories in the *maquila* system paid no local taxes, so while the town attracted more workers, the infrastructure to support them didn't follow. In the case of the garbage, neighbors in Flores Magon organized and sent a delegation to the mayor's office to demand the service. According to Sandoval-Pérez, in the office the mayor pointed up to a map of the city and said, "You don't exist." Sandoval-Pérez gave him a look. "We exist," she said. The mayor looked at the map, and said "I don't see you here." The neighbors returned to Flores Magon. They filled up a truck with mounds of garbage. They went back to the mayor's office and dumped half of it there. They dumped the other half at the front door of the mayor's private residence. Then they left a letter: "Do you think we exist now?" Flores Magon was part of the Global Palestine.

"We are living in a time of extreme and extraordinary inequality," writes Chuck Collins, senior scholar at the Institute of Policy Studies.[14] Today, the richest one percent have more wealth than everyone else on the planet, in a trend that's only increasing. In 1960, people living in the world's richest countries were 33 times wealthier than those living in poor countries, but by 2000, the difference had quadrupled. "The absolute gap between the average incomes of people in the richest and poorest countries," anthropologist and author Jason Hickel writes in *The Guardian*, "has grown 135 percent."[15] Between the United States and Latin America, the figure is 206 percent; between the Unites States and sub-Saharan Africa, 207 percent; and South Asia, 196 percent. "The global inequality gap has tripled in size," in what the International Monetary Fund has warned could be the "defining challenge of our time."

"Wealth, power, and resources are becoming ever more concentrated in the hands of the rich and the super-rich, who increasingly sequester themselves with gated urban cocoons and deploy their own private security or paramilitary forces for the tasks of boundary enforcement and access control," writes Stephen Graham in *Cities Under Siege*.[16]

In Nogales, this enforcement apparatus stares people like Marycruz Sandoval-Pérez and her daughters Brisa, Lluvia, and Neblina—who all work in the factories—right in the face from the U.S. side. A towering twenty-foot wall dominates the landscape; through it, U.S. Border Patrol agents have shot and killed Mexican citizens on Mexican soil. Less visible is the network of sensors and cameras that feed into a command and control room at the nearby fortified U.S. Border Patrol station. All of it is part of the Israeli-inspired "smart wall."

The one time I got a firsthand glimpse into this control center, it was full of men looking up at various monitors showing different angles of the boundary wall and Elbit Systems' Integrated Fixed Towers. They weren't the "girl soldiers" in the Israeli control rooms (that day there were no women at all, that I saw), but it was clearly the same concept, United States–style. The setup here was not as cut-and-dry as the one aimed at by University of Arizona's Global Advantage program—a direct connection with a manufacturing base through a clearly set preexisting program—but instead reflected the normal operation of NAFTA and a neoliberal economic system and its perennial search for cheap labor to do the hard work.

The top four sectors for *maquilas* in Nogales were computers and electronic products; apparel; transportation equipment, including components and parts for the aerospace industry; and electrical equipment.[17] At the time, for national security reasons, U.S. military and border systems were assembled in the United States. Even so, Bruce Wright of Tech Parks told my research assistant, Nora Collins, in 2017, he thought there was an opportunity for an entire national security system to be built in another country, "but it's just a growing area that we're starting to look at." He added, "Now components, if they assemble a radar system or a detector or something like that, might be made in Mexico and then it's brought back in and installed in a system, like a jet or a submarine."

Just a random drive through Nogales and its industrial parks shows a wide array of factories. The town, deficient in infrastructure, is crammed with traffic going up and down its vast hills, some with *colonias*; some with housing projects for *maquila* managers; some with older *maquila* parks of windowless concrete slabs, where workers go for ten-hour shifts, inhaling god knows what; some with post-NAFTA industrial parks and their newer, more modern structures. In between these are crammed in every cheap U.S. fast-food restaurant and Sam's Club–style box store, ready to suck up whatever meager wages stay in Nogales. Charles Gilman, Weiser Lock, and Amphenol Optimize Mexico manufacture computer cables and connector assemblies; Arrow Electronics makes electronic components; Subsem Inc. turns out wires and electric cables; and Curtiss-Wright Controls de Mexico specializes in "military police, search and rescue, border protection, coast guard." The factory's website says, "Customs personnel use our video systems on helicopters in a variety of countries."

Global border enforcement apparatuses are also made in Ciudad Juarez, Tijuana, Reynosa, and other high-tech cheap labor assembly zones around the world. The CEOs of the outsourcing companies, of course, are paid dramatically more than their employees. One FTSE-100 CEO, for example, makes as much as 10,000 garment workers in Bangladesh.[18] Perhaps this striking inequality explains today's global matrix of borders better than anything else.

The average pay for a line worker in a Nogales *maquila* is about 800 pesos per week. With the exchange rate hovering in 2017 at around 18 pesos to the dollar, that amounts to $44 for a whole week on the assembly line. To buy a gallon of milk and a carton of twelve eggs, each costing about 43 pesos ($2.40) at the Nogales supermarket La Ley, you would have to work four and a half hours. To understand what that means in U.S. terms, it would be like spending $32 for your eggs and milk, on a minimum wage of $7.25. In Nogales, a whole chicken costs 34 pesos, a little under $2, the U.S. minimum wage earner's equivalent of more than $13, paid for by some two hours of hard work. The *maquila* worker's pay doesn't even come close to filling a market basket, and much less when you begin to add utilities, clothing, and, increasingly in this climate-shifting world, water. More than terrorism, this is fundamental to understanding today's borders. People like Marycruz Sandoval-Pérez will organize to demand justice in a world that is fundamentally unsustainable and a status quo that separates her and her neighbors in Flores Magon from the mayor. And Sandoval-Pérez was not alone. Globally, 4.2 billion people live on less than $7.40 per day—a number that has, according to Hickel, "increased dramatically" since 1981. This was the conservative estimate of the minimum wage for people to achieve "basic nutrition."

Nogales was not Palestine. But if one of these workers dared to cross into the United States without papers, as many indeed do, like a Palestinian, he or she will become enmeshed in an Elbit-built cyber-physical wall.

The term "border security" effectively blinds us to the deeply personal decisions an individual or family must make to cross a heavily militarized border. Even when parents are skipping meals so the children can eat, want the kids to have a good education instead of going to work at an early age, or simply be warm on a frigid winter night, the decision to sacrifice life in their country to migrate for the greater good of their family is not easy, never lightly taken. It is this sacrifice that is superseded by the term "border security," which designates everyone who breaches a border without proper documents a criminal. The rhetorical nature of the word choice stunts the empathy most would have for people traveling through dangerous situations. Framed by "border security," the story begins when a person becomes illegalized. What life is like in Nogales doesn't matter. What life is like in Beit Itja doesn't matter.

In such a way, I begin to understand the lack of empathy exemplified by DOGO and the suicide drone. In such a way, I begin to understand both the differences and similarities between the Sandoval-Pérezes and the Sabri Gharibs. In both cases, their images have surely appeared in Elbit Systems–designed control rooms.

Part Three

Borders of Empires:
The Colonial Creation Story

In vain do we march with unprecedented strides to empire so colossal, outvying the antique, beyond Alexander's, beyond the proudest sway of Rome. In vain have we annex'd Texas, California, Alaska, and reach north for Canada and south for Cuba. It is as if we were somehow being endow'd with a vast and more and more thoroughly-appointed body, and then left with little or no soul.

Walt Whitman

We are still waiting for our welcoming ceremonies.

Colleen Cardinal

5.

Maps of Empires

You wouldn't have known it was an international border. The only reason I knew was that John Ole Tira, the Maasai man who was driving, came to a stop. "We are at the border," he said. We'd been driving for over an hour on a network of bumpy dirt roads through the Maasai Mara, and this place looked like everywhere else. We had seen herds of zebra moving in long lines in a migration pattern over the vast, flat plain. In the distance was a mountain, called the Sleeping Maasai, shaped like a person lying face upward in blissful rest. There was tall grass all around, swaying gently in the breeze—grass that people warned you harbored snakes. I could see the distant silhouettes of three large elephants and four giraffes, part of a landscape that was becoming golden in the setting sun. When we got out, Tira pointed down to a somewhat crumbling small marker off to the side of the road: the international border.

"So that grass is in Tanzania and this grass is in Kenya?" I asked, pointing to either side of the road. "Yes," Tira said. "And those elephants are Tanzanian?" Tira smiled. Yes, my joke was mediocre. We were only a couple of weeks from the great wildebeest migrations. They would cross the Sand River into Kenya in a huge looping path that made international political boundaries look silly. The Maasai themselves were pastoral and semi-nomadic and had historically negotiated boundaries with the animals and peoples of this gorgeous landscape. Borders, to the Maasai, were things that were always moveable, porous, never fixed, never hardened, never militarized. And the negotiation of a border happened between peoples, peoples and the biosphere, or peoples and animals meeting on equal ground.

Before I'd arrived in the Kenya-Tanzania borderlands, a few days earlier, I'd been in Israel and Palestine, where "boundaries" marked by gigantic concrete walls had been imposed, not negotiated. And I lived near the U.S.-Mexico border, only 60 miles from where the 20-foot border wall snakes up and down through the city of Nogales. To my eyes, this African landscape seemed much more open and free, devoid of the intense surveillance systems and armed patrols I'd grown used to seeing. Unlike the pronghorn antelope in the Sonoran desert, the wildlife of the Kenya-Tanzania borderlands—including lions and leopards and ostriches—did not have to come head-to-head with a border wall imposed on their habitat. There were dirt roads, but not the national security F150s that ripped through the landscape in Arizona, creating thousands of miles of wildcat routes. It wasn't too long ago that most political borders around the globe were invisible, like this one.

But things can change quickly. On the way to the border we drove by a surveillance tower Tira had not seen before. "I know the Mara like the palm of my hand," he told me. Earlier, we'd passed within feet of panting golden lions to get a close-up view of their muscular jaws and sharp teeth, but he wanted to keep his distance from the technology. We rumbled through a pack of zebras on the move, but drew off some fifty yards before, as if the tower could attack. The zebras ignored it completely.

At the crumbling monument, however, there was an illusion of nothingness, no sign of surveillance at all. It wasn't until later, when I talked to Meitamei Olol-Dapash that I realized this border was a much more powerful impediment than appeared at first glance. Olol-Dapash was a respected Maasai elder long-involved in a boisterous land-rights movement; and while I was in Kenya in June 2017, a candidate for parliament in an election that was only a few months off. Even without walls, barriers, obvious surveillance systems, the rumbling vehicles of border guards, or any other such markers of an international boundary line, Olol-Dapash said, the border was a "tool of oppression."

Olol-Dapash—whose Maasai mother had been born on the other side of this arbitrary line, in Tanzania—called the boundary a "product of colonial power when they were partitioning Africa, with their own political and economic interests." By *they* Olol-Dapash meant the European colonial powers, "a bunch of white guys sitting around the table," at the 1884 Berlin Conference.

Where borders were "visually indistinct," wrote geographers James Anderson and Liam O'Dowd, "they are typically the bearers of a wider symbolism as the material embodiment of history."[1]

The borderline we saw in the Maasai Mara was established at the conference, convened by German Chancellor Otto Von Bismarck. Representatives of European powers met for months in a room dominated by a large map of Africa. They carved up the continent as if it were a slab of meat. The British got Kenya, along with present-day Egypt, Ghana, Nigeria, South Africa, and Uganda. Today Kenya has two official languages, English and Swahili, and 60 other languages besides, including Maa (the language of the Maasai), but English dominates the billboards and political gatherings. In cars, the steering wheel is on the right-hand side. Kenya gained independence in 1963, so the colonial period is relatively recent history, still widely remembered and talked about. Everyone in Maasailand knows that fixed boundaries are a legacy of colonial days, imposed by colonial powers. Germany snagged Tanzania at the Berlin Conference, the other side of the divide where I saw the elephants and giraffes. The French maintained dominance over huge swaths of land in Africa's north and west. Angola and Mozambique went to Portugal. And Congo to Belgium. The "Dark Continent," as the Europeans called it, acquired its international boundaries without most people who lived there even knowing it.

"Just as the partition of British India paid little attention to the linguistic, economic, or ethnic communities of South Asia," Reece Jones writes in *Violent Borders*, "the boundaries established in Berlin did not consider local conditions such as tribal affiliations, language communities, or traditional economic networks." Jones also writes that the Berlin Conference was one of the historic foundational events of the "movement restrictions" we see at borders today.[2] Olol-Dapash took this idea even further when I spoke with him at the Maasai Education and Research Institute, which he helped found in 1987:

"Technocrats designed the whole thing to disenfranchise Africa." The drawing of borders—the Kenya-Tanzania border specifically—was a "gross injustice," a violation of indigenous rights. The impact has "left lasting psychological and economic suffering," he said. "We don't see it ending unless the United Nations enforces the Declaration of Indigenous Rights."

While post-9/11 U.S. border externalization did represent a modern paradigm shift, in another way, it was deeply rooted in this imperial and colonial past. The Berlin Conference demonstrated that border externalization first emanated from colonial power when the nations of Europe—and later the United States—sliced up Africa, the Middle East, Asia, and Latin America. As Olol-Dapash concluded, the colonial line of division that slashed through indigenous communities on his land was not unique to the Maasai: It was a human rights violation and historic injustice perpetrated worldwide.

THE NATURALIZATION OF NATIVISM

Shut your eyes for a moment and imagine a map of the world. Most likely, you see it divided as it was at the Berlin conference, in a series of straight lines. Imagine that Kenya-Tanzania border as a straight line from Uganda to the Indian Ocean. Imagine the Syrian divide with Turkey or the Egyptian land borders, which look as if they'd been drawn with a ruler, much like a good swath of the U.S. border with Canada. On maps, what Jones calls "arbitrary borders and artificial states"[3] overshadow the majestic mountain ranges of the world, overshadow its networks of rivers and beautiful lakes. On the map you imagine, countries within these lines of division may even be color-coded. On most maps, the lines around countries are so prominently drawn as to give a sense they were present from time immemorial, as if international borders rose from the earth's tectonic plates, like mountains, or from its fissures, like rivers. Yet political borders, the ones that today are considered sacrosanct, almost always came from colonial powers. And this context of colonial domination has been seared into maps and minds and worldviews.

In other words, political boundaries between nation-states are relatively new. And hardened, militarized borders are a very recent development.

It wasn't until the late nineteenth century, around the same time as the Berlin conference, that governments began to make distinctions "between their own citizens/subjects and others, a distinction that could be made only on the basis of documents," as historian and sociologist John Torpey puts it.[4] Prior to World War I, passports were only required during times of war, to prevent the unchecked movement of possible enemy agents or sympathizers. However, Torpey writes, the documents "sharpened the line between national and alien"—"alien" is the official term used to describe undocumented outsiders—and contributed to a dynamic now omnipresent in discussions around borders: "the naturalization of nativism." The United States did not have a peacetime passport requirement until after World War II. And yet, since lofty (though selective) declarations of rights found their first expression in the famed American document of 1776, "citizenship" has depended on where you were born and, originally, whether you paid property taxes. The first U.S. Constitution upheld slavery, denied women the right to vote, and distinguished between the citizen and noncitizen—creating a precedent for applying the term *illegal* to human beings. Jones notes, "the category for slaves was eventually abolished, but the distinction between citizen and noncitizen remains, and the constitutions of newly independent countries continued to incorporate these distinct categories and reserve the majority of rights for citizens, not all humans." This has created a huge number of illegalized and stateless people, randomly disenfranchised by the geographical location of their birth. Citizenship, as Branko Milanovic has shown in his extensive research on inequality, has been one of the greatest determinants of life outcomes.[5]

The imposition of a border in the first place, Anderson and O'Dowd wrote in their discussion of border contradictions, creates a "paradox of origins." The "origins of democracies are generally undemocratic," because the imposition of a new nation usually involves physical force or other coercion. "Typically it is violence or the threat of force, rather than democracy, which is embodied in state borders." Hand in hand with this paradox goes the "politics of forgetting." For the "democracy" to appear legitimate, its brutal origins must be forgotten.[6]

Look at a map of the world and think how many of the borders you see came with their own set of distinct historical events exemplifying the paradox of origins and the politics of forgetting. Most of those border histories originated in a world dominated by European imperial powers and, before that, by private property—a concept unknown in most of the world before the seventeenth century, and not recognized even in Europe until the end of the Middle Ages, although arguably Europe had been preparing for it with its monarchist system administered by kings, lords, vassals, and the church. The Midlands Revolt of 1607, which Reece Jones calls one of the four events of world historic importance behind today's global system of militarized border zones, was one of the first insurrections against privatization, in this case, the enclosure of common lands in rural Great Britain.[7] The end result exemplified the brutal politics of border origins: State forces massacred fifty people and captured and imprisoned hundreds more, and then imposed their new system of bounded private property.

When the European concept of private property was "exported," it was quite baffling to people like the Maasai in southern Kenya, Olol-Dapash recalls in his still unpublished autobiography, *London is Burning: The Life of a Maasai Activist*. He writes that private ownership is inefficient: "When you share, you have more yourself. When land, water, housing, food is privately owned, everything must be replicated—I will need my own set of tools, which sit idle most of the time, my own store of food, which might become moldy with age, and my own pasture, where grasses will die before they are eaten." He describes the common land: "In Maasailand we travel without carrying anything because moving between villages is like moving between rooms of a very large house; it is all 'home.'" And the land is also shared with "wildlife and trees and water, with all the natural world." And although this worldview was en route to a head-on collision with the British colonial freight train after the Berlin Conference, it remains a powerful counterpoint today to the view that accepts a world fraught with lines of division.

It is safe to say that those seventeenth-century British "commoners" —the small farmers of rural England—felt much as did Olol-Dapash and the Maasai when state powers sought to divide their communal land into private territories. More than 5,200 enclosure bills, worth some 6.8 million acres, were enacted in the English Parliament between 1607 and World War I. As Britain's land became more and more enclosed, says geographer Ian G. R. Shaw in *Predator Empire*, "commoners were brought inside a growing technological civilization, stripped of their land and the rights attached to it."[8] The result, in Shaw's analysis, was inevitable: "The war machine and the machines of war, that military-industrial complex," he writes, "arise from attempts to destroy the world's commons." Not only did enclosure lay the general foundation for the system of separate nation-states, but it was also a way to successfully manage and operate a global empire.

The moment of transition followed another seventeenth-century calamity, the Thirty Years' War. The Peace of Westphalia, the series of treaties that concluded that war, besides consolidating state authority and a system of international diplomacy, also marked the emergence of a system of boundaries drawn to designate the new nation-states that "claimed absolute authority over all land, resources, and people in a territory based on borders drawn on a map."[9]

The first boundary stones were laid between Sweden and Brandenburg, much like the crumbling marker I saw on the border between Kenya and Tanzania. The kingdoms of Spain and France were divided along the Pyrenees. Nation-state by nation-state, Europe began to institutionalize the post-Westphalian system. Anderson and O'Dowd point out that the borders of nation-states were "coercive, disabling, and limiting, including and excluding many people against their will," but also "benign and enabling, providing the basis for security, dominant forms of identity, and conventional representative democracy. 'Prison' or 'refuge,' they can facilitate oppression or provide an escape from it."

With the implementation of bounded countries also began the most intense and expansive period of colonization in world history. In the seventeenth and eighteenth centuries, the new European nation-states overran the rest of the world from the Americas to Asia, "removing local leaders, mapping the land, and creating European-style political systems."[10]

By the time these powers got to Africa in the late nineteenth century, the integral relationship between drawing political borders and colonization went hand in hand. Comparing the pre–Berlin Conference maps with those drawn post-Berlin sharply illustrates this dynamic. At the Maasai Educational Resource Center office where Olol-Dapash worked and Prescott College ran a program, there was a series of maps on the wall. The first depicted Maasailand in 1890, after the Berlin Conference but before the implementation of the lines of division. This map shows no political borders, only networks of rivers connecting with lakes extending from today's Kenya to Tanzania; that is, boundaries defined by the natural contours of the land, by waterways and mountain ranges, divisions imposed by the earth itself. The international boundary where the grassy plain on either side still looks the same, where the zebras, giraffes, elephants, and wildebeest still cross freely, didn't exist.

But by the first decade of the twentieth century, it did exist, slicing through the heart of the map in one incisive line, dividing Maasailand and the Maasai population in half, and incidentally disabling the Maasai as a political force. "I know that this was done on purpose," Olol-Dapash told me. On top of that, a series of fragmented interior borders and enclosures had been established, including the first Maasai "reservations," modeled on the South African Bantustans of the apartheid era and the reservations for Native Americans in the United States. This system not only facilitated the seizure of previously common lands and resources by colonial settlers, but also was a mechanism to control and pacify the native population. Borders, as Olol-Dapash reiterated time and time again, are from the indigenous perspective a human rights violation. Suddenly the Maasai had to carry identification, and could not leave the enclosures without risk of arrest.

Although the reservation system with its internal boundaries was abolished in 1963, the Kenyan Independence (from Great Britain) brought a new, international boundary, dividing the countries of

Kenya and Tanzania. To many Maasai, independence meant next to nothing. The creation of the Kenyan nation-state, like the Peace of Westphalia and the Treaty of Berlin, expressed a world of lines and divisions that came directly from the colonial powers. And along with the international border came a whole new set of boundaries and private property enclosures that hindered and limited the Maasai's mobility on their traditional land. All of this Olol-Dapash explained to me as we sat before a crackling fire on that cool June morning. Hitching his red checkered *shuka* over his shoulder, he assured me that his people would continue to resist these fixed, non-negotiated lines of division that impeded them.

6.

The Caribbean Frontier

After spending several minutes painting a dreary picture of Caribbean drug routes, Michael McCaul, chairman of the Subcommittee on Oversight, Investigations, and Management of the House Committee on Homeland Security, pulled up a chummy photo of then–Venezuelan President Hugo Chavez and then–Iranian President Mahmoud Ahmadinejad and showed it to his audience at a 2012 congressional hearing titled "U.S. Caribbean Border: An Open Road to Drug Traffickers and Terrorists."[1] He paused to let the image sink in.

"Iran and the Bolivarian states [at that time Venezuela, Bolivia, Ecuador, and Nicaragua], which are major drug producers, bring a dangerous new set of threats to the Western Hemisphere as they work together with transnational organized crime enterprises and terrorist groups," he said, emphasizing the threat of "asymmetrical warfare" against the United States and the use of weapons of mass destruction. "This is not a regional problem that won't reach our shores—these *are* our shores."

McCaul was evidently aware that most people don't realize the United States extends so far. Indeed, after Hurricane Maria eviscerated Puerto Rico in September 2017, one poll revealed that only 54 percent of people in the United States knew that the Caribbean island, which was seized by the United States in 1898 during the Spanish-American war, is a U.S. territory or that its people are U.S. citizens.[2] McCaul was forcing his listeners to reckon with the much more expansive notion of the United States. The case of Puerto Rico shows not only the elastic nature of the U.S. border but also how the idea of an expanding "frontier" has played an integral part in U.S. history.

The Spanish-American War and the U.S. seizure of not only Puerto Rico but also the Philippines, Guam, and Cuba offer an initial glimpse into the expansion of U.S. imperial power in the Pacific and the Caribbean. Geographers Jenna Loyd and Alison Mountz, in their book *Boats, Borders, and Bases: Race, the Cold War, and the Rise of Migration Detention in the United States*, write that the U.S. "empire of military bases" in these regions from the Cold War era "would remain fundamental to [U.S.] economic and political objectives."[3] And further, while the United States deployed some bases on the "periphery of empire," their placement also had a more aggressive objective and a forward-reaching operation. These bases were called "lily pads" by the U.S. military and were used to facilitate strategic movement and "exercise control in decolonizing regions." On a trip to Puerto Rico in 2012, I was able to connect this history with a system of militarized border enforcement. In fact, it was during this trip that my idea of the U.S. border radically changed.

THE LILY PAD

The distance from Ponce in Puerto Rico to Caracas is approximately 500 miles, half the distance Puerto Ricans must travel to get to the United States. There is only one U.S. Border Patrol sector outside of the continental United States, and that is the Ramey sector, which covers Puerto Rico and the U.S. Virgin Islands. It is worth mentioning here that the United States security forces consider the Caribbean to be a climate-change hot spot—a 2003 Pentagon-commissioned report describe the potential impact of global warming there as "particularly severe"[4]—as seas continue to rise and vicious hurricanes spin more strongly over heating ocean waters.

It was on my 2012 trip that I met with Wilfredo Ramírez, the law enforcement agent for the Puerto Rican Department of Natural and Environmental Resources who worked on Mona Island in the Mona Strait—the stretch of water that separates Puerto Rico from the island of Hispaniola. The moonscape island was more than a nature preserve and a U.S. territory, I found; it was also a small fragment of U.S.

border, a "lily pad" that allowed U.S. Homeland Security—including the U.S. Border Patrol—to operate just 30 miles from the Dominican Republic. That's excruciatingly close—the same distance as San Diego is from Tijuana.

Ramírez connected with me in Aguadilla, near the Border Patrol, Coast Guard, and DHS stations on Puerto Rico's west coast, a Homeland Security cluster that had replaced the Ramey air force base. At first I was astonished to see the green-striped Border Patrol vehicles so familiar in Arizona rumble to and from their Puerto Rican station surrounded by coils of concertina wire, presumably for detention of migrants. Before Ramírez's deployment to Mona Island, he'd worked in Aguadilla and paralleled the general region. As we drove, he showed me the places along the shore around Mayaguez where he used to search for unauthorized migrants. He showed me stretches of beach where the Dominicans might land. I was quickly taken with Puerto Rico's west coast, with the sweeping view of the Mona Strait and the dark green canopy that hung over the coastal road as we drove. I asked Ramírez whether he—although he was an environmental police officer, whose job was to search for environmental hazards— also had the power of the Border Patrol to arrest people without documents. He told me that an officer who didn't arrest an undocumented person could be fired. Non-arrest was considered an "omission." The mere fact that undocumented people were here was a crime, he said. Later, sociologist Michael González of the University of Puerto Rico in Mayaguez would tell me that an "Arizona law" already existed in Puerto Rico, and it was uncontroversial.

That very year, Ramírez told me, a 185-foot freighter carrying some 80 Haitians had run aground on Mona Island. He figured the captain of the boat had "fallen asleep." Before the freighter scraped the shore, the Haitians had been in international waters heading to St. Martin, one of the British Virgin Islands. They had "papers to work there," Ramírez said. The moment they set foot on Mona Island, however, they became "aliens" under U.S. immigration law. Even so far away from any logical conceptualization of what the United States is, the U.S. border had swallowed them whole.

Ramírez said, "If they had stayed on the boat we would not have arrested them." But the Haitians had—understandably—abandoned the wrecked ship and swum in through the sharp coral reefs to shore, only to be corralled by two Natural Resources police fulfilling their border-enforcement role. As was standard, the two agents called the U.S. Border Patrol. It took them "two days to get there." He said that it was because there were too many people already stuffed in the Border Patrol's jail, which was located right at the station in Aguadilla. The United States government charged the Haitians with "illegal entry," an administrative misdemeanor—but enough to justify their incarceration. This was the precise moment when my concept of the U.S. border, my idea of where it was and what it meant, drastically changed.

HOW THE EMPIRE'S BORDER ARRIVED IN PUERTO RICO

Puerto Rico was a good place to start to understand how U.S. territorial expansion in the nineteenth century set the blueprint for today's empire of borders. As journalist Juan Gonzalez notes in *Harvest of Empire: A History of Latinos in America*, U.S. expansion did not "climax with the closing of the western frontier;" in 1890; "rather, it reached its culmination with the Spanish-American War of 1898."[5] The war was the first U.S. foray into European-style colonial expansion overseas. It would not only forever change the true location of the U.S. border from the one recorded on the map, but also in important ways lay the foundations for twenty-first-century international border policing.

In the nineteenth century, the U.S. border on the North American continent was already malleable, changeable, and arbitrary. In 1821, the U.S.-Mexico border was where modern-day Louisiana ended and Texas began. During Donald Trump's 2016 presidential campaign, people joked that he should build his wall along that earlier border. Then the towering concrete edifice he envisioned would have followed the southern edge of today's Oklahoma, cut right through the center of Colorado, and stretched north all the way to southern Oregon. Imagined in the context of today's borders, that region would have constituted 55 percent of Mexican territory.

In 1821, the U.S. map included Florida for the first time. Before the Adams-Onis treaty of 1819, a particularly contested part of the U.S. southern border was the divide between Georgia and New Spain. Intense waves of European and Anglo colonial settlers had constantly attacked and often viciously displaced indigenous people in the area, undermining Spanish rule. One such settler was a speculator named Andrew Jackson, who eventually became a U.S. army commander and then president of the United States. This seizure of control over Florida, which the treaty legalized as the Florida Purchase, was one of three phases of development in the nineteenth-century U.S. border, which constantly shifted and remade itself, cumulating with the 1898 Spanish-American War.

In the nineteenth-century U.S. lexicon, the term *frontier* had multiple, changing meanings, and the rhetoric it produced was very different from the black-and-white, legal-or-illegal, criminal-or-innocent rhetoric that surrounds it today. The idea of frontier was a prism through which the world's newest expanding empire viewed its prerogatives and its future. "Facing west meant facing the Promised Land, an Edenic utopia where the American as the new Adam could imagine himself free from nature's limits, society's burdens, and history's ambiguities," historian Greg Grandin writes, "No myth in American history has been more powerful, more invoked by more presidents, than that of pioneers advancing across an endless meridian."[6]

To protect that potential, cross-border policing and military patrols have been in existence since the origin of the United States. According to Ethan A. Nadelmann in his book *Cops Across Borders: The Internationalization of U.S. Law Enforcement*, *frontier* referred to "lands outside the jurisdiction of the United States, claimed by various European powers and inhabited by assorted Indian nations, that would be eventually purchased, seized, or otherwise acquired by the United States."[7] And even after the U.S. acquired them, those territories were still defined as frontier, regardless of who was or had been already living there, until they were "settled" by European immigrants. The doctrine of Manifest Destiny in this nascent nineteenth-century empire, and the idea of white supremacy associated with that doctrine, still courses through the veins of today's United States as American exceptionalism, according to border historian Guadalupe Castillo, who described the superiority complex as the "psychology of patriotism of the nation-state."[8]

One could say that the U.S.'s southwestern border was finally fixed after the Treaty of Guadalupe Hidalgo in 1848 and the Gadsden Purchase in 1853–54. Although history often refers to "treaties" and "purchases," it was a blood-soaked war, famously denounced by Henry David Thoreau, that imposed today's U.S.-Mexico border. The division was fixed with little negotiation, most notably none with the indigenous people who had lived on the land for thousands of years. The true history of the Mexican-American War and of the Gadsden "purchase" embodies the "violence of origins." It wasn't as much a purchase as the seizure by the United States of today's southern Arizona and Tohono O'odham land from Mexico at gunpoint. And overall, once that 55 percent of Mexico was seized, in came the private property mentality reminiscent of the enclosures of early seventeenth-century England. U.S. Senator John Logan in 1883 explained to the Lakota Chief Sitting Bull how Manifest Destiny was effectively parceling up land: "the government feeds and clothes and educates your children now, and desires to teach you to become farmers, and to civilize you, and make you as white men."[9] Similar were the sentiments of colonial settlers in nineteenth-century Mexico (now Texas) who considered Mexicans to be racially inferior, "a mongrel race."[10]

The United States, like almost all colonial powers, those of the Berlin Conference being one example, drew borders without consulting those whom they would enclose and divide. The new power did not conceive of the border as something to be negotiated, in good faith and with respect, between one people and others, between humans and the living earth. The U.S. border was, instead, an expression of one nation's Manifest Destiny.

Every schoolchild knows the contours, and the contents, of U.S. territorial boundaries, but not necessarily what lies outside them. There are maps that show the other North American nations, Mexico and Canada, as featureless tracts, with transfrontier rivers and mountain ranges abruptly ending at the U.S. borders. There are meteorological maps that do the same, as if weather systems didn't cross from the U.S. into Mexico or vice versa. Certainly this insular view has helped develop the sort of nationalism that pervades most public life in the U.S., fueling a rhetoric of a unified people despite the many, and often major, differences in the lives and histories of the various individuals and peoples who inhabit the nation-state. A July 4, 2018 tweet about the "American people" by Professor Tom Nichols of the Naval War College is just one example: "We are generous. Emotional. Brave. Quick to act. We look for the right and we do it. We produce bravery that is unrelated to the soil beneath our feet and we fight like wolves far from home. We are a remarkable people."[11] As Nichols' unifying exceptionalism implies, the United States is much bigger than what is within its actual territorial boundaries. There is the United States on a map whose "sea to shining sea" shape everyone knows. And there are the borders of the United States empire, which make a completely different shape, invisibly extending farther than once seemed possible, where we will nonetheless "fight like wolves ..."

How often in the modern lexicon, especially in sports, does *world* stand for the United States. The World Series is one example. And we call the team that wins a title in a national league, such as the NBA or the NFL, "world champions," not U.S. champions. In Latin America and the Caribbean, no one speaks of North America and South America: "America" is used to refer to an entire connected continent. Yet in the United States "America" is often used to refer only to the United States, much to the chagrin of many Latin American scholars and activists. Whether intentionally or not, this way of speaking expresses Latin America's historic subjugation by the United States, as if the whole land mass to the south, with its wide variety of countries, peoples, languages, and traditions, were only the North's "backyard"—a subordinate part of the U.S.'s gigantic sphere of influence, an exploitable part of its empire. The "backyard" concept dates to the early nineteenth-century Monroe Doctrine, when, in 1823, President James Monroe declared Latin America a place appropriate for the United States, not Europe, to colonize. "Backyard" has survived nearly two centuries and was repeated as recently as 2013, by

Secretary of State John Kerry.[12]

How can a country such as the United States be at once so claustrophobically confined to its own echo chamber and ubiquitous in the world outside? Such is the challenge to understanding both the delirious beginnings of U.S. empire building and how the current U.S. empire is managed and maintained today.

William Walker, a U.S. mercenary and freebooter, attempted to invade Mexico in 1853, hoping to establish a new English-speaking slaveholding colony, and declared himself ruler of the country of Sonora (a state in northern Mexico). After the Mexican army booted him out, Walker usurped the presidency of Nicaragua, where he actually did "rule" from 1856 to 1857, before being expelled by allied Central American military forces. Walker's adventures in the region ended when the Honduran government executed him in 1860. Nevertheless, he embodied the dynamics that would fuel Washington's zeal that resulted in the 1898 Spanish-American War.

To trace these beginnings of U.S. empire and how it relates to today's expansive border building dynamic, I made an early morning drive through the pouring rain on Puerto Rico's west coast to the home of Ricardo Padilla Matos, the retired *comandante* of Puerto Rico's 2,000-strong Joint Force of Rapid Action unit (FURA), part of the Caribbean Border Interagency Group (CBIG). I traversed a beautiful stretch of land where red-flowered tamarind trees had overgrown the rolling hills that fell into the sea. With no GPS system on my flip phone, I was dependent on Matos's old-fashioned directions. As I was navigating the crisscrossing roads through the Puerto Rican landscape, sometimes in a complete state of confusion, he would say, on the phone, in Spanish, "Stop at the baseball diamond, call again, and I will give you directions." When I finally arrived at his small aqua-painted house, I hurried on to the patio, past several cars and a small boat in the driveway. The early morning smell of rain was intoxicating. Matos, or Chalete as he preferred to be called, had been a boat captain for FURA for many of the 27 years he spent in the Puerto Rican Police Department. Most of that time he worked with the 1,000-strong border enforcement unit. On this day he wore a blue cap and a blue shirt emblazoned "Chicago." He jumped right into it.

He said the migrants had no life-saving equipment. He said there were sharks in the Mona Strait. He said it was a long journey; the quickest run was three days. If the migrants reached the shore, they proceeded to San Juan.

On the job he'd encountered not only *indocumentado*s, mainly Dominicans, but also Colombians with "*cargamento*," drugs. They used to capture 2,000 to 3,000 people per month, he told me, but this number had come down in recent years. It was good to catch the undocumented as part of his outfit's partnership with the U.S. Border Patrol, he told me, because if they didn't, then the government would have to give the migrants benefits.

"If they don't have papers," Matos said, "they aren't supposed to get these benefits."

The day before, I'd stood on the coast in Aguada, a couple of hours to the north, with community activist Juan Junior Santiago. Santiago had pointed to an antenna tower supposedly used for surveillance and said, with a bit of a chuckle, that Dominican migrants used this antenna as a landmark. The beach where we stood had a beautiful view of the Mona Strait. Santiago described how the *yolas*—the name given to the rickety boats used in unauthorized crossings— crashed onto the coast, scratching the sand, and everyone jumped off and ran into the *monte*, the dense vegetation around the beach. Normally, they then connected with someone in town. In Aguada, Santiago told me, there were a lot of people who did humanitarian work, but now the Border Patrol had arrived in their green-striped vehicles, and walked around town knocking on doors. They do that randomly? I asked, shocked. To get *inteligencia*, he said, pointing to his head.

Less than two minutes later, Santiago told me that this beach was where Christopher Columbus landed when he "discovered" Puerto Rico. Aguada celebrated this every year, although admittedly there was a controversy about where the landing actually took place. From where we were standing we could see all along the beach up to Rincon, a popular surfing destination. I looked back up at the antenna. Santiago said it had been put up by the *marina de guerra*, the Navy.

It was a hard juxtaposition—in 1493 Columbus had come to

the same place, and in much the same way, as the refugees of 2012. Later on that sultry hot afternoon, Santiago and I visited the Ermita de Espinar. The crumbling stone structure was a remnant of one of the first churches left by Spanish Franciscans for European worship and for the conversion of the Tainos (Arawaks). The Tainos, who numbered in the millions in the Caribbean when Columbus's first expedition arrived, would be almost completely wiped out by the mid 1500s, by disease, brutality, and enslavement. Columbus wrote in his log about the Arawaks, "They willingly traded everything they owned. They do not bear arms ... They have no iron. Their spears are made of cane. They would make fine servants. With fifty men we could subjugate them and make them do whatever we want."[13] In Puerto Rico, the Spanish empire drove the remaining Tainos into the mountains. The crumbling ruins of the old monastery had been covered by a new church.

To add to this strange juxtaposition, looking five miles down from the shores where Columbus arrived, I could see the town of Aguadilla, the location of the Homeland Security cluster and the U.S. Border Patrol. In the Puerto Rican capital, San Juan, the connection between Columbus and the Border Patrol was both more obvious and more visceral. In old San Juan, I was stunned by the beauty of the building that lodged CBP, a pink Colonial-style edifice completely different from the plain, often fortress-like structures used for the same purpose across the mainland United States. Behind the antique entrance gate, a white flag with the logo of Homeland Security waved softly in the late afternoon breeze. Right off the coast, a Coast Guard red-striped cutter—patrol boat—bobbed in the waves. CBP spokesperson Jeffrey Quinones told me that their handsome headquarters stood on the site of the old Spanish Customs House. It was painted pink because of Jean Whitmore, the "first female to be appointed customs administrator" by the Roosevelt administration. "She liked pink," he said. The United States government had built it in 1924, the same year that the Border Patrol was created, ornamenting its European and colonial architectural elements with symbols of U.S. nationalism—flags, ships, a coat of arms, an eagle.

The building almost looked friendly, as if you could walk right in and somebody would give you a history lesson about old San Juan. But there was no front door. And the sidewalk was barricaded. As I walked around snapping pictures, I saw a carved eagle puffing its chest patriotically over some large windows behind the semi-militarized barricades; the bird seemed to be leering down at the surrounding cobblestone streets. It was like watching the collision of the old crumbling empire with the new one on its way to twentieth-century world hegemony: the U.S. building blending in with the Spanish Fortaleza, the huge brick wall that circled old San Juan, raised to fend off other nineteenth-century imperial powers with its cannons. Now the once formidable Fortaleza was buzzing with tourists.

And that's because the wall was not formidable enough to withstand a U.S. invasion in 1898 during the Spanish-American War. The terms of resolution that followed made Spanish-speaking Puerto Rico a U.S. territory. Later it became a commonwealth, but it has never attained full statehood, remaining a shackled semi-colony with boisterous independence movements. Puerto Rico's "second class" status in the eyes of Washington was made brutally evident in 2017 in the aftermath of Hurricane Maria in which approximately 3,000 people died.

The 1898 Treaty of Paris gave the United States control not only of Puerto Rico but also of Cuba, the Philippines, and Guam. And 1898 was the year that the United States annexed Hawaii. This was the first time that the United States appropriated overseas colonies, and they created a conduit for U.S. businesses, such as the Boston-based United Fruit Company. In 2011, Juan Gonzalez wrote, "More than any other U.S. company, United Fruit became the twentieth-century symbol of U.S. imperialism. It would evolve into a corporate octopus, controlling the livelihood of hundreds of thousands and toppling governments at will."[14] In 1902, ninety years before Gonzalez and just four years after the Treaty of Paris, U.S. historian and political scientist Brooks Adams wrote of the United States that, "the union forms a gigantic and growing empire which stretches half round the globe, an empire possessing the greatest mass of accumulated wealth, the most perfect means of transportation, and the most delicate yet powerful industrial system which has ever been developed."[15]

THE THIRD BORDER

What I saw and heard in Puerto Rico in 2012 left no doubt that this U.S. semi-colony had become part of the extended U.S. border. One thousand miles away in Washington, DC, Michael McCaul told a congressional hearing, "This Caribbean region is America's third border, an open door for drug traffickers and terrorists." McCaul was deploying the rhetoric typically used to justify border buildups. Geographers Loyd and Mountz see the issue in a much different way: Puerto Rico is among the very "racialized, colonized, and militarized grounds [where] we locate the United States' transnational migration-detention and deterrence regime."[16] It was the colonial bases on these "'edges' of American empire," they write, that provided the foundation for "building up today's historically unprecedented detention, deportation, and border apparatus."

Ramey Air Force Base is not Puerto Rico's most famous military installation. That would be Vieques, where in 2003, a large, forceful social movement finally stopped the United States Navy from using a large swath of the small inhabited island off the eastern coast as a bombing range. (The Navy had been bombing there since the 1940s.) As for the Ramey base on the other side of the *isla*, my *Lonely Planet* guidebook described it as obsolete, "a relic of the Cold War," glossing over its transition to a concentration of Homeland Security buildings. This was one example of the many, as Loyd and Mountz note, both active and decommissioned U.S. military bases in Guam, Cuba, Panama, and Puerto Rico that have become the "material grounds of refugee and migration-control operations," fusion centers of the security wars.

The U.S. Border Patrol's Ramey Sector has its own explanation:

The Ramey Sector was established in 1987 to combat the rising tide of illegal aliens arriving from the Dominican Republic located some 90 miles to the west on the island of Hispaniola, which it shares with Haiti. Citizens and government officials alike expressed great concern in the mid-1980s to the rising tide of illegal aliens.[17]

This can be read in the context of the 1980 Mariel boatlift, when 125,000 Cubans arrived in southern Florida, and of the increasing political turmoil in Haiti under the Jean-Claude Duvalier dictatorship, which was notorious for locking up people for political reasons in a network of prisons and beating and banning journalists. Alison Mountz and Nancy Hiemstra write, "these arrivals, occurring as migration from Mexico and Central America also surged, were viewed with increasing alarm among the US public in ways that provoked enforcement policies that grew incrementally more restrictive."[18]

Indeed, much of the historic precedent for U.S. border externalization is found in the Caribbean, on the "third border," whose enforcement and deterrence apparatus served as a model for the Prevention Through Deterrence strategy used on the U.S.-Mexico divide since the 1990s. For example, as Loyd and Mountz note, based on years of boat interceptions by U.S. border guards, in the 1990s presidents George H. W. Bush and Bill Clinton began to establish a "transnational deterrence infrastructure" or an "offshore detention archipelago." This culminated in Operation Safe Haven, in which both the Clinton and Bush administrations made agreements with a variety of countries, including Panama, Dominica, Suriname, Grenada, St. Lucia, the United Kingdom for the Turks and Caicos, and the Bahamas, to provide temporary "respite" for people fleeing Haiti and Cuba. The result was a system of refugee camps that immigration attorney Harold Koh said "rank among the most startling, yet invisible, features of United States foreign policy in the post–Cold War era."[19] He described tent cities that held "thousands of men, women, and children, surrounded by rolls of razor-barbed wire, amid the sweltering heat of the U.S. Naval Base at Guantánamo Bay, Cuba, and the former Panama Canal Zone." By 1996, the number of Haitian and Cuban asylum seekers in Guantánamo peaked at almost 48,000 people. This was not sanctuary, but rather an offshore, transnational mass incarceration. It was deterrence.

Indeed, historian Adam Goodman notes, it was basically an outsourcing of deportation. The policy of interdiction was meant "to skirt the asylum process" by redirecting boats with migrants to other countries, and then was expanded even further from the Caribbean with Operation Global Reach. In order to combat "illegal immigration through emphasis on overseas deterrence," this $8.2 million initiative of the Immigration and Naturalization Service established 40 overseas offices between 1997 and 2001. According to Goodman, Operation Global Reach trained 45,000 officials around the globe, from Africa to Asia to Latin America. "It is much cheaper to deter people from migrating illegally from abroad," two *Los Angeles Times* journalists wrote about the operation, "rather than attempt to find, detain, and deport them once they are here."[20]

Ramey is the Border Patrol's smallest sector, and it started out even smaller, with a single agent in the San Juan immigration office tasked with processing apprehended migrants. When I was there in 2012, the number of agents had increased to 60. Although that's still small compared with forces on the U.S.- Mexico border—the Nogales station alone had 621 agents—Ramey used a wide variety of what Homeland Security calls "force multipliers," referring to technologies and agencies outside of DHS. In Puerto Rico, the Caribbean Border Interagency Group, a fusion of CBP and the Coast Guard with Matos's FURA, had a meeting every morning, CBP representative Jeff Quinones told me over the phone. In the meeting, he said, agents would speak "of the plans for the day and you basically figure out the problems you are going to address." They shared information, determined who would be in the water, who would be on land, who would be in the air. This deployment followed the CBIG "mantra for border security": "force multiplication and multilayered enforcement at the border." Though Puerto Rico's western coast did not look like the physically walled U.S.-Mexico border, there was a virtual wall there—a human wall, with a formidable web of agencies and a long history of interdiction.

Each agency represented a layer in this enforcement web. The web's center was the interior of Puerto Rico with Immigration and Customs Enforcement, and its coils extended outward. Customs and Border Protection's law enforcement arm was the Border Patrol, whose jurisdiction included the coast, particularly the west coast, and the sea up to twelve miles out from there. Quinones called those twelve miles the water border, and the Border Patrol agents worked it alongside agents like Matos at FURA. Outside of that jurisdiction was another coil, patrolled by the Coast Guard. The web extended into the Mona Strait itself, making it seem like one big border trap. In addition to the web of enforcement agencies, there was an intense concentration of "assets" and enforcement technologies on this U.S. "third border" that in some ways mirrored the cyber-barriers of the U.S.-Mexico border. Mona Strait border policing equipment included Predator B drones (Guardians), two AS-350 Light Enforcement Helicopters, two UH-60 Medium Lift Helicopters, and two De Havilland DHC-8 Maritime Patrol Aircraft, all state-of-the art aircraft for detecting vessels.[21] This didn't even count the Midnight Express Interceptors, according to CBP the "fastest, most capable law enforcement vessels in the world."

Matos had the wrinkled, weathered face of a sage, but his gestures and tone were those of a lawman. Mid-conversation he paused, looked at me, and asked, "Do you want a cup of coffee? Do you want a sandwich?" which added an unexpected homely note to his character. So did the leafy plants spread throughout the patio. The nice breeze continued smelling of rain and the sea.

While we ate, Matos told me that he had three children, one of whom was in Bahrain on a detail with the U.S. Coast Guard. He wasn't sure why his son was in Bahrain or what that had to do with guarding the U.S. coast, but there he was. He had been in the Coast Guard for twelve years and had trained for one year in the academy in Virginia. Matos told me his son had also worked out of the station in San Juan, and would pass in front of the house on runs down the coast.

When I brought up the "Wet Foot/Dry Foot" policy—which automatically awarded Cuban nationals who set foot on U.S. soil the right to pursue residency (this policy ended in January 2017), Matos said he didn't think it was strange that Cubans were "home free" and other nationalities were not. Ramírez had told me earlier that if it had been Cubans who'd crashed into the shore of Mona Island that day instead of Haitians, they would have been also sent to Aguadilla but then released on their own recognizance. Matos didn't have a problem with that. He said, "It's a communist country."

Toward the end of our conversation, his tone grew dark as he spoke of a boat carrying ninety-three Dominicans that ran out of fuel and then capsized. A fishing boat spotted them. "I went out there and helped even though it was my day off," Matos said. "Many of them didn't swim, and there were ninety-three crowded onto a small boat." Eight people drowned, he said. He was shaken; I could tell from his tone. They didn't have life-saving equipment. There weren't any liquids on the boat; everyone was dehydrated. The rescuers had to give them first aid. "It was very sad," he admitted, as if he profoundly understood how fatal the deterrence policies could be.

That year, 2012, the journalists Luis Barrios and David Brotherton reported that more than 50 percent of people in the Dominican Republic were un- or underemployed, and 57 percent of Dominicans wanted to migrate from Hispaniola. There was a sense of hopelessness on their island, and Barrios and Brotherton underscored that this hopelessness had developed under the regime of the Dominican Republic Central American Free Trade Agreement, CAFTA-DR, implemented in 2005. Dominicans owned almost none of their country's resources. Every resort on the DR's "extraordinary coast" belonged to foreigners. Further, Barrios and Brotherton wrote, "The nation's entire energy system, i.e., its gas, electricity and petroleum, is controlled by U.S., Spanish, Canadian or Italian corporations. Meanwhile the manufacturing sector is almost entirely owned by corporations in the United States, Korea, Taiwan and Canada with the country's so-called Free Trade Zones providing unlimited cheap labor."[22]

After Puerto Rico, I would head to the Dominican Republic, where the walls of Santo Domingo were covered with graffiti condemning the Canadian mining company Barrick Gold, which had been exploring and exploiting the countryside. Much on Hispaniola had changed in the more than five centuries since Columbus's arrival, but the foreign quest for gold had stayed the same.

Matos told me another story of a boat that ran out of gas. He was even more emotional as he described how the captain of a *yola* had become disoriented and the boat was lost at sea for twelve days. Most of the sixty people aboard perished, and when they were found their bodies were already decomposing. Twelve people survived, he told me, because a woman gave them milk from her breast for eight days. Some say only 40 percent of the boats make it to Puerto Rico. Others say it's less.

In the same year I learned these things, McCaul testified in front of U.S. Congress about the "third border" and that "this is a wide-open back door to the United States and we need to shut it."[23] He uttered not a word about the palpable violence that Dominicans and Haitians experienced every single day, or the perils they endured to escape it. His words expressed Latin America's and the Caribbean's both historic and future position in the United States empire, as another critical coil of razor wire in its extended border.

7.

The Philippines and the
Periphery of Empire

The National Coastal Watch Center looked out of place. The other buildings in the Philippine Coast Guard complex in Manila Bay blended into the ramshackle port; the U.S.-funded building, large and gray, built by Raytheon Corporation, was conspicuously new. Out of the Coast Guard barracks spilled an endless stream of cadets in navy blue uniforms, some of them running through the complex in straight lines. Just the day before, the head of the U.S. Pacific Command, Admiral Harry Harris, had entered that building for a meeting, but it wasn't open to everyone.

One of my interviews with the Coast Guard took place on one of the boats gently rocking in the harbor, where Philippine officials had sent me and video journalist Alex Devoid. From the boat we could see a billboard advertising the Philippine Coast Guard: "Serving our Nation by ensuring a Safe, Clean, and Secure Maritime Environment." This text was surrounded by pictures of the Coast Guard in action, including one of its members in maritime camo, crouched with automatic weapons in all-out national security mode. Another sign enlarged on the mission statement of the first: "To promote safety of life and property at sea, safeguard marine environment and resources, and to enforce all applicable laws," including the 1994 Law of the Sea.

"At the turn of the twentieth century," writes Reece Jones in *Violent Borders*, "the oceans were one of the last bastions of free movement and unclaimed resources on earth."[1] The Law of the Sea, then, divided the waters into exclusive economic zones that extended anywhere from 12 to 200 miles from the coastline. Although international ships could freely sail on the surface of the sea, everything below it

—any resource or sea life, sea-floor minerals, fossil fuels—were under control of the coastal states, often through contracts with multinational corporations. For example, the BP deepwater mobile rig responsible for the catastrophic 2010 oil spill was drilling in the U.S. exclusive economic zone about 42 miles off the coast of Louisiana. The 1994 Law of the Sea was the last of the four historic events that Jones identified as fundamental to today's global border surveillance regime and the enclosure that it relies on, after the 1607 Midlands Revolt, the 1648 Peace of Westphalia, and the 1885 Berlin Conference. From a specific U.S. perspective, another merits attention: the 1898 Spanish-American War.

On the boat there was a plastic laminated map showing the Coast Guard's twelve stations and seventy substations, spread across this country of more than 7,000 islands. The commander, Armando Balilo, would joke the next day that there was one Coast Guard agent for each island. Our guides took us into the helm, where we were able to stand over a confusing (at least to me) steering and tracking system. Behind us, a Coast Guard crew in orange uniforms prepared a rubber boat. Above, the Philippine flag gently waved in the breeze. And hovering over all of this, like the epitome of a vast, global, surveillance apparatus, was the National Coastal Watch Center. Its walls looked even grayer under the overcast sky, which threatened rain in spite of the pleasant breeze. Beyond the Watch Center we could almost see the massive United States Embassy just up the coast. Even though I was on the other side of the world, I felt firmly planted in the archipelago of U.S. power.

"THE TASTE OF EMPIRE IS IN THE MOUTH"

Once the United States finalized its territorial international boundary, in the late nineteenth century, it began its outward overseas expansion, through seizure of territory, as with Puerto Rico and through occupation, as with the Philippines. The Raytheon Watch Center on Manila Bay represented not only that historic occupation but also the present-day U.S. surveillance apparatus, in one of the very places where it was first developed.

In 1890, the year of Wounded Knee—when the U.S. Army massa-cred hundreds of the Lakota in Pine Ridge, South Dakota—the U.S. Bureau of the Census declared the nation's "internal border" closed. After the dozens of changes to the U.S. international boundary over the nineteenth century, the country had finally taken the shape that now appears on today's maps. And this limitation had an immedi-ate impact in the eyes of Washington. The decade that followed was one of social turbulence in the United States. There was an economic depression. There was "underconsumption." There were strikes and protest movements. With its terrestrial borders finally set and a dan-gerous imbalance of wealth and opportunity within them, the United States in the 1890s needed either a new system of economic distribu-tion or a new way of extending its economic frontier. As Howard Zinn wrote in *A People's History of the United States*, "the profit system, with its natural tendency for expansion, had already begun to look overseas."[2]

Up to this point, the U.S. had not yet launched a colonial war, although it had invaded other countries—mostly Latin American countries, including Argentina, Uruguay, and Nicaragua (several times), but also Hawaii, Japan, and even China. Now, however, an ideology of overseas expansion really began to take hold, especially among the elite, and especially with regard to foreign markets. Captain A.T. Mahan of the U.S. Navy even suggested that not the meek, but rather the countries with the biggest navies, would inherit the earth. Senator Henry Cabot Lodge wrote, "The great nations are rapidly absorbing for their future expansion and their present defence all waste places of the earth. It is a movement which makes for civili-zation and the advancement of the race."[3]

In 1897, on the eve of the Spanish-American War, *The Washington Post* captured the sensation quite well with an editorial on the "new consciousness":

Ambition, interest, land hunger, pride, the mere joy of fighting, what-ever it may be, we are animated by a new sensation. We are face to face with a strange destiny. The taste of Empire is in the mouth of the people even as the taste of blood in the jungle ...[4]

The consciousness of an American colonial imperative was encouraged not only by the newspapers but also by scholars. John Burgess, arguably the most influential political scientist of the day, wrote that the "Anglo-Saxon" races were "particularly endowed with the capacity for establishing nation states."[5] And nation-states—such as those that had just been carved out of Africa at the Berlin Conference—were the "political civilization of the modern world."

After the U.S. invasion, the proper destiny of the Philippines came to President William McKinley as a revelation after a conversation with God. The treaty signed with Spain in 1898 gave that archipelago along with Puerto Rico and Guam to the United States in exchange for $20 million. During negotiations, there had been some debate surrounding the Philippines. "I went down on my knees and prayed to Almighty God for light and guidance," McKinley said. The Lord's answer came in bullet points: The United States couldn't give the Philippines back to Spain. The U.S. couldn't turn the Philippines over to France or Germany, who were commercial rivals. Finally, "we couldn't leave them to themselves—they were unfit for self-government."[6] His conclusion? "There was nothing left for us to do but to take them all and to educate the Filipinos, and uplift and civilize and Christianize them." U.S. historian and senator Albert Beveridge reached a similar conclusion about the Philippines without divine guidance. He noted, "there are not 100 men among them who comprehend what Anglo-Saxon self-government even means, and there are over 5,000,000 to be governed." He also professed less lofty motives than McKinley for assuming such a task, speaking openly about U.S. dominant economic interests, the "fertility in the plains and valleys of Luzon," the woods that "can supply the furniture of the world for a century to come," and the mountains on the island of Cebu that were "practically mountains of coal." Beveridge also claimed to own " a nugget of pure gold picked up" from the banks of a Philippine creek. But he also called the Filipinos a "barbarous race," and said that God had "marked the American people as his chosen nation to finally lead in the regeneration of the world."[7]

Howard Zinn notes, "The Filipinos did not get the same message from God" as President McKinley—or Senator Beveridge did.[8] It took three years and 70,000 U.S. troops to crush the Filipino insurrection that followed Washington's takeover of the islands.

"We have pacified some thousands of islanders and buried them; destroyed their fields; burned their villages, and turned their widows and orphans out-of-doors," wrote Mark Twain. "And so, by these Providences of God—and the phrase is the government's, not mine—we are a World Power."[9]

FROM THE CRUCIBLE OF COUNTERINSURGENCY TO THE STORMS OF CLIMATE CHANGE

From the Coast Guard boat, I looked out at the rolling waves. It was like watching the planet breathe, and the boat rocked back and forth. But in the twenty-first century, this water—and the thought of its unleashed power—is less calming to Admiral Sam Locklear, former head of the U.S. Pacific Command, who has said that a significant upheaval as a result of a warming planet "is probably the most likely thing that is going to happen" in the Asia region, and that this should be of greater concern to the United States than a Chinese hegemony or the North Korean nuclear threat: "You have the real potential here in the not too distant future of nations displaced by rising sea level. Certainly weather patterns are more severe than they've been in the past."[10] In 120 years, the Philippines has gone from being the front line of U.S. colonial expansion to being the front line of climate change, and according to the U.S. military, climate change is a "threat multiplier."[11] The Philippines, indeed, were the convergence point of the most daunting geopolitical dynamics of the twenty-first century.

Back in the office of Armando Balilo, I asked the Philippine commander about the one thing that had perplexed people when I'd told them that I was going to the Philippines to learn about border policing: How did border enforcement work in this country of thousands of islands? There'd been particular interest in this point in Arizona, where we had a land border and large, clearly marked walls. The first thing that Balilo said was that he had been to Arizona, an assertion that no longer surprised me, since so many other commanders I'd interviewed—from Jordan to Israel to Guatemala—had said the same thing. Balilo had visited Scottsdale, the affluent Phoenix suburb. He'd gone there for a Coast Guard–related conference, but he wouldn't say more about it.

"You know the Coast Guard is in charge of the coastline," he remarked. It was the "first line of defense." The Coast Guard was not only deployed in strategic border areas, but also in the "exclusive economic zone" designated by the Law of the Sea. To look at that zone on a map was like looking at an expansive blue shroud—one that extended significantly into the South China and Philippine Seas and surrounded the Philippine archipelago, giving it a shape as if it were a single giant land mass.

It reminded me of the border between Kenya and Tanzania: Something significant existed on the map, where nothing was visible on the surface of the vast sea.

The Philippines' border-policing apparatus centered on the National Control and Watch Center. When U.S. Ambassador Philip Goldberg cut the ribbon on the building in 2015, an article written by the U.S. Embassy called it an "action that underscores the U.S. commitment to helping the Philippines manage and secure its maritime domain."[12] To support the "enhanced awareness" afforded by the Watch Center, the U.S. supplied $20 million, and so began a multi-year partnership funded by the Defense Threat Reduction Agency of the U.S. Department of Defense, as part of the WMD Proliferation Prevention Program's Maritime Security project. In fact, the Defense Threat Reduction Agency has been and continues to be involved with border-building projects around the globe, including on the borders between Lebanon and Syria and Syria and Jordan. Other locations include Ukraine, Kenya, Kazakhstan, and Singapore.

According to a document produced by the Raytheon Corp., "Border Security and Critical Infrastructure," the multinational company, too, was developing, implementing, and operating "integrated end-to-end border security solutions" not only in the Philippines, but also across the globe.[13] This activity was central to the strategy behind the war on terror; Raytheon, through contracts with nations involved, had deployed border "solutions" in more than 24 countries across

Europe, the Middle East, Southeast Asia, North America, and South America, covering more than 10,000 miles of both land and maritime borders. This included designing and deploying more than 500 mobile surveillance systems, training more than 9,000 members of security forces, and building 15 "sustainment centers." Indeed, Raytheon was committed to building a "host nation capability," providing "intelligence and surveillance solutions that help detect intruders and illegal materials such as narcotics and weapons of mass destruction." The purpose was to "deter, detect, and interdict illegal activities that threaten regional and global security."

In the Philippines, the National Watch Center connected more than a "dozen stations and sensors, as well as ships of the Coast Guard, to provide a more comprehensive picture of ships and vessels operating in or near Philippine waters," as the embassy put it. This system extended throughout the Philippines, in Palawan, Cebu, and Mindanao—a place that has had historic U.S. military presence, a place that the George W. Bush administration called the "second front" of the global war on terror.[14]

The National Watch Center was the most modern embodiment of a process that began on Philippine soil more than 100 years ago, at the end of the Spanish-American War. What the United States got from the Philippines was much more than natural resources and a market for surplus goods. The Philippines was the cradle of the U.S. surveillance state. As Alfred McCoy writes in *Policing America's Empire: The United States, the Philippines, and the Rise of the Surveillance State*, the U.S. information and intelligence infrastructure was developed in three phases, and the first was in the Philippines from 1898 to 1907, in a "crucible of counterinsurgency."[15]

The Spanish-American War was fought soon after the invention of Edison's two-way telegraph, the first commercial typewriter, and Bell's telephone—the information revolution of the 1870s. Textual data was being recorded and transmitted at what were then breakneck speeds and in unparalleled quantities, and with unprecedented accuracy. There were also innovations in data storage—the Dewey Decimal System in the 1870s and the electronic tabulating machine of the U.S. Census in the 1890s. George Eastman invented his film roll in the 1890s. These precursors of today's biometric systems and databases were key elements to the Philippine "experiment."

In the first ten years of the Philippine pacification, to create compliance, the United States formed three agencies in the country crucial to the development of this intelligence apparatus: the Division of Military Information; the Philippine Constabulary, charged with pacifying the population through persistent and persuasive surveillance; and the Manila Metropolitan Force. These three departments pursued three results: basic intelligence on leaders and movements; "scurrilous"—potentially scandalous—information about the derelictions of local leaders, to keep them in compliance with the occupation authority (the United States); and the enhancement of a vast imperial, panoptical gaze. The Division of Military Intelligence created a sort of Dewey Decimal system of its own for filing information cards on every influential Filipino. Like a nascent National Security Agency without the computers, authorities indexed these cards in alphabetical order for different military zones. The first U.S. civil governor of the Philippines, William Howard Taft, established the 5,000-agent Constabulary, which was tasked with colonial intelligence and counterinsurgency. The Information Division of the Constabulary formed a sort of blueprint for today's homeland security state and intelligence apparatus, deriving data from "intensive surveillance, covert penetration, and monitoring of press and public discourse,"[16] according to McCoy. The Philippine Constabulary was the model for the United States' Military Police, established in 1918 and tasked with managing the post–World War I occupation. And in 1921, when 10,000 striking mineworkers in West Virginia took up rifles and shot at military and private security forces, the United States turned to psychological tactics learned in the Philippines to quell the uprising.

Colonel Ralph Van Deman, known as the father of U.S. Military Intelligence, was the first commander of the Philippine Division of Military Information, creating a network of surveillance that included telegraph line "knitting nets" around guerrilla zones and then transmitting information from 450 intelligence officers.[17] Such experience was not only fundamental to Van Deman's role in later establishing the Military Police, but also to the vast surveillance done in the United States by the House Un-American Activities Committee and the anticommunist witch hunt led by Senator Joseph McCarthy. A report written by Van Deman naming Hollywood stars such as Charlie Chaplin, Orson Welles, and Frank Sinatra as "red appeasers" was 709 pages long.[18]

The Philippines' pre-computer surveillance state paved the way for the second "information regime," which developed during the Vietnam War. This was when the U.S. government began to use IBM computers, as then–Defense Secretary Robert McNamara, said, to "tell us the status of control in the countryside."[19] Going into the surveillance industry was a profitable decision for IBM. Years later, U.S. Customs and Border Protection gave the company a highly lucrative new contract: helping CBP operate its "data support services."[20] The Vietnam War also saw the first use of rudimentary drones, which the U.S. employed for surveillance in both China and Vietnam, and the construction of a 48 kilometer electronic intrusion system deployed between the north and south known as the McNamara wall, a sensor system later reapplied to the U.S. Mexico border in 1970.

According to McCoy, the true beginning of the third robotic information regime was with the Iraq War in 2003 that continues today.

When we first stood outside the gray Watch Center, we could see the silhouettes of people inside what looked like a modern lobby. The Coast Guard headquarters had buckets in the hallways and paint peeling from the wall that gave it somewhat of a charming character, in my opinion. By contrast, the Watch Center seemed ahistorical, utterly new. But when we were denied entrance, suddenly the place didn't seem ahistorical at all. Rather, it was the product of a long history that began with the U.S. seizure of the Philippines after the Spanish-American War and ended with the global border regime of today. The Philippines had become, as McCoy put it, the "periphery of the U.S. empire." It was a place where the U.S. border was not only physically present, but also, when you considered the monitoring and tracking aspects of the border apparatus, where it had been invented.

THE CENTER PERIPHERY MODEL

Although the U.S. occupation of the Philippines ended long ago, and U.S. military bases were removed in 1991, the influence of the United States on the island nation is still evident, even prominent. This includes, aside from the incrementally increasing military aid, the presence of U.S. Customs and Border Protection, which maintains an attaché office in the U.S. Embassy along with its network of trainers and advisors. One aspect of CBP training is streamlining the agencies in foreign countries, getting them to work together in a whole government approach to immigration policing. It's also about pushing countries to give border forces a type of authority and power that follows the model of U.S. enforcement.

It is important to reiterate what this means: In the United States, Customs and Border Protection has not only firepower and the ability to make arrests, but also extra-constitutional powers. As the CBP official of the International Affairs Office I spoke with in Washington, DC, pointed out, the U.S. Department of Homeland Security is "exempted" from following the Fourth Amendment. The U.S. government has also exempted CBP and DHS from the restrictions on racial profiling imposed on all other federal departments. A DHS official told the *New York Times*, "We can't do our job without taking ethnicity into account. We are very dependent on that."[21] The American Civil Liberties Union calls the 100-mile border jurisdiction zones around the contour of the United States a "Constitution-free zone." And there is a push to implement and reinforce such zones of exception worldwide.

In May 2017, I spoke on the phone with a U.S. CBP trainer—a trainer with considerable experience in the Philippines—who told me that other countries are "hampered by the lack of regulations, by the lack of authority that allows certain agencies to do things." The Philippines was one of many examples of this. A lot of these countries were like "the US, 15 years ago, fragmented." At CBP, he said, "We have a lot of authority." In other countries, customs agents are seen as "tax collectors, revenue generators." We are trying, he said, to get them to "move forward in increasing their authority so that they're able to do what they need to do."

He told me he conducted one weeklong training a month on average, a sort of "School of the Americas" for the world's border guards. Well, he added, it used to be one week, but now, to save money, the Export Control and Related Border Security—the State Department's border program, much like the Bureau of International Narcotics and Law Enforcement—was doing back-to-back two-week trainings. His job was 80 percent training and 20 percent border assessment. All in all, they did hundreds of trainings in a year.

He had trained agents in Mindanao, in Cebu, in Manila. The Philippines had clearly taken a central role in what could be called the U.S.-Asian border, which included U.S. border programs in Vietnam, Laos, Cambodia, and Indonesia.

Indeed, the day before we spoke with Commander Balilo of the Philippine Coast Guard, Admiral Harry Harris of the U.S. Pacific Command had arrived, escorted by the Coast Guard, on his first trip to the Philippines "to discuss matters of partnership and future engagements." The Philippines was a critical part of what the United States described in "The Asia-Pacific Maritime Security Strategy: Achieving U.S. National Security Objectives in a Changing Environment." The first sentences of that document read, "The United States has enduring economic and security interests in the Asia-Pacific region. And because the region—stretching from the Indian Ocean, through the South and East China Seas, and out to the Pacific Ocean—is primarily water, we place a premium on maintaining peace and security." Things hadn't changed much from the proclamations of Senator Beveridge in 1898, or President McKinley's insistence that God had commanded the United States to "civilize" the island nation.

In 1948, two years after the United States ended its almost 50-year occupation of the Philippines, U.S. strategist George Kennan told an audience at the National War College that the "most important determinant" in the relationship between the United States and the world remained "the fact that this country has 50 percent of the wealth of the world and only 6 percent of its population."[22] According to the scholar of American Studies, Edward P. Hunt, Kennan was one of the first to identify and understand how "the United States came to dominate the postwar world as a powerful empire."[23] Kennan viewed the

U.S.'s vast concentration of wealth as "vulnerable" amid a "jealous and embittered world," making "our real task" one of "devis[ing] a pattern of relationships which will permit us to maintain this position of disparity" with no "detriment to our national security."

Noticeably absent from Kennan's discourse were the lofty, blatantly racist declarations of Manifest Destiny. Indeed, they were replaced by a more pragmatic and concise expression of empire building: "We have to accept a certain unchallengeable antagonism between 'him that has' and 'him that has not' in this world," he said, as I mentioned in the introduction, during a conference with the Central Intelligence Agency in October 1949.[24] Kennan's words expressed—tacitly acknowledged—the empire's underlying fear: that the world's poorer countries would develop an alternative political and economic system; that the poor would challenge the status quo. By the time he finished his term as Director of Policy Planning in 1949, Hunt writes, Kennan had "introduced a bold new vision in which U.S. officials secured the dominant position of the United States in the world shaping the main contours of global order." This marked a major turning point in U.S. history. What Kennan promoted was what was called a "center periphery model" of world organization, featuring what sociologist R.D. McKenzie described in 1927 as a "dominant center and subordinate integrated parts."[25] Here is the blueprint of today's U.S. globalized border apparatus: its vast international scope of "subordinate parts" have emerged wedging hardened and harsh lines of division between the global north and global south.

Leaders talk of border security as if it were as natural and timeless as a mountain or a river. It is not. The hardened militarized borders insisted upon by politicians are a recent phenomenon, as are political boundaries between nation-states, as are nation-states themselves. True, if you count those first days of the development of the modern surveillance apparatus after the U.S. seized the Philippines, the Raytheon National Coast Watch Center—with its fixed and mobile command units, its common operational pictures, its tactical radios, maritime radar, camera systems, and ground sensors—has been more than 100 years in the making. Kennan and his preoccupation about the *have nots* from the "embittered" world would be proud.

Part Four
Extreme Vetting

Nationalism is often expressed as a kind of love: love of the abstract nation and of abstract people, living and dead, associated with a place. Supposedly, we do not let bad things happen to those we love. In the same way that we are usually conditioned to think about love in terms of scarcity— that there are limits to our love—the border acts as a kind of organizer of the limits of love.

Fiona Jeffries

8.

"We've Got Big Brothers and Sisters All Over the Place"

When Canadian photojournalist Ed Ou walked into the Vancouver, British Columbia airport in October 2016, he probably didn't think that agents of U.S. Customs and Border Protection were going to ask for his three cell phones and their passwords. He expected to get on his plane to North Dakota, where he was going to cover the protests against the Dakota Access Pipeline at Standing Rock, on contract with the Canadian Broadcasting Corporation. Ou is an award-winning journalist who began his career when he was a teenager by documenting Israel's 2006 attack on southern Lebanon. Since then, he had worked for Reuters and the Associated Press and interned at *The New York Times*. He had lived in Kazakhstan and had covered the uprisings of the Arab Spring. In one of his award-winning photo essays, "Escape From Somalia," he captured people becoming refugees, backpacks slung over their shoulders and plastic jugs in hand as they traveled through driving rain to the Gulf of Aden, where they would get on rickety boats to Yemen. One photo showed a group of refugees sitting in an intimate circle, the stars and swirling clouds soaring through the night behind them.

In Vancouver, the U.S. CBP agent signaled that Ou needed to go to secondary inspection. According to Ou, the agents there immediately asked him about the last time he'd been in Iraq. They asked why he was so interested in covering Standing Rock. They asked him if he had any claims to Indigenous status. They asked him who he knew at Standing Rock. They asked him why he would travel there all the way from the Middle East. Ou responded that he was not working in the Middle East right now, that he was a journalist and traveled on different assignments. They gave him a list of every single country he had been to for the past five years. They asked him to write in detail what he'd been doing on each trip. Ou said, "I answered quite openly, because all my travel could be matched with a published article." Ou had been there for several hours when the CBP agents asked him to unlock his phones. They said, "We need to look to be sure there's no photo of you posing next to a dead body somewhere."[1] Technically Ou was in Vancouver, British Columbia. He was miles away from the U.S. international divide. He had never left Canada. And yet he was at the U.S. border, up against a cyber border wall of extreme vetting.

Ou was one of 2.3 million air passengers who pass through the second-largest preclearance site in Canada each year. An article from the CBP magazine *Frontline* described the Vancouver preclearance experience as if it were a friendly amusement park. The inspection area "hummed" with travelers wheeling luggage and "speaking" with the 85 CBP agents who worked there. At one of the 18 computerized kiosks, where passengers scanned their passports and had their photos taken, "one older woman laughed at her image in the kiosk camera," as if she were in a fun house looking into a wacky mirror.[2] Once cleared, you could walk under the WELCOME TO THE USA sign. Once you got across that "border," you could visit an array of shops and restaurants in the "United States."[3] Vancouver Port Authority vice president Steven Hankinson called the preclearance travelers "customers." He raved about the efficiency of the preclearance experience, as if being questioned by armed, uniformed agents on intimate, private matters might even be joyous.

When agents asked Edward Ou to hand over the passwords to his phones, he resisted. He told them that would be a breach of journalistic trust and integrity. By then, he had already missed his flight to North Dakota.

Another man, a few months later, did hand over his phone password and also missed his flight. Thirty-year-old Andre—a set designer from Vancouver who for his own protection used a pseudonym in telling this story—was on his way to New Orleans to visit his boyfriend when CBP demanded his phone and password. "I didn't know what to do," Andre told journalist Rob Salerno. "I was scared, so I gave them my password and then I sat there for at least an hour or two."[4]

Andre was hardly the only person who'd had an electronic device confiscated and searched by CBP. Cell phone searches were becoming much more common. In 2015, 8,503 arriving international travelers had their electronic devices searched, up from approximately 5,000 annually in previous years. And then in 2016, the number skyrocketed to 19,033, more than doubling in one year,[5] and then almost doubled again to reach 30,000 in 2017.[6]

According to Andre, the CBP agent returned and grilled him. He asked Andre if an email that was attached to a Craigslist account for sex ads was his. The agent asked if an account on Scruff, an app for chat, dating, and social networking for gay men, was his. The agent asked, "Is this you, on BBRT," a similar app. "Yes," Andre told him, "this is me."[7]

Then the agent asked Andre what he meant by "looking for loads." Andre said that although he tried to explain to the CBP agent what that term meant, the agent kept hammering him with questions. "Humiliating" was how Andre described the experience to Salerno. Finally, he gave up, and asked if he could just go back to Canada. If he did, would he be barred for life? The agent said no. A month later Andre tried again. This time he wiped clean his sex apps, browser history, and messages from his electronic devices beforehand, but CBP knew who he was. The cleared phone made CBP even more suspicious. Andre said they went through his computer. They looked at his word documents. There was a nude photo of him on the phone and they asked who this person was. They didn't let him through; they accused him of being an escort. When I tried to follow up on this story, Salerno wrote me that Andre was so traumatized that he wasn't responding to any more journalists.

In August 2016, during his presidential campaign, Donald Trump promised to impose "extreme vetting" on people desiring to enter the United States. This would include an "ideological test." Trump said that only people that "shared American values" would be let in. "We will be tough," he said, "and we will even be extreme."[8] Trump had first called for a "Muslim ban" in 2015, after the December San

Bernardino mass shooting, when he issued a statement calling for a "total and complete shutdown" of Muslims entering the United States until the government could "figure out what is going on."[9] The Trump campaign's website used the language "Muslim ban" up to May 2017, when they finally removed it. Even so, Trump soon thereafter issued a number of tweets doubling down on the policy: "That's right, we need a TRAVEL BAN for certain DANGEROUS countries, not some politically correct term that won't help us protect our people!"[10]

One of the Trump administration's first executive orders in January 2017 mandated "new vetting measures" to keep "radical Islamic terrorists" out of the United States. The countries it covered were Iran, Iraq, Libya, Somalia, Sudan, Syria, and Yemen.

There was an immediate response from prominent Democrats condemning Trump's order. New York Senator Chuck Schumer said, "Tears are running down the cheeks of the Statue of Liberty tonight. A grand tradition of America, welcoming immigrants, that has existed since America was founded, has been stomped upon."[11]

And Senator Dick Durbin, from Illinois: "History will judge where America's leaders stood today. Faced with the humanitarian crisis of our time, the United States cannot turn its back on children fleeing persecution, genocide, and terror."[12]

Yet the United States had been turning its back on such children for more than a century, and since the 1990s it had been building up a border-enforcement apparatus that turned truly formidable post-9/11. The U.S. annual budgets for immigration and border enforcement, as I mentioned in the introduction, have grown almost eighty-fold since 1978 to approximately $23 billion in 2018, if you combine CBP and ICE.[13] I have seen with my own eyes the abandoned plastic suitcases of children in isolated stretches of the Arizona desert. The U.S. international push has included not only the forceful outward extension of its border through training, supplying, and arming border patrols and creating surveillance systems in other countries, but also a system of vetting, even extreme vetting, that targets people of certain nationalities and religions and income brackets thousands of miles away from U.S. borders. But the vetting is even more broad and extreme, as the cases of Ed Ou and Andre demonstrate. Perceived political sympathies, sexual orientation, or even setting foot in one of the United States' targeted countries could leave a person blockaded at the border, even if that border is in Vancouver.

THE SILHOUETTE

In November 2015, I went to Paris to attend Milipol, one of the largest homeland security conventions and exhibitions in the world, and saw how extreme vetting might evolve into the future.

Moranne Yaari, product marketing director of the cyber intelligence company Verint, was about five minutes into her presentation when she stopped and insisted that the international audience of security people and executives watch a clip from the movie *Lucy*. Originally, she said, she'd meant to begin the presentation with this clip, a science-fiction depiction of how extreme vetting could look in the future. Lucy, played by Scarlett Johansson, is living in Taiwan when she's kidnapped by a criminal organization that forces her to work for them. Meanwhile she ingests a substance that gives her mental and physical superpowers.

The substance-enhanced Lucy is able to identify anyone's digital footprint. She can sense people's digital footprints all over Paris. She can see long, thin lines rising from people's bodies to the sky above. She holds them, then opens them with her fingers, as if she were using an iPad. Then she makes what Yaari called "actionable decisions." In the movie, "actionable decisions" seem to include driving a car full speed the wrong way, causing countless crashes and running over human beings in order to overtake the "bad guys."

That wasn't the movie's main point of interest, however. Yaari was focusing on a world where Big Brother was everywhere. In the extreme vetting of the future, she said, people in the public thoroughfare will be analyzed and classified and targeted in one digital glance.

At times it was difficult to hear Yaari's voice. There were so many attendees at that year's Milipol that whenever the door opened the speaker was drowned out by thousands of voices that swept into the room like a swarm of drones. At this point in my research on homeland security I had been to quite a few of these types of conventions, and none had even remotely matched this one. The exhibition hall, packed with vendors and surveillance equipment, was so large that I literally could not see to the end of it. And Yaari was not the only presenter using stories and characters from fantastical fiction. For much of the time, a person in a dinosaur costume wandered amid the thousands of people in the hall. When I finally got up the nerve to ask what the dinosaur signified, a Taser representative told me it meant that security was in the "stone ages" and needed to modernize. Taser's electrocution guns, the rep added, were one way into a new era. Another company, IR Defense, was displaying a "predator" with a frightening monster face and hanging mandibles—external mouthparts used for biting, cutting, and sawing. The creature was tall, had a layer of armor as skin, and held a spear in one hand and the leash of a guard dog with a spiked collar in the other. I thought I was in a *Terminator* movie. The first time I saw the "predator," there was a big group of men in navy suits and ties standing behind it deep in conversation, as if the monster weren't even there. Above them was a billboard that showed a large black-and-white photo of soldiers posed ready for action. I was trapped in the bizarre imagination of the global security apparatus.

The conference had brought in almost 1,000 vendors and 100 delegations from different countries, altogether some 30,000 people. The sheer numbers were surprising because Paris was on emergency lockdown. It was November 18, 2015; coordinated attacks by ISIS had killed 130 people only five days before. Other large-scale events, including what was to have been the world's largest climate march at the end of November, had been canceled for security reasons. The night before I'd woken to the automatic gunfire of the French National Police, pounding 5,000 rounds into an apartment building less than two miles from my hotel, in the nearby suburb of Saint-Denis, where two of the attackers were hiding. From the open window of my hotel I could hear the progress of the seven-hour "kill or capture" operation.[14] There was martial law, a state of emergency. In Paris, the bouquets of flowers were still fresh, and the candles were still flickering in front of the Bataclan theater and other blasted locations.

The Paris attacks had inspired Moranne Yaari to change her

presentation on her product. Yaari's company, Verint, an Israeli firm founded by Jacob "Kobi" Alexander—a former IDF intelligence officer —has 800 employees, half of them in Israel and half in Melville, New York, the site of its worldwide headquarters. (Verint was also a sponsor for Guy Keren's Israeli Homeland Security (IHLS) incubator that organized the unmanned systems expo in Tel Aviv.) Now in Paris there was a tangible example of what Verint's products were meant to forestall, an example so close that you could feel the fear in the air. Before the clip from *Lucy*, Yaari showed us a slide of people leaving the European Union for Muslim countries, "traveling to jihad." Another showed men with kaffiyehs on their heads, "returning from jihad." The last simply showed a group of migrants, as if they, too, were part of a river of terrorists, out to get "us," the good guys. The borders of Europe were transparent, she said, and this was how the "terrorists" were getting in. Yet the borders she called transparent had been forti-fied by massive EU investments, visible right there at Milipol.

Yaari explained how Verint's product, like Lucy, would open up a person's "digital footprint." Times had changed, she said. People were doing everything on the Internet. They were making calls. They were buying clothes. They were buying food. They were buying airplane tickets. They were doing banking transactions. They were finding love. There were digital footprints everywhere. "What is a digital footprint?" she asked. It was "the data left behind of users on digital services internationally or nationally, intentionally or unintentionally." Verint was able to glean information, she said, to form a "silhouette." And a silhouette allowed you an "insightful lens." It allowed you to "get the target's interests, habits, workplaces, relationships, associates, communications through devices, location activities." This would help you with your investigation. This would, she said, allow you to understand where to "apply the heavy cannons." It would allow you to apply a "counterposition" to your "target." Indeed, it formed the basis of a system of targeting, the brains of the preclearance site and the U.S. National Targeting Center and extreme vetting. And if Verint bore a strong resemblance to the National Security Agency, it was because this very private company had an NSA contract to tap lines through Verizon to accumulate metadata.[15]

On top of its NSA contract, between 2008 and 2018 Verint had nearly 50 other contracts with the U.S. government, worth more than $2 million, primarily through the Departments of Defense and Homeland Security.[16] At the end of 2018, the company reported eight percent revenue growth, a profit margin that it expects to continue into the future.[17]

Yaari clicked on a slide. A picture appeared of a person with cross-hairs between his eyes, as if he were the target of an execution, not surveillance. Verint can get the metadata, Yaari explained. It can see how people use their applications; it can see how they use their web browsing. We can, she said, "extract a lot of information." The private company started by an Israeli intelligence officer could see what audio you were listening to, what media sharing you were doing, what news groups you were looking at, what social networks you were active on, if you were following a religion, if you were building weapons, or if you were interested in violence. There were also apps with built-in leaks, according to Yaari. Shazam, the song-identifying app, was one example. Every time a person attempted to Shazam a song, the app sent out their "exact GPS coordinates." "Most people don't know that," she said. Their targeting system could also bust through some encryption, and was able to "harvest" information from Facebook and Twitter.

She ended full circle, showing the pictures of migrants fused with pictures of the Paris attackers. That they were the same people at whom the police were shooting the bullets I'd heard from my hotel room surely helped Yaari's point. If the French government had had the Verint tracking system before the attacks, she implied, "maybe we could have figured it out."

When Yaari finished I bee-lined over to ask her a question. I played the naïve reporter, infusing my voice with excitement, exuding the sort of technological fetishism that these companies like to hear in those who ask about their products. What were the applications of Verint on border control, I wanted to know, and was any country using Verint on its borders?

Yaari gave me a cold look. Who are you? she asked. It took only a few moments for the "director of marketing" to pop up from a sitting position in the front row. She walked quickly behind Yaari, as if one journalist were causing an emergency situation. In fact, I knew that besides having the NSA contract to tap into Verizon lines, Verint had supplied Mexico with what was known as the Reliant Monitoring System that since 2006 had been intercepting "virtually any wired, wireless, or broadband communication network and service," as the company noted in a 2012 article.[18] Essentially, the U.S. State Department had supplied a surveillance system to the Mexican government through Verint. The department had additionally awarded the Israeli company a contract for the Communications Intercept System for the Mexican Federal Investigations Agency. This was jointly run by the United States and Mexico, through the INL—the same agency that provided financing for CBP training and creation of border patrols throughout Latin America and beyond. Indeed what Yaari had been describing was an aggressive border, a ubiquitous border, a border with teeth, a border that didn't respect borders—the border of the future.

According to Verint, their "solutions" were deployed in more than 180 countries and used by more than 10,000 organizations. The company said it was "making the world a safer place."[19] Now, as Yaari and the marketing director looked at me, I wondered if I was being vetted and classified in the same way, if these "solutions" were prying information out of me like Lucy in the Paris plaza.

The marketing woman said, "We don't talk to journalists."

"We are," she said, "an intelligence company."

"WE GOT BIG BROTHERS AND SISTERS ALL OVER THE PLACE"

Perhaps Yaari's "future" is already arriving.

The "massive paradigm change" in the early 2000s redefined borders "not only as lines, but also as movements—flows of people and goods on a global scale both legally and illegally," according to former CBP commissioner and DHS official Alan Bersin. He pointed to the "underwear bomber," Umar Farouk Abdulmutallab, who intended to blow up a Northwest Airlines flight over Detroit in 2009, as one example of the shift:

Border security in this context requires that Abdulmutallab be prevented from boarding the plane in the first place. For these purposes, the border became Schiphol Airport in Amsterdam, and the goal changed to identification and preemption of high-risk individuals in the flow of passengers at their last point of departure toward the United States.[20]

In comes the hidden army of "nerds" of U.S. enforcement: the thousands of agents who are able to navigate twenty-first-century computer systems and break into people's Facebook, Twitter, and email accounts. Ted McNelis was one of them. He was not CBP, but worked for the private company Deloitte under contract. At the eleventh annual Border Security Expo, in San Antonio in April 2017, he told a packed room of border industry executives and representatives that he worked for the Counter Networks Division at the U.S. National Targeting Center, where "one of the goals is to extend the border beyond the physical border."

This border was not passive, but rather "proactive," aggressive, he said. This aggressive enforcement apparatus could shut down illicit networks, criminal networks, "before they actually get to the border and do something bad." They created this continuous immigration-vetting loop, according to one of his co-panelists, Al Davis from the United States Citizen and Immigration Services, by using biometrics.

The National Targeting Center was founded on September 11, 2001, according to former acting CBP commissioner Thomas Winkowski, when "two people jumped in a booth or cubicle and began targeting." To understand the monumental growth of the CBP vetting apparatus, you just have to look at the sweeping expansion of the Targeting Center, which grew from those two agents into today's massive apparatus that every day sifts through tens of thousands of profiles of people bound for the United States. If you are on a U.S.-bound flight, in other words, DHS scrutinized you before you got on the plane. Winkowski said the Targeting Center has become even more important during the age of Trump.

We've been talking about "extreme vetting," he said, and that really involves one question: "How do you get good people in quickly and stop bad people from coming into the country?" Before 9/11, he explained, although the United States did have Immigration and Naturalization Service (INS) offices abroad, "we hadn't gotten to the next level."

"And so we started off small, but have gotten big," Winkowski said, perhaps too modestly. The National Targeting Center had grown from a cubicle in CBP to a building the size of three football fields, full of workstations and agents pouring over computers. From 2002 to 2012 the NTC staff had increased from 60 employees to 714,[21] more than a 1,000 percent jump. Now, they analyze the data of 250,000 passengers per day.[22] And every day generates thousands of "targeting hits" that prompted "meticulous research." The center is filled to the brim with all kinds of constantly evolving, state-of-the-art surveillance equipment manned by agents with concentrated faces, pouring over data. ("It was also nice building," commented one visitor on Yelp, "but it has no deli." It did, though, have a workout room.) It resembles an extra-large U.S. border command and control center, in Nogales or El Paso or Iraq or Afghanistan. But from here the surveillance gaze is not on a single stretch of land or coast, but on the whole planet. Every airport, indeed, as Bersin asserts, is a U.S. border zone, one where every traveler, every piece of luggage is scrutinized.

The National Targeting Center is "a prime example of how CBP continues to push our zone of security outward," says CBP spokesperson Mike Pope in a short video promoting the NTC—available on YouTube—"working closely with our international partners to disrupt threats as far from the homeland as possible by identifying high-risk passengers and cargo well before they would cross our land borders, sail into our ports, or touch down on our tarmacs."[23]

"The NTC," Pope assures us, "is on duty to protect our people and economy 24/7," protection that extends to the intellectual property rights of corporations and the securitization of the global economy.

"Listen, there is no margin for error," NTC Enforcement Operations representative Thomas Sutton chimes in, looking solemnly into the camera. "Terrorists only have to be right one time. We have to be right every time." As Sutton speaks these words, an image appears of a woman in a black hijab and her male companion speaking with a CBP officer, one of many images throughout the video depicting people of apparent Middle Eastern descent. The video ends with Pope lauding NTC workers like Sutton as heroes, and the center itself as a "model" for other countries to emulate.

The 2008 visit of a Turkish delegation to the NTC gives a fair example of how this model is demonstrated to other countries. The delegates met with NTC representatives who took them to the operation's "nerve center." There they learned not only about software but also about personal radiation detectors. Then, according to a leaked U.S. Turkish Embassy cable, "they discussed how to set up such a targeting center for passengers and cargo in Turkey that would include officials from TAEK [Turkish Atomic Energy Authority] and Ministry of Interior organizations." On the same visit, the delegation visited the CBP Advanced Training Center in Harpers Ferry, West Virginia, the center that turned down my request for an interview. The Turkish delegation, however, were not journalists but potential clients, and then-director Jim Cobb invited them to the facility where they talked about future expansion projects, visited "tactical facilities and expressed an interest in acquiring training materials for physical training (training items such as batons, knives, guns, etc.). The delegation also expressed an interest in sending some of their officers to this facility for advanced training."[24]

The NTC was not only keeping track of people entering the country, but also on those who were leaving, an example being the 2010 operation to prevent Faisal Shahzad—the Times Square bomber—"from fleeing the country" by identifying his flight out of John F. Kennedy Airport in New York. Another success story, according to the NTC's video, was an unnamed "serial killer" the center had identified before he or she could board a flight from Atlanta to the Middle East. The video offered no details about this person, not even nationality.

One case the video didn't mention was that of Haisam Elsharkawi, whom CBP agents stopped when he was boarding a flight to Saudi Arabia in Los Angeles. The six agents said he had been "randomly selected." The agents asked Elsharkawi, a naturalized citizen—born in Egypt, and Muslim—for his cell phone. When he refused, they slapped handcuffs on him and detained him in the airport. Then, three hours after his plane departed, he was released without charges.[25]

These were the nuts and bolts of the CBP National Targeting Center, the brains behind preclearance and other airport operations, the ways a person can end up in the CBP interrogation room facing questions about their intentions, religion, profession, even sexual orientation.

When the Trump administration initiated its executive action on vetting in 2017, and added an explicit nationality-based exclusion imperative, it actually came from a long history. There was the Chinese Exclusion Act of 1882, the first law excluding people of a specific nationality from entering the United States. The immigration act of 1917 targeted for exclusion those who were "morally undesirable"—including anarchists, idiots, and beggars. The Immigration Restriction Act of 1924 capped the number of immigrants based on their country of origin, favoring those from European and Christian backgrounds. And as Trump said himself: "In the Cold War we had an ideological screening test. The time is overdue to develop a new screening test for the threats we face today."[26] Most likely Trump was referring to the 1952 McCarran-Walter Act that not only called for restricting ideological leftists but also LGBTQ people. CBP was able to implement Trump's 2017 travel ban order as quickly as it did because a vast international infrastructure of exclusion was already in place. The countries specified in the travel ban were already categorized as "Special Interest," and travelers from those places already received extra scrutiny. To fully implement a "travel ban," all CBP had to do was flip an extra switch. And although the executive order itself has been contested in legal battles, and Iraq was removed from the list, the larger, very discriminatory vetting system it rests upon has not been challenged at all.

Some of this targeting work was being carried out by people like McNelis of Deloitte, the "number one global consulting organization."[27] Deloitte's extensive contracts with DHS, more than $1 billion worth in services through more than 250 task orders and contracts, are just another example of the ever more commonplace privatization of border enforcement. [28]

During his talk in San Antonio, McNelis stressed that the strength of private industry was not in law enforcement, nor in dismantling criminal networks, but in targeting. It was in social media analysis—the same specialization Moranne Yaari had promoted, for Verint, in Paris. Social media analysis enabled agents to "build out a 360 view of an individual, a criminal." They were the "deep web crawlers," using advanced Google searches and other data sets. They were able to get to watch lists and sanction databases that might not be available to government. They could get the corporate records, the litigation records, the shipping history and data records, the personal identifiable information—information that could be used on its own or with other material to identify, contact, or locate a single person. Think of Cambridge Analytica, the data mining and voter-profiling company hired by the Trump campaign that had gained private information on more than 50 million Facebook users and then "offered tools that could identify the personalities of American voters and influence their behavior."[29] In the case of CBP, McNelis implied, the agents were like detectives. Listening to his even, polished monotone as he explained all this was like listening to somebody tell you he could break into your privacy, violate your civil liberties, and learn all kinds of personal information about you, and then assure you it was for not only the greater good of the country, but also your own greater good.

Big data was now "THE THING," former CBP commissioner and Border Patrol chief David Aguilar had said earlier in the day. "Wasn't this getting kind of Orwellian?" Aguilar paused, almost laughing. "We got big brothers and sisters all over the place."

Listening to McNelis, I knew he was exactly what Aguilar meant.

The private industry vetting sleuths also examined international news sources—they wanted to know what was being said in each country in the language of that country. They shared this with the governments who were their international partners. McNelis listed potential red flags, why people would be targeted: "Somebody is sending money to someone they shouldn't be sending it to, or somebody travels to some place they shouldn't, like Syria." From there, agents began to identify larger networks. So who else was sending "him" money? And why would somebody with no "familial or travel history to Syria—why are they sending money there?"

Then they would turn to social media to build out "a view of the target." They would see if certain people knew each other on Twitter or Facebook, "or various other social media websites."

Jim McLaughlin of the CBP Targeting Center, McNelis's co-panelist, backed him up: Fifty years ago, he said, if someone went to the town square and screamed they were going to do harm, "you had to pay attention to it." Now, he continued, it's just as likely that will come in "146 characters" or a "chat room."

"One of our goals at the Counter Network Divisions," McNelis said, "is to identify, disrupt, dismantle, and then remain vigilant."

Agents could pounce on a target at preclearance sites, which exist at Vancouver and every other major Canadian airport; at airports in the Caribbean, the Bahamas, Bermuda, and Aruba; at Shannon and Dublin; and at the Abu Dhabi International Airport (where the United Arab Emirates picks up 80 percent of the costs). In 2016, CBP "precleared" 18 million travelers.[30] All in all, there are more than 600 agents stationed at 15 preclearance sites in six countries.

At the end of 2016, CBP signed an agreement with airports in Stockholm and Punta Cana Dominican Republic, to create two more sites, and have identified other countries such as Colombia, Argentina, United Kingdom, Iceland, Mexico, Italy, Japan, Brazil, and St. Maarten for future expansion.[31]

Where preclearance sites didn't exist, plainclothes CBP agents of the Immigration Advisory Program could interrogate people bound for the United States at airports in Paris, Madrid, Amsterdam, Frankfurt, Manchester, London, Doha, Tokyo, Mexico City, and Panama City.[32] These agents worked directly with the airline companies and local governments, as well as with the National Targeting Center, to identify and stop "high-risk" travelers from boarding U.S. flights. While their role was advisory—they couldn't directly deny boarding or inspect a person's belongings—they could issue a "no board recommendation."

And then there's the Transportation Security Administration's Quiet Skies program. *The Boston Globe* reports that since 2010 "thousands of unsuspecting Americans have been subjected to targeted airport and inflight surveillance, carried out by small teams of armed, undercover air marshals." The marshals document whether a person sweats, trembles, or blinks rapidly during the flight, whether they change clothes or abruptly change directions while moving through the airport, whether they talk to other travelers. As Michale Bilello, assistant administrator of public affairs for TSA, told NPR, "These are people who perhaps haven't done anything previously to put them on a terrorist watch list, but perhaps there are things ... that make us concerned about their future activities or actions."[33]

Like Trump's promised "wall," which would not be built upon nothing, but rather on the foundation of a historic fortification of the U.S. southern border that has a wall and barriers that extend hundreds of miles, Trump's targeted extreme vetting follows an established history of sanctioned discrimination and structural exclusion (backed by billions of dollars). In June 2018, the U.S. Supreme Court upheld the travel ban. Chief Justice John G. Roberts proclaimed that Trump had "ample statutory authority to make national security judgments in the realm of immigration."[34]

Who knows what information the National Targeting Center had already pulled on Ed Ou when he arrived at the Vancouver airport on his way to Standing Rock? Had CBP scoured his Facebook or Twitter or other social media accounts? Was there something about his award-winning photography in the deserts of Somalia, in Egypt, in Libya, in Iraq, in Lebanon? Did he blink excessively at the CBP kiosk? Whatever the reason, one thing is clear: He'd run smack into Yaari and McNelis's future border.

When CBP asked him for his password, Ou declined. He politely explained that he had sources that he was obligated to protect, "much as doctors have a responsibility to patient privacy, and lawyers have to protect their clients' confidentiality." The agents told him they had the right to search everything he brought through the border. They said that included passwords and phones. That was true: a 2012 ruling by the U.S. Supreme Court stated that Customs and Border Protection could search electronic devices at the border. People have had their laptops seized. There have been thousands of such cases.

"Pocket trash was some of the most valuable stuff we used to use," David Aguilar explained at the Border Security Expo. "Little slivers of paper, little receipts and stuff." He held up his cell phone. "This is today's pocket trash."

In Ou's case, they threatened to deny him entry. They searched through his bags. They photocopied his documents and personal journal. They asked what extremist groups he had met with abroad, how many people he had seen die, and whether he had been "approached by government agencies in the Middle East."

Ou offered to put them in touch with his editor. He was, after all, a professional journalist. Perhaps that would do the trick. The agents told him that it wasn't necessary. In a piece he wrote for *Time.com*, Ou said in that moment he recalled when he'd swallowed a SIM card a few years before in what he called an "authoritarian country," to protect his sources, and another incident, when he was in Crimea and Russian Special Forces invaded a Ukrainian military base where he had been filming. They rounded up the journalists. They seized the memory cards. They said they were doing it "for security." When the journalists protested, the soldiers told them, "You're in our country now; we can do whatever we want."

In Vancouver, the CBP agent told Ou, "Everything you bring through here is mine to go through and take." When Ou brought up the example of a U.S. journalist going to Russia or China only to have their electronic device confiscated, the agent retorted, "Stick to being a journalist—and don't tell us how to do our jobs."

An article that recorded this incident mistakenly described it as life in the "Constitution-free zone," the 100-mile jurisdiction Homeland Security holds over the U.S. borders it patrols.[35] But Ed Ou was in Vancouver, not the U.S. However, one could faithfully argue that by then the zone had extended outside of its territorial borders.

After six hours, the U.S. Department of Homeland Security told Ou that he would be denied entry to the United States. The reason was "classified." His name perhaps matched a "person of interest." The fact that he hadn't handed over his phone password "didn't help."

When the baffled Ou left the interrogation room, a CBP supervisor said, "You're probably going to write about this. Well, we're not scared of you. You can say what you want. It won't change anything."[36]

9.

The Global Caste System

In February 2017, in the U.S. preclearance zone of the Abu Dhabi International Airport in the United Arab Emirates, CBP agents seized the passports of Nigerian bank executive Popoola Olayemi and his pregnant wife and two children, and sent the family back to Nigeria. It wasn't until he reached Lagos, Olayemi said, "that I discovered that our visas had been cancelled."[1]

CNN was in search of a Trump administration extreme-vetting story, and reported the incident in a story headlined, "Africans wary of U.S. travel after series of border denials." The lead paragraph read, "Nigeria is not on the list of countries affected by the U.S. government's temporary travel bans. But several Nigerian citizens claim to have been denied entry since they were introduced." Many paragraphs later, the real story emerged. When the reporters contacted CBP, the DHS agency had "indicated that the details were down to established practice rather than new policies of the Trump administration."

In other words, the global classification system was already in place. And to be able to classify and ban so broadly and at the same time efficiently, the United States not only needed to build infrastructure and implement its policies and practices (the grounds for inadmissibility), as it has done with the targeting center, but also establish cooperation across borders with other nation-states. As an agent of Interpol, the largest international police organization on the globe, put it, create a "global border system." In order for that to happen there has to be agreement between countries about who can and cannot move across borders, who will be included and who excluded, that is, agreement not only on a global border system, but on a global caste system.

The same Abu Dhabi airport and preclearance zone where CBP rejected the Olayemi family left air-travel blogger Ben Schlappig—known as "Lucky"—unimpressed when it first opened in 2014. He called it a disaster, "possibly the most dysfunctional facility I've ever seen."[2] But his complaint was not that he had been rejected—quite the contrary. Schlappig, who claims to fly 400,000 miles per year—that's sixteen times around the globe—is a member of CBP's Global Entry, a trusted traveler program for "low risk" individuals. According to 2018 statistics, Lucky was one of five million people in the program who were able to breeze through international borders.

To get Global Entry, you fill out an application, and then CBP does a background check. If you pass that, you attend an in-person interview with an agent. Global Entry expedites people for preapproval clearance upon arrival in the United States, regardless of whether the "United States" means an airport preclearance zone in the United Arab Emirates, Canada, or Ireland.

Although Schlappig complained that the security checkpoint in Abu Dhabi was the "most superficially detailed and rude" he'd ever been through, Global Entry helped him more than he realized. It put him on the other side of the divide, on the other side of the U.S. border that both visibly and invisibly extends throughout Planet Earth. The vetting system epitomized by Global Entry exposes the internal functioning of the global classification system—the sorting of people into categories of admissability and inadmissability, of low and high risk, that exist even among the relatively privileged, like Popoola Olayemi and his family. If Schlappig and Olayemi stood in the same line at the Abu Dhabi airport, the border between them would be as clear and vivid as the U.S.-Mexico border wall.

VIRTUAL GATEWAYS AND HAPPY FLOW

How does the United States plan to classify passengers efficiently?

A high official at the International Air Transport Association (IATA) made an impressive declaration at a Washington, DC, forum in 2018: "Seventy percent of people would be happy to give up their biometric data" to facilitate their travel. The public, he declared, wants "unobtrusive security." Basically, what seemed to be the demand of "Lucky" Schlappig.

I was present at the forum, but organizers kept tight rules and asked journalists not to reveal the names of any of the panelists.

Unobtrusive security is what the World Travel and Tourism Council is demanding as well. According to the council's statistics, as rattled off by a rep at the same forum, in 2017, travel and tourism made up 10.4 percent of the global GDP, representing one-tenth of all jobs in the world. Tourism was 30 percent of global exports. On any given day, the equivalent of the entire population of Portugal—10 million—was in the air, and four billion were flying per year. Despite the fact that less than 10 percent of people in the world have ever flown at all, these numbers were expected to double in coming years, to 20 million a day, 7.8 billion per year.

In a world of ever increasing militarized borders, both in terms of fortification and extension across the globe, how can you ensure that people like Lucky don't have to endure security shakedowns? The answer: biometrics. Biometrics is going to "revolutionize" what the IATA rep called the "virtual gateways." Biometrics, he said, are going to "harmonize" the world. Indeed, if market analysts are to be believed, the Global Automated Border Control systems are going to grow substantially, at a projected rate of 18.7 percent—between 2018 and 2025. The market will more than triple during this time—from USD $470.9 million in 2017 to USD $1.7 billion in 2025.[3]

In the future, said the rep, the world will operate on "one ID," and not only will officials capture data at airports and at borders, but "down the chain." In other words, everywhere. The goal is to create a "seamless trip" where biometric data not only efficiently facilitates the entrance of a person at a border, but also is transferred to the "hotel companies" and "cruise ships."

"You could go to the Marriot," said one person in the audience, dreaming of a future devoid of even baggage claims, "and have your bags delivered to you."

The biggest barrier to the realization of this dream, the IATA rep insisted, would be one state withholding data or information. He suggested a four-prong plan for a global border system that included common standards among countries, shared technology (primarily facial recognition), harmonized applications, and trust and cooperation across borders. Implicit in the dream are open borders for the elite and a caste system for everyone else.

How could this be done? One answer, according to a representative from the private company Vision-Box, is Happy Flow, in which people would be a part of the process. He might have been talking about an innovative new form of democracy. Vision-Box describes itself as the number one "provider of automated border control systems." And Happy Flow, as its website states, is "the first 100% self-service passenger experience, based on traveler-centric biometric technology, from curb to boarding!" With biometrics, your face becomes a "token." You go to a "touch point" that condenses the border process from twenty-nine steps to five or six. Vision-Box, he said, was already testing Happy Flow in Aruba, a "real-world environment."

Happy Flow is an "ecosystem of technology" bounded by a platform called Orchestra, a term that rang like Orwell's "Ministry of Love"—that place of terror where dissidents guilty of "thought crime" are taken to be tortured and reformed.

"The process at each Passenger Touch Point only takes a few seconds! No queues, no uncomfortable identity verification processes, a happy journey all the way from check-in to boarding!"[4]

This is not science fiction. This is happening now. According to Patrick Nemeth, DHS's director of Identity Operations, biometrics for CBP "went big time"[5] after 9/11. The number of "subjects" CBP keeps in the DHS database has increased from 10 million to 212 million. They keep digital fingerprints, facial recognition, and iris scans corresponding to individual records and big data. DHS has the second-largest biometric system in the world, according to Nemeth, "right behind India's citizen system."

In June 2018, the Orlando airport became the first U.S. airport to commit to monitoring all arriving and departing international passengers with facial recognition technology.

"WHY DO YOU HAVE A PRAYER MAT AND QURAN IN YOUR LUGGAGE?"

When I contacted Hassan Shibly, Florida's executive director of the Council of American Islam Relations (CAIR) to ask about CBP treatment of Muslims, he immediately told me that he himself had been detained and interrogated by the CBP more than twenty times. CAIR documented a long list of questions that CBP agents have asked Muslim-Americans: "Are you a devout Muslim?" "Are you Sunni or Shia?" "What school of thought do you follow?" "Which Muslim scholars do you follow?" "What current Muslim scholars do you listen to?" "Do you pray five times a day?" "Why do you have a prayer mat and Quran in your luggage?" "What do you think of the USA?" "Have you ever delivered the Friday prayer?" "What are the names and telephone numbers of parents, relatives, friends?"

In early January 2017, CBP agents put Hassan Shibly's brother, Akram Shibly, into a chokehold after he refused to give them his telephone password while crossing the border into Buffalo, New York. While he was restrained, they forcibly removed the phone from his pocket. Shibly's case and 24 others, were documented by NBC in a report in March 2017.[6]

Muhammad Ali Jr., the son of the legendary boxer, entering the country at the Ft. Lauderdale airport, was detained and interrogated for two hours by CBP agents, who asked him if he were a Muslim. Ali Jr. told *The Nation*, "it takes Trump getting in office to be treated like this."[7] However, the abusive behavior shown by CBP to Muslims, and Muslim-Americans, and the confiscation of telephones and demanding of passwords, started long before the Trump administration.

In 2012, I interviewed Egyptian American Abdallah Matthews (a pseudonym) for my book *Border Patrol Nation*. He described ugly interrogation scenes in back rooms of the Port Huron port of entry in Michigan, including questions about his religion and beliefs. On one occasion, agents asked him in an aggressive manner why he had been in Canada, and kicked his ankles while trying to remove his shoes. In 2012, CAIR Michigan was receiving five to seven complaints a week exclusively from Muslim-American men, all of whom had been interrogated at length about the details of their religion, their mosque, their imam, their prayers. According to CAIR, CBP had used hand-cuffs, conducted invasive body searches, and detained people from two to twelve hours, and in one case had handcuffed a man to a chair. In 2012, CAIR filed a lawsuit against CBP, alleging violation of rights under the First Amendment and Religious Freedom Restoration Act. A federal judge dismissed the claims, "saying the plaintiffs did not prove that federal agents had prevented the free exercise of religion." The plaintiffs had also stated that border agents, in subjecting them to invasive searches and interrogations, had violated the Equal Protection Clause of the U.S. Constitution; those claims were still being litigated. During the discovery phase of the trial, Immigration and Customs Enforcement released a heavily redacted document high-lighting the same invasive questions about religion listed by CAIR, which included "Do you have any relatives or friends who have been martyred fighting in the defense of your beliefs?"[8]

If you are somebody like Lucky Schlappig, an algorithm allows you a swift entry into the United States, and perhaps your luggage dropped off to your hotel room. If you are Muslim, another algorithm gets you precisely the opposite treatment. There have been advances not only in automation, but also in discriminatory automation. Abdallah Matthews told me in our 2012 interview that he'd asked a CBP agent whether, if he crossed the border again and came back, he would receive the same treatment. The agent said yes.

Muslims like Matthews have certainly borne the brunt of the CBP vetting system, but CBP's classification system goes much further. Indeed, Homeland Security has developed an entire global classification system.

GROUNDS FOR INADMISSIBILITY

A CBP spokesperson told CNN that having a "valid visa" did not guarantee entry into the United States. A valid visa only allowed a "foreign national to come to an international U.S. airport and present themselves for inspection, where a CBP [agent] will determine the traveler's admissibility." According to the Immigration and Nationality Act, Act 212, "General Classes of Aliens Ineligible to Receive Visas and Ineligible for Admission; Waivers of Inadmissibility," there are more than 60 grounds for exclusion. Travelers who may be refused admission to the United States include people who are deemed to have mental disorders or drug abuse or addiction problems, and people who have been convicted of "certain crimes," including prostitution, or are deemed to be going to the United States for reasons of sex work—the ground on which CBP restricted Andre's travel from Vancouver.[9] The same list of grounds that would make a person ineligible for a visa is invoked a second time at the port of entry. While a major part of inadmissibility stipulations are intended to ban potential terrorists, there are also criteria blocking "an alien whose entry or proposed activities in the United States the Secretary of State has reasonable ground to believe would have serious adverse foreign policy consequences for the United States." That could mean any type of activism, really. There are even criteria left over from the Cold War: an immigrant who has "been a member of or affiliated with the Communist or any other totalitarian party (or subdivision or affiliate thereof), domestic or foreign" is also inadmissible. The list goes on and on, including stipulations regarding pregnancy; a CBP agent can deny you entry if "the government must provide medical care because you do not have medical coverage."[10]

Popoola Olayemi can confirm that: "One of the immigration officers told my wife to go and deliver her baby in Nigeria and that she can visit the U.S. afterwards."[11]

Then there is the Immigration and Customs Enforcement Visa Security Program. Agents with the ICE Homeland Security Investigations unit specializing in counterterrorism and immigration law, located in different posts around the globe, investigate and interview visa applicants and scour documents submitted with the application. According to The New York Times in an article titled "Why It's Already Difficult to Gain Entry Into the U.S.," from 2015 to 2017 agents looked over two million applications, using the classifications detailed in the grounds for inadmissibility document.[12]

Worth mentioning are the vast numbers of people either denied visas to enter the United States or put on long wait lists. Abroad, U.S. consular offices have "sole authority to approve or deny" visa applications. In one case that came to light in Brazil in the 1990s, consular agents were classifying applicants "LP" (looks poor), "TP" (talks poor), "LR" (looks rough), according to testimony by a dissenting, fired employee in a court case.[13] While using such overt, crude classifications as a screening process were deemed "illegal" by a judge, it still adequately describes a process normally couched in more sterile, bureaucratic language that systemically denies marginalized and poor people visas. As the U.S. Embassy in Morocco warns prospective applicants, "Our immigration law requires consular officers to view every visa applicant as an intending immigrant until the applicant proves otherwise."[14]

For immigrant visas and permanent resident applicants, the web of rules becomes even more intricate and complicated. Jane Guskin and David Wilson in their book *The Politics of Immigration: Questions and Answers* describe one, the Seven Percent Rule, that stipulates that no single country can receive more than 7 percent of the immigrant visas given out by the U.S. government. In 2012, because of that rule, only 47,000 of the more than 1.3 million Mexicans on the waiting list (by far the largest nationality in line) received a U.S. visa.[15] And for permanent resident applicants: sometimes even close family members of U.S. citizens face waiting periods of ten to twenty years.

The United States does have a visa waiver program for the citizens of 38 countries, mostly in Europe, who may go to the United States without a visa for visits of ninety days or less. In 2016, however, the Obama administration began to implement restrictions for people who had dual citizenship with Iran, Iraq, Sudan, or Syria, or had "traveled to those countries in the last five years."[16] Later, the administration added Libya, Somalia, and Yemen. The classification system is subject to constant modification.

Indeed, what the United States has developed as part of a border enforcement apparatus is much more than a wall. It was, as top advisor and National Defense Institute professor Celina Realuyo put it, "a cyber-physical wall," and a bureaucratic wall. It involves not one simple "line of defense," but a multitude of lines and many layers, from old-fashioned barbed wire and bullets to twenty-first-century virtual barriers, including a vetting system unlike anything seen before.

RECONFIGURING AN EMPIRE OF BORDERS

I arrived at the entrance of the Ronald Reagan Building near the National Mall in Washington, DC, and found a protest gathered at the entrance. The headquarters of U.S. Customs and Border Protection was located here, along with many other agencies, companies, and nonprofit organizations. The June 2018 International Border Summit was about to take place, during the heavy media and political scrutiny the Trump administration received after it announced its decision to fully prosecute all border crossers, which would necessarily involve the forced separation of families. After a long period of almost no detailed coverage, the U.S.-Mexico border had taken front and center stage in the 24/7 news cycle, and this demonstration of 200 people was one result. I saw signs demanding that ICE be abolished and the border wall torn down. Upstairs, in Pavilion 2 of the summit, officials from all over the world had convened to talk about international partnerships and the global proliferation of borders. There were plenty of CBP high brass at this gathering, including many former commissioners. Corporate sponsors, each with a representative, included Elbit Systems of America, Accenture, Gate Keeper, and General Dynamics. There were officials from Singapore, Australia, Bulgaria, Saudi Arabia, the United Kingdom, Uruguay, and Canada, among other places.

In these meetings, while each country spoke from the perspective of its own "sovereignty," it was clear that something much grander was emerging: a global border system. This apparatus in its totality included more than 77 border walls, billions upon billions of dollars' worth of surveillance technology—including biometrics—and tens of thousands of armed agents guarding the dividing lines between Global North and Global South. From the United States to Europe to Australia, the planet was filled with detention centers crammed with hundreds of thousands of people, families, groups, even full communities who had dared to cross lines, often because of hardship or persecution, evils established by colonial powers and enforced by their successors. The Global Detention Project has identified approximately 2,250 detention centers worldwide. While those numbers are in fluctuation, given the constant closure and opening of such prisons when seen visually on a map, these detention centers cluster in and around the United States and Europe and around Australia.

As I witnessed these meetings, I realized that it is no longer sufficient, when thinking of borders, to simply think of one individual country's enforcement efforts. This was the same point that historian and former soldier Justin Campbell made in Guatemala about "border sets." The border apparatus has to be looked at as a global regime, reconfiguring before our eyes, a developing arsenal of the Global North sorting, classifying, and repelling or incarcerating people from the Global South, while employing and deploying countries of the Global South as enforcers.

Australian Secretary of Home Affairs Michael Pezzullo took the concept a step further as he explained the divisions to attendees at the summit as they ate a catered meal off clinking plates: He suggested that a reorganization of the nation-state system might further the goal of a more efficient global border apparatus. First, Pezzullo spoke of the days following the fall of the Berlin Wall in 1989, calling them "five minutes of strategic sunshine."[17] He recounted the overly optimistic idea of the so-called "new world order," that George H. W. Bush proclaimed soon after, noting that officials and elites failed to realize that when the world opened up with the fall of the Soviet Union and the end of the Cold War, the "risks" didn't disappear, they simply changed. He described those first days when corporate globalization was unleashed, how the result was expected to be a utopia, a world of "liberal economic systems" to support a world of liberal democracies. The map would be "filled out to the edges" with "prosperity." What "we" failed to reckon with, he said, was the "dark" realities of globalization —the world that lay underneath. Now, we had to "recalibrate" for a "darker, more realistic view of the global order." Now that the Soviet threat was gone, our problem was the "transnational criminal networks" that "threaten our economies." The problem was the "ungoverned spaces."

There were positive relationships in our new world, he said, but they were built atop "a dark world of misery."

He could have been describing us, where we sat up in Pavilion Two of the Ronald Reagan Building, behind dozens of interior checkpoints, shielded from the street below where a few hours earlier the protest had gathered. This was just a few days before the increasing public pressure forced the Trump administration to end the policy of taking children from their parents at the border, and as Pezzullo talked, I was haunted by the voices of the children. That day, *ProPublica.org* had published a report that featured a recording of Central American children crying out "Mami" and "Papa" from the jail where the United States Border Patrol had put them after they had been forcibly separated from their parents. Many of the children were young, under five; there were infants who were expected to represent themselves in court. As a father of a toddler, I found the cries unbearable. I had to turn the recording off. [18]

But what I already heard could not be erased. When Pezzullo spoke of "misery," I heard the children's voices crying for their loved ones, asking if their mommy or daddy would come for them, asking if they could go. In the sweep of what Pezzullo was describing, though, the children were but one solitary glimpse into something much bigger and more brutal. The routine separation of families was intrinsic to the border and incarceration apparatus; it was happening not just at the Mexican border but worldwide, and has been for a long time, under the cover of the media's long, complicit silence. Now, it was as if for just a few weeks that silence had been shattered, revealing the violence and suffering of the border with a level of detail not heard or seen before by the public at large, and a huge swath of people had become excruciatingly aware of it.

Pezzullo continued his lecture:

Rather than the map being filled out to the edges, perhaps we need a completely different metaphor and image: Perhaps we have built "Gotham," where wealth, prosperity, and positive human connections and relationships sit atop a dark underworld, where beneath the elevated roads, trains, and high-rise buildings resides misery, dysfunction, and the dark heart of evil.

But despite all that, he assured us, there was "good news." Security was becoming transnational. Everybody here at the conference had seen the "increased level of transnational collaboration" in customs and border protection, in law enforcement, in aviation security, in cyber security. The border of the future would be heavily dependent on digital systems, contingent on biometrics such as facial recognition to mitigate risks. We would have secure global supply chains, armoring the status quo.

While Pezzullo talked, and I listened from the press table at the back of the pavilion, I thought how strange it was, given the amount of attention that the border was getting from the media, how little media was there to cover this forum about the global border and the expansion of U.S. policy and practices around the world. I shared the table with two young interns from *Homeland Security Today*, two representatives from *Tactical Defense*, a reporter from the *Arizona Republic*, and a small film crew from Israel. Yet outside of the forum, in my more than fifteen years reporting on the border I had never seen such incessant mainstream coverage. Not on the advent of DHS in 2003, not on the 650 miles of border walls and barriers constructed after the Secure Fence Act of 2006, not on the combined 5 million deportations during the George W. Bush and Barack Obama administrations. The 5,100 children permanently separated from their families, reported by the Applied Research Center in 2011, caused barely a peep in the 24/7 news cycle.[19] Prevention Through Deterrence and the remains of 8,000 people found in the desert, the thousands of families in search of lost loved ones, the ultimate family separation of death got no national coverage at all, and only cursory local coverage, if that. Even in 2014, what the media called the unaccompanied child crisis didn't get the same attention as what was happening outside the hall on that day in June 2018. A reporter from National Public Radio had been there for CBP Commissioner Kevin McAleenan's opening keynote, and had asked whether forcibly separating children from their parents wasn't akin to "child abuse." After McAleenan gave her the standard answer, blaming violent criminal networks and the parents who put their children in danger, she got up and left. She did not return.

Ethnographer and researcher Gabriella Sanchez said in a July 2018 interview:

> For the people who call the U.S.-Mexico border home, none of the practices we are witnessing is either new, extraordinary, or unfamiliar. For generations, we have attested or been the target of family separations, of the spread of the immigration detention complex and of the systematic criminalization of our communities. The wire, concrete, steel barriers and long crossing times have been a constant in our experiences as *fronterizos*: they are not a recent invention.[20]

What Sanchez is saying can be applied to the entire global border system, from the migrants caged in the Australian archipelagos, to the capsizing boats in the Mediterranean, to the notorious train on Mexico's southern border with Guatemala, where I witnessed Gerardo's painful glance at the photo of a beloved child he hadn't seen in seven years. Extreme vetting is an intrinsic part of hardened militarized borders, in the air or on land, on the United States frontier or on the West Bank. For one month, the media captured the pain and violence of the borders, and it provoked an outrage about them I had never seen before. Sociologist Douglas Massey once wrote, "undocumented migrants are not perceived as fully human at the most fundamental neural level of cognition, thus opening a door to the harshest, most exploitative, and cruelest treatment that human beings are capable of inflicting on one another."[21] Finally, people were recognizing that dynamic as an innate part of the immigration system, as the normally obscured securocratic wars were suddenly, vividly, astoundingly revealed. I reflected on the NPR reporter's abrupt exit for several days. It was as if the national media had landed in the forest and fixated on a few trees, telling the same story over and over again. If that reporter had stuck around, she would have discovered that the forest was even bigger, more geographically expansive, more savage, and horrifying. What media outlets were reporting at the time was only a fraction of the cumulative violence committed by a global border regime that most of the time goes unchecked.

Pezzullo said, "we have to secure aviation, transportation, and global supply chains generally through the creation of ever thicker collaborative, transnational inter-locking layers of security." What he was suggesting was the securitization of the global economy through his emerging "harmonized" global border system.

It was at this point that I realized that I needed to shift my definition of "empire" beyond its traditional meaning of territorial expansion. As Pezzullo pointed out, the "risks" had changed, and now so had the empire. The United States was still a superpower. But individual countries now meant less than did the harmonized relationships between them, officials, and the transnational corporate nexus. This cross-border complex, taken together, wielded a power stronger than any individual nation. I didn't come to terms with this just because of Pezzullo's keynote, or because of the many indications that this was the case during the two days of the summit, with its constant talk about the global harmonization of border systems. It was also fundamental to the homeland security system. It was what Israeli Colonel Danny Tirza, architect of the West Bank border wall system, stressed over and over again that day in West Jerusalem. Tirza underscored that the key to an effective homeland security system was to get military and security forces to work together, to break the old chains and divisions to create the new juggernaut. This was also what was happening at the global level. Countries were breaking old divisions and even animosities and working together at a governmental and corporate level. This was a constant message at the International Summit. Much more than between countries, "border security" was between the transnational elite and the rest of the world.

Pezzullo was so convinced of this, he even said there might be a dissolution of the nation-state itself as we moved into the future, or at least "a transformation of the state itself will be required." And part of this transformation would be in the "transnational model of security." As a key example, he described how the border and immigration ministers of Australia, Canada, New Zealand, the United Kingdom, and the United States had been meeting "to address issues of common concern." These were the countries of the storied "Five Eyes" military and intelligence partnership, he pointed out, that had grown out of the Second World War. Yet it had taken this grouping of white-dominant, English-speaking countries years to come together on border, homeland security, and law enforcement issues. "Future historians," Pezzullo said, "will be puzzled by this delay." Yet the reason for the delay was obvious: The "transnational cooperation had been consigned to the margins." Now this had changed.

Anthropologist Jeff Halper put what Pezzullo was saying another way: "Securitization plays a key role in perpetuating the hegemonic relationships through which the world-system operates, promoting a certain social order while also ensuring the smooth flow of capital."

That was what Pezzullo and so many others were suggesting. The harmonized global border system was not necessarily attached to the nation-state, but rather to the global economy; the elite world was not beholden to the flags of individual countries, but rather to the banner of Walmart, Boeing, Google and the power structure that sustains such corporations. Nation-states served to confine and control the masses, aided by the harmonized border regime and its patrols, while allowing the elites of the world to move in "happy flow." Border walls divided the global elite from the global poor, but, even more, so did all the layers of a caste system that could judge your religion, political ideology, and the state of your pregnancy, using your face as a token.

Part Five

Armoring Capitalism: "Teaching The Mexicans How to Fish"

Voy a crear un canto para poder exigir
Que no le quiten a los pobres lo que tanto les costó construir
Para que el oro robado no aplaste nuestro porvenir
Y a los que tienen de sobra nos les cueste tanto repartir.

Voy a elevar mi canto para hacerlos despertar
A los que van dormidos por la vida sin querer mirar
Para que el río no lleve sangre, lleve flores y el mal sanar
Para el espíritu elevar y dejarlo vivir en paz.

Natalia LaFourcade

10.

Armoring NAFTA

Behind a podium at Mexico City's Expo Seguridad, Commander Benjamin Grajeda spoke about the relationship of Mexico's newest federal police force, the Gendarmería Nacional, with U.S. Customs and Border Protection. He said the force had agents "trained by CBP in order to be able to deal with border issues." Just the day before, "in coordination with CBP in the city of Reynosa," across the border from McAllen, Texas, "a shipment of marijuana was stopped." They got "seven packets," measuring a cubic meter. For the Gendarmería, the border mission was a central one, Grajeda said, vital for guaranteeing "the rights of the citizenry, of the Mexican citizenry, to rely on secure borders." However, soon it would be clear that the security goals of the Gendarmería were much loftier than securing the rights of one nation's citizens. They were part of the global economy's iron fist.

It was March 2017, and the words of newly inaugurated U.S. President Donald Trump were still in the forefront of people's minds in Mexico, since he'd called a good swath of migrants from their nation "rapists." At this point, Trump still spoke confidently about Mexico funding a 2,000-mile concrete wall, which President Enrique Peña Nieto categorically denied would happen. (It's now even more unlikely under President Andrés Manuel López Obrador.)

But although Mexico declined to finance a border wall built on the U.S. divide, it was already funding another sort of "wall" by helping police its own southern borders with Guatemala and Belize, in cooperation with the U.S. multilayered border strategy.

When asked if there was a fractured relationship between the two countries, Grajeda said the complete opposite was true. His navy coat with golden buttons gave him a military look, and he spoke at a fast clip that was all business. "I believe that the coordination that we have institutionalized, the trust that Mexican authorities have generated with the daily work with U.S. authorities will continue," he said. (A CBP official in Washington, DC told me something similar a month later: "I bet you there are fifteen phone calls going on with Mexico at this very moment.")

So it shouldn't have been a surprise when a man in the crowd, who identified himself as Daniel Arvayo, stood up during the question-and-answer period and said, "I belong to the mining sector, the company Goldcorp, a Canadian company," and then recapitulated a central point of Grajeda's talk, the creation of security coordination between different industries, public security, and private security—what he called a "business front." Arvayo said Mexico had initiated a similar type of regional security council in the "semi-arid zone of Zacatecas," a state in central Mexico. However, so far it had been ineffective; the "challenge" they faced was from the delinquent groups who were still operating in the area. My first thought when he said "delinquent groups" was that he was referring to organized crime in Zacatecas. However, after a little research I saw he was more likely referring to the local social movements that had shut down mining operations in massive protests on multiple occasions, and threatened to continue to do so.

I have been to many such homeland security conventions, and I have seen the public and private sectors interacting to form an apparent security-industrial complex. But I had never witnessed such a moment: A corporation from a foreign country that had a large mining operation was asking a federal police agency to help protect it from a community protest.

Peñasquito, the Goldcorp operation in Zacatecas, is Mexico's largest gold mine. It also produces silver, lead, and zinc. The early projections of extraction were gargantuan: 500,000 ounces per year of gold, 28 million ounces per year of silver, 450 million pounds a year of zinc and 200 million pounds a year of lead, over a 22-year lifespan.[1] According to a 2010 assessment, the company could expect to earn around $598 million per year; most of that money would leave Mexico and enrich Canada's private sector.[2]

Through the open gates created by NAFTA, Goldcorp arrived in

Zacatecas in 2005, bearing grandiose promises of jobs for people who live in one of Mexico's most marginalized areas. And after several years in operation, the problems that the Peñasquito mine had were not with the "cartels" but with Mazapil, the local community, which among other actions led a series of *plantones*, or occupations, to protest the company's low wages: $800 pesos—$66—per week, with no benefits.[3] In October 2016, community members blockaded the gold mine again.[4] This time, the protest followed a leaked report that Goldcorp had excessively contaminated the local water supply, and had had knowledge of this contamination since 2013.[5] This was arguably the worst of a list of grievances that spanned the years of Goldcorp's operation in Zacatecas: the seizure of water in the arid land, the low wages for the dangerous work, the profits that without impediment headed north, out of the community. Journalist and photographer James Rodriguez reported that one commissioner said the mining company used in one hour "the amount of water a local family would use in twenty-five years."[6] The contamination of water was predictable. Toxic substances such as cyanide are used in mining to separate precious metals from the earth, and they remain in the tailings at the end of the extraction process. And spills are frequent— in 2014, 10.5 million gallons of concentrated sulfuric acid and heavy metals spilled from a holding pond in Cananea, Sonora, from a copper mine owned by Grupo Mexico, and flowed into the headwaters of the Sonora River, "affecting 24,000 people who live in forty-five towns along its banks."[7] In 2015, a Canadian company, Great Panther Silver, spilled 1,200 gallons of toxic waste into a river in the state of Guanajuato.[8] These are just two of many examples.

Companies were effectively sneaking across Mexico's borders in the middle of the night and causing significant damage to the health and well-being of populations. Yet not with this mining company nor with the hundreds of others that have crossed into Mexico and Central America have there been border issues—no calls for towering border walls manned by a regiment of armed agents to stop them, no campaigns by influential politicians and presidents to criminalize their operations, no talk of drones or surveillance towers. The mining proprietors have not been forced into the desert to struggle with thirst and hunger on their journeys to sites all across Mexico, from Chiapas to Sonora. And despite the longstanding environmental damage, sustained water contamination, and food supply contamination they cause, there is no interior police force searching them out, rounding them up, incarcerating them, and then expelling them from the country.

Precisely the opposite has happened. While global border enforcement enters an unprecedented phase of tracking, arresting, and incarcerating people, the world has never been so wide open to multinational corporations. These entities can roam the world and set up shop wherever they please, almost regardless of the consequences to local communities. For the Goldcorps of the world, there are comparatively very few impediments to crossing the border, few regulations, little red tape. NAFTA has not only opened the border to foreign companies' merchandise, chopping off tariffs and quotas and all obstacles to profit, it has opened the border for foreign business operations, and mining is just the tip of the iceberg. Other megaprojects include hydroelectric dam construction, tourism and infrastructure, energy-generation projects, water privatization, and oil exploration. There are hordes of foreign businesses crossing borders today, and they are after the most essential of their host countries' resources.

"We saw it coming, but we didn't realize the utter force with which it was coming at us," Marco Leyva of Oaxaca's Services for an Alternative Education (EDUCA) told me in a 2008 interview about this influx of such capital-intensive projects. Leyva said that in Oaxaca alone, the Mexican federal government had given out more than eighty mining concessions in three years, covering 1.5 million acres of land. By 2015 in Mexico there were 927 mining operations run by 267 foreign companies.[9]

When people think about free trade, "they think about reducing tariffs, quotas, etc., but it has expanded much beyond that to become a delivery mechanism" for corporations in other countries, Public Citizen's Melinda St. Louis told me. "It is about deregulating and investment to be able to maximize profit." She added that when Washington talked about "investment, it often is really talking about taking natural resources from other countries." Multinational corporations are doing exactly what nativist groups accuse undocumented people of doing in the United States: invading, taking over swaths of territory with little local consultation, and destroying the well-being of local people. And they are coming through the wide-open gates of what are otherwise heavily policed borders.

NAFTA didn't come out of nowhere. It traveled the long road of structural adjustments made to Mexico's economy since the country's 1982 debt crisis and the requirements attached to loans Mexico received from the International Monetary Fund. These requirements included deregulation; opening public entities such as water, electricity, and oil to privatization (Carlos Salinas de Gortari, Mexican president from 1988 to 1994, privatized 85 percent of state-owned businesses);[10] and cutting back on social spending such as education and health. Part of the IMF's Structural Adjustment Program obliged Mexico to cut the subsidies and price guarantees once given to the country's many small farmers. Also setting the stage for NAFTA were more than 100 modifications to the Mexican constitution, including the cancellation of Article 27, the prized provision in the constitution that protected the communal land system, and the subsequent parceling of land for sale in the free market. Article 27 carried a heavy historical punch in Mexico, as one of the key accomplishments of the early twentieth-century revolution that made Mexico's constitution one of the most progressive in the world. This was the equivalent of carving up of the commons in seventeenth-century Great Britain.

NAFTA tore down the metaphorical walls protecting Mexico's small farmers, small businesses, and workers piece by piece. The walls had to fall to make way for the great U.S.-Canada-multinational migration to the south that not only eluded border control in a direct physical sense but also in terms of political, social, and media scrutiny, scrutiny that instead has been exclusively focused on the unauthorized individuals who try to breach the border in the other direction.

One set of people, including members of the media and politicians, breezes over the border in airplanes; another set faces walls and guns.

Under NAFTA, which was essentially a closed-door deal between governments and hundreds of corporate advisors, companies could sue if something—such as local resistance—were an impediment to future profit. The U.S. landfill management firm METALCLAD did just that when local authorities would not issue a permit for a hazardous waste dump in San Luis Potosi in 1995. Not only was METALCLAD permitted to cross the border and "manage" hazardous waste on Mexican soil, but when it was kicked out by the local community, it could also claim a "right" to pollute.[11] And the NAFTA tribunal didn't send it to a detention center as a threat, but instead awarded the U.S. company millions for future lost profit. Indeed, as Public Citizen points out, NAFTA's "investor-state dispute settlement" (ISDS) system created "a parallel and privileged set of legal rights for multinational corporations to own and control other countries' natural resources and land, establish or acquire local firms, and operate them under privileged terms relative to domestic enterprises." Other U.S. companies that have won NAFTA Chapter 11 cases since the METALCLAD ruling include Corn Products International, Archer Daniels Midland, and Cargill the same companies that constantly undermined small Mexican corn producers.[12] And still another example was Trans-Canada's $15 billion NAFTA suit against the U.S. government over the Keystone XL pipeline (poised to deliver 800,000 barrels of crude oil per day), which was blocked by the Obama administration but restarted under Trump (after which Keystone canceled the suit).[13]

Important to note that NAFTA 2.0, otherwise known as United States-Mexico-Canada agreement (USMCA), was signed by the three countries in November 2018. The deal awaits domestic ratification in each country including the U.S. Congress, which could be years in the making. While in many ways it continues the NAFTA system of opening up the otherwise militarized borders to corporate interests and powers, it does offer revisions that would curtail corporate rights in the "investor-state dispute settlement system" outlined above. However, according to the Sierra Club, it would then uniquely offer "those egregious rights to notorious corporate polluters," U.S. gas and oil companies such as Chevron or ExxonMobil who have had, at least at some point, offshore drilling, fracking, refinery, or pipeline maintenance contracts in Mexico.[14] That means that the "largest corporate climate polluters in history and repeat users of ISDS [investor-state dispute settlement system]—would be allowed to challenge environmental protections in Mexico by relying on the same broad corporate rights that they have used to successfully challenge public interest policies" in other places across the hemisphere. The Sierra Club calls NAFTA 2.0 a "pro polluter" deal that would continue to outsource U.S. jobs.

At the Expo Seguridad, I noticed that the Goldcorp representative, Arvayo, wore a black vest with both a patch of the Mexican flag and the red maple leaf of the Canadian flag. Twenty-first-century homeland security had met the world's free-trade regimes, where the transnational surveillance police state met economic neoliberalism, where borders were simultaneously closed down and opened wide depending on your classification. Imagine a future, as envisioned in the transcripts of NAFTA 2.0, of Exxon oil drilling and pipelines but now surrounded by homeland security troops. All of this is indeed more evidence of a long process that began in 2005 when the presidents and prime minister of the NAFTA countries—George W. Bush, Vicente Fox, and Paul Martin—after a meeting in Waco, Texas launched a regional initiative called the Security and Prosperity Partnership, dubbed NAFTA Plus. It called for "greater cooperation" to "increase security and to enhance prosperity" of the region. At a North American Trilateral Summit in April 2007, Thomas Shannon, the U.S. assistant secretary of state for Western Hemisphere affairs described the SPP as understanding "North America as a shared economic space," one that "we need to protect," not only on the border but "more broadly throughout North America," through improved "security cooperation."

"To a certain extent," Shannon said, "we're armoring NAFTA."[15]

Although the SPP of that era has dissolved, it now embodied the multibillion-dollar security package known as the Merida Initiative. And at the Seguridad Expo, the armoring of NAFTA was happening right before my eyes. Benjamin Grajeda of the Gendarmería, considering Arvayo's question, spoke of the *"frente empresarial"*— "business front"—between the government and the private sector as "for security and against the criminality that affects companies and transnationals in the country." This was already in robust formation in Mexico, through what he called "supply chain security," a key part of the CBP mission and the global border system. The Gendarmería coordinated with private security companies to guard freight trains, to protect the petrochemical industry, the extensive Mexican fossil fuel industry, and the automobile industry, and, to appease Arvayo, he talked about preventing the robbery of silver and gold from corporations like Goldcorp. With frankness, he discussed the detailed practicalities of opening the armored gates and then protecting those entities—the corporations—that could cross the border so freely.

Even the name of the convention center where the Seguridad Expo took place, Centro Citibanamex, expressed the corporate nexus between the United States and Mexico, fusing Citibank with Banamex, formerly the National Bank of Mexico, which Citibank had bought in 2001. In the Centro, I was in the physical manifestation of the financial merger of the two countries, surrounded by 400 vendors from 19 countries selling security products to an estimated 17,000 visitors. The armoring of NAFTA was a booming business in its own right.

At one point, I found myself staring at a large armored mobile home made by the company CT Defense. Off to the side they had popcorn. I waited in line behind ten people watching an employee in camo pants who was wearing goggles in order to fire a gun virtually. When I got to the front of the line, the kid in the booth asked me if I had been in the CT Defense vehicle. I looked at him. He said, "I can only give you popcorn if you go in." I climbed the stairs. Inside it was all white, with monitors glaring from the walls. I stared at the twenty bunk beds, stared at the command and control center, and had an uncomfortable sensation that I was looking at the future. I left the Citibanamex center without the popcorn.

Outside, I walked on the *Paseo de la Reforma*, Mexico City's beautiful, wide boulevard toward my hotel. I passed the tents of a protest encampment in front of the Procuraduria General de la Republic, the Attorney General's building. The photographs of the faces of the forty-three disappeared students from Ayotzinapa stared out towards the traffic. All evidence indicated that the students disappeared at the hands of the police in 2014. And in another case, the headline indicated that very morning in March 2017 that another mass grave was found in the state Veracruz. The paper pointed out that there was no way that the authorities could not have known about the bodies. Were they some of the corpses of the tens of thousands of disappeared Central American migrants or of dissidents like the activist students?

Mexico was becoming a country of mass graves, but all the security technology was not to protect the victims. Nor was it for the homeless families—near the Alameda—who were clustered off to the side, wrapped in old blankets. One young man, with seemingly no other choice, was crouched and taking a shit in full view of the public.

Mexico was a country where four multimillionaires accounted for nine percent of the country's GDP, and one percent owned forty-three percent of the country's wealth according to OXFAM, while almost half the population lived below the poverty line.[16] In Mexico City, this poverty was visible in the neighborhoods that swelled after people from the countryside—from the south: from Puebla, from Oaxaca, from Chiapas—began migrating to the cities, post-NAFTA. While the government slashed budgets for basic necessities, it was simultaneously pumping up security and military budgets. From 2001 to 2013 security spending in Mexico increased 200 percent. "The sum was greater than investment in other areas, like health or science," wrote Arturo Angel in *Animal Politico*.[17] In 2016, there was another upsurge in public and national security spending—that totaled 154 billion pesos (using an exchange rate of 19 pesos to the dollar, that amounts to approximately $8 billion USD), three times and $100 billion pesos more than Mexico's spending in 2006,[18] following a prominent global trend.

"A paranoid nervous system fuses us together inside a hyperactive technological civilization obsessed with mitigating risk," writes Ian Shaw in *Predator Empire*. "We live under the most complex and pervasive apparatuses of surveillance, enclosure, and killing in human history."[19] But how to sell it?

Back at the conference in Mexico City, David Prall, a former U.S. Air Force pilot and now a field application specialist from the company Aeryon Laboratories, advised officials and corporate representatives to avoid the word "surveillance," which the general public doesn't like. Instead he recommended that law enforcement agents use the phrase "high-risk overwatch," and that officials highlight its "passive uses," such as fighting fires and search-and-rescue. "Nobody," he said, "is going to complain." Then the armoring of NAFTA, and its brethren counterparts across the globe, would be a breeze.

11.

"A Return on Our Investments"

It didn't take long for Mexican authorities to pull somebody off the bus, in this case a child. I was traveling with historian and former soldier Justin Campbell from Mexico's southern border in Tapachula, Chiapas, to Tucson, where we both lived, a trip of more than 1,000 miles. It was January 2017. We were seeing firsthand the extraterritorial extension of the U.S. border in layers—what Campbell argued was a "border set." We would count twenty-four checkpoints between Tapachula and the Mexican city of Puebla, almost 650 miles away.

The child was not pulled off at one of the biggest U.S. border investments in the region, the "mega checkpoint" in Huixtla, twenty-five miles into Mexico's interior in the state of Chiapas, where National Immigration Institute (INM) officials forced everybody off the bus. This multi-building checkpoint complex was the size of a shopping mall and was one of several that Mexico had built on major inland roads going north from the border in Comitan and Tenosique. Two others still remain to be built, all with U.S. support. I had never seen a checkpoint so large in my life. While soldiers cradled machine guns in their hands, everyone pulled out their luggage, as if we'd reached an authentic border crossing. We streamed into a spacious, bright room that looked like a port of entry, where a man in a brown INM shirt stared us down. I gripped my passport in my pocket, thinking he would ask for it, but he just continued to stare with a grimace, not only at me, but at everybody. I put my luggage through the X-ray machine—another "donation" to Mexico from the United States.

Former Immigration and Naturalization Service commissioner Doris Meissner confirmed my suspicions about the significance of the

United States international border policing shift symbolized by that Huixtla mega-checkpoint. Speaking in a panel on Central American migration in Washington, DC in May, four months after the incident in Huixtla that I will return to shortly, Meissner said that while much of the U.S. discussion on immigration "is limited to what is happening on our southwest border," it was only possible to understand the total effectiveness of U.S. border enforcement by "looking at the numbers that are manifest in both U.S. data and Mexican data."

Meissner was the official who oversaw the shift in U.S. border policing to Prevention Through Deterrence in the early 1990s, and her words should not be taken lightly. She understood when huge strategic changes were in the works, and the numbers bore this out. Former CBP commissioner David Aguilar noted in June 2018, "The last three years, Mexico has removed more Other Than Mexicans than we have." Other Than Mexican or OTM is accepted Border Patrol vernacular, describing people from countries that weren't, of course, from Mexico. In 2015, bankrolled by U.S. funding from the Merida Initiative, Mexico for the first time expelled more Central Americans than the United States had in the same period. The third pillar of the $3 billion dollar military aid package (since 2008) is the creation of a "twenty-first century U.S.-Mexican Border."[1] This significant strategy shift barely made a peep on the U.S. media radar. Mexico had essentially become the U.S. Border Patrol's newest hire. But it was also a result of many years and many attempts by the United States to get Mexico to "carry out its dirty work," as historian Adam Goodman put it. The efforts had been under way since 1981, when U.S.-funded wars were ravaging Central American countries, and U.S. Border Patrol chief Larry Richardson said that "the United States ha[d] quietly been paying Mexicans to deport Central Americans to Guatemala."[2] Even in the early 1990s, Meissner's INS offered immigration enforcement training to Mexico for at least three years.

The 2014–15 strategy shift had taken this to a new level—according to Meissner's Migration Policy Institute, thanks to Mexico's "increasingly muscular enforcement." MPI reported that many migrants "who previously would have made it to the U.S. border and been apprehended by the Border Patrol are being intercepted by Mexican authorities."

Here the "paradigm shift," as Alan Bersin, former commissioner of CBP called it, was palpable. However, Bersin was quick to point out that it wasn't just about deportations. In a 2012 keynote speech to the U.S.-Mexico Chamber of Commerce, Bersin said that cooperation and collaboration between the United States and Mexico was incredibly strong and would ensure "prosperity" for both countries—and for the North American region in the years ahead, thanks in part to the oil and gas resources in the three NAFTA nations. The armoring of NAFTA was very much part of U.S. policy calculations, for multiple reasons.

Meissner knew this, too: In 1992, as INS commissioner, she testified at a congressional hearing that there would be a significant increase of migration from Mexico because of the newly signed NAFTA agreement —a prescient observation, since after 1994 migration from Mexico doubled. Meissner argued that the United States needed to implement a stronger enforcement apparatus, modeled after Operation Hold the Line, which had concentrated agents, technologies, and eventually walls and barriers in highly transited urban areas extending across the U.S.-Mexico divide in El Paso. Rerouted unauthorized migrants often crossed into dangerous and desolate places, circumventing the enforcement apparatus. Nature's "mortal" harshness became a deterrent—a weapon. And the harrowing and horrifying stories of people crossing these isolated borderscapes, relegated to oblivion.

Meissner, in other words, presided over this simultaneous closing of the border to individuals and the class of the poor and undocumented, and opening of the same border to merchandise, capital, factories, and complex corporate operations—what CBP calls "legitimate trade and travel." As geographer Joseph Nevins writes, this simultaneous opening and hardening of the border illustrates "the two-tiered system of humanity in a political-economic era many describe as neoliberal."

Programs such as the Central American Free Trade Agreement and the Alliance for Prosperity and even Programa Frontera Sur, which I witnessed firsthand at the Huixtla mega-checkpoint, fused southern Mexico with Central America into a "borderless" Mesoamerica, while simultaneously enacting the strongest border enforcement zones ever known to the region. Very palpably the region was becoming what anthropologist Elana Zilberg might call a "neoliberal security scape."

After Meissner spoke, I proceeded to the CBP International Affairs office, which was in the same Ronald Reagan building in the heart of DC, but I had to go through several security checkpoints to get to a long, well lit hall that led to where three officials waited for me. They had agreed to speak with me on condition of anonymity. Two wore U.S. Border Patrol uniforms; the third wore a suit and tie. This was the meeting where they talked about how the international operations had expanded "exponentially" in the post 9/11 era, and made a key assertion: "The leadership understands that the U.S. border does not start at the U.S. border." This bolstering and expanding strategy and policy shift was just as important as the early 1990s shift to Prevention Through Deterrence under Meissner, they implied. "We are always trying to open new [CBP attaché offices], but it's always trying to find the place where there is more bang for our buck." Together, they talked about the global advisory programs, the focus on the Americas, the Middle East, the Caribbean, and the "large U.S. presence throughout Central America."

Then there was a sudden slight yet revealing disagreement. The civilian official said that there was "a large effort to capacity-build the Central American partner, in both Mexico and the United States, in terms of gifts of equipment, gifts of vehicles, trainings, and even personnel we have in the country." The uniformed official sitting by his side looked at him with some disbelief.

"Gifts?" he said. "They are not gifts." He paused, then said: "We, in fact, expect a return on our investment."

After our inspection in Huixtla, we were all allowed back on the bus, but less than 30 minutes later, the bus came to a halt again. Now night had fallen. An INM agent boarded and walked the narrow passageway, staring into everyone's face until she reached the back. She asked Campbell and me for our papers, then walked several rows up, and turned to a woman with long, slightly graying braids and the boy sitting next to her. There was a long pause after she asked for their documents, and the bus was silent; almost everybody was watching. I could hear papers shuffling, and after a while, the woman with the braids stood up. I thought she was the target, but she was simply making way for the child. He handed the hovering agent a long piece of paper. The agent unfolded it as she stood in the aisle. She gave it a quick glance. She gestured with her hand for him to get up. He looked 10 years old, maybe even younger. He walked off the bus alone. I waited for someone to join him. Nobody did. The INM agent followed him. Seconds later, the lights went off. The bus shifted into gear and as we sped by, I could no longer see the child.

"WE HAVE TAUGHT THE MEXICANS HOW TO FISH"

Since Mexico started Programa Frontera Sur in 2014, there has been a "dramatic increase in security operations," according to the Washington Office on Latin America (WOLA).[3] U.S. twenty-first century border assistance has supported the Mexican National Immigration Institute with a training program to enhance its capacity to "identify and interview vulnerable populations" and teach it deportation "best practices." In May 2017, thirty INM agents began a thirty-day pilot-program training course with the U.S. government to "improve baseline skills." The International Bureau of Narcotics and Law Enforcement Affairs, the INL, has also supported the presence of CBP and ICE "mentors" in Mexico's immigration detention prisons to help interrogate people "of interest." The "return" on this investment has been an 85 percent increase in arrests of northbound migrants in the first two years.[4]

As for the drug war, U.S. General Lori Robinson said in April 2017 that Northern Command worked "closely with the U.S. interagency community and the Mexican interagency organizations to support the Government of Mexico's Southern Border Strategy to improve security on their border with Guatemala and Belize."[5] Robinson also stated that Northcom was focusing on "ensuring the timely delivery of a record Foreign Military Sales of over a billion dollars in UH-60 Black Hawk helicopters and High Mobility Multipurpose Wheeled Vehicles."

That wasn't the only equipment and training the U.S. Department of Defense has provided to the Mexican military patrolling the country's southern borders. Other U.S. investments have included backscatter X-ray vans and contraband detection equipment;[6] funds for the INM, the Mexican Marines, and the federal police for facility construction, patrol boats, night vision, communication equipment, and maritime sensors; and helicopters, which, according to WOLA, have been spotted near Mexico's southern border. The U.S. has also supplied K-9 units, drug- and contraband-sniffing dogs.[7] "Dogs are very popular. Everybody wants dogs," the CBP International Affairs officials told me.

Antonio Trindade, director of the U.S. Border Patrol's Enforcement Systems Division, in April 2017, told industry and high-level government officials at the San Antonio Border Security Expo:

> We are looking to expand our reach at the border … It's very big to us. The largest one is actually the project that is going on in Mexico. Basically, DHS with Northern Command and the Department of State is building a biometric solution similar to IDENT [the biometric system CBP already uses in the United States] in Mexico, and it is starting at the Tapachula border crossing—at the southern tip of Mexico.

He concluded, "So, it's a great time for biometrics."

Tony Crowder, commander of the U.S. CBP Air and Marine Operations Center in Riverside, California, speaking at the same Border Security Expo, probably explained best what the United States was doing not only in Mexico, but also worldwide: "We are fusing over 450 sensors that are looking out into the entire Western hemisphere." He said Air and Marine Operations was the world's largest aviation and maritime law enforcement agency. It employed more than 1,200 agents and had offices in seventy locations. It had 260 aircraft of twenty-six different types and approximately 300 "maritime vessels." He said the agency was often called to work in the Baltic and Middle Eastern nations, and that it had gone into Mexico and "built technology."

In Mexico, CBP gave Mexican officials "domain awareness capability." He said, "we coordinated with them directly in their country, with as many as 600 to 800 tactical responses in a year's time with sharing domain awareness with them." By this he meant that CBP shared a considerable amount of real-time, actionable information with Mexico from an air, land, or maritime domain.

Then Crowder got to his main point: "We have taught the Mexicans how to fish, is how I describe it." But this hardly means, to him, that the U.S. can now pack up and go home. "Even though we have all this surveillance capability, we don't have enough, we need more."

Nelson Balido, CEO of the Border Commerce and Security Council—a council representing more than forty companies—told me during a phone interview that the problem was "the weed. And the weed, the roots are coming from Mexico and south. So how do you start cutting the weed from the root? You can't just trim the tips. We got to eradicate the weed." By "the weed," I thought at the time, Balido almost certainly meant criminal organizations, but, in retrospect, I couldn't be sure. He might have been talking about the blowback—about Mazapil protesting Goldcorp, about individuals and groups fighting and resisting the increasing inequalities, about the strong social movements pushing for a new world, even about individuals on a daily basis subverting border enforcement.

According to Balido, despite the spectacular growth of its apparatus, what Mexico was doing was not enough. When I asked him how much more he thought was needed for Mexico to achieve "security," he said, "You know we need to continue what we are doing today, and we should double our efforts ... Because at the end of the day we are going to save more in the U.S. if we do more there. Then we should measure it."

Balido asked me a series of rhetorical questions.

"Are we apprehending more bad people?"

"Are we putting more people in jail?"

"Maybe it takes triple or quadruple, I don't know," he finished.

Back at the Seguridad Expo in Mexico City, a zealous U.S. Embassy representative approached me at the U.S. Commerce Department booth, speaking in Anglo-accented Spanish. When I responded in English, he told me Commerce was there to help U.S. companies connect with other countries in the global market. There was a purple magazine on the booth's counter with the cover line, "EXPORT USA, THE GLOBAL ECONOMY: WHERE DOES YOUR COMPANY FIT IN?"

When I asked him what Commerce was doing at the expo, he told me that they were trying to advance "U.S. interests."

He pointed toward the companies in PABELLON USA, the U.S. pavilion, as if such interests were right before our eyes. There was the red, busy booth of Stalker Radar. There was Identicard, which specialized in ID badging programs and identification solutions. There was 6K Systems. There was Crossmatch Biometric Security. There was Alvarado, which specialized in turnstiles and gates. There was even the outdoor-gear store REI, among others, many others. The Embassy representative was friendly, but became a bit nervous when he realized that I was a journalist. I asked him how the whole thing worked. He said that if Mexico announced a "platform," in this case a security platform, the Commerce Department could suggest that a U.S. company come in.

Mexico's security, he said, is a concern for us and vital for our security.

Plus, we get to promote U.S. businesses and "create jobs."

It's a "win, win, win," he said, a huge return on the investment, which is only expected to grow.

"THE HIDDEN HAND OF THE MARKET WILL NOT WORK WITHOUT A HIDDEN FIST"

"The hidden hand of the market will never work without a hidden fist—McDonald's cannot flourish without McDonnell Douglas, the builder of the F-15," New York Times columnist Thomas Friedman wrote in one of his most prescient columns in 1999. "And the hidden fist that keeps the world safe for Silicon Valley's technologies is called the United States Army, Air Force, Navy and Marine Corps."[8] Friedman quoted historian Robert Kagan, "Good ideas and technologies need a strong power that promotes those ideas by example and protects those ideas by winning on the battlefield." Friedman's description is more fully developed now in 2018: a world whose battlefields are at the edges of where the rich and powerful meet the poor and marginalized, who must be managed, confined, and pacified.

These were the places where the global supply chains needed to be maintained and protected.

Leslie A. Bassett, former deputy chief of mission at the U.S. Embassy in Mexico, was very clear on the issue:

> A lot of things we count on every day for our fast food, for our commodities, for Walmart, for anything else, come across that border from Mexico. And they [CBP] make sure it gets there on time. So that's a very important part of our economy. So we need free trade and we need safe trade. And what CBP does for us is make sure both things are possible.[9]

Matt Vega, former in-house senior counsel of Federal Express, agreed: "We believe in the globalization of CBP initiatives."[10] Or, as writer and journalist John Washington—who has covered border and immigration issues extensively—put it, CBP and its international programs have become "global capitalism's bouncers."[11]

Borderlands historian Guadalupe Castillo told me in an interview, "The nation-state has become the policeman for the corporate world," creating borders to "clear the landscape for those in the world for whom borders don't exist"; that is, the "1 percent." As Alan Bersin notes, expediting trade and heightened security are complementary elements of a single process in what has become "the cornerstone of our system of border management in the United States." The result is a "co-created regulatory regime," a sort of empire of partnerships, involving foreign governments, client regimes, and the private sector, to ensure the free flow of Western civilization,[12] precisely what Australian Department of Home Affairs secretary Michael Pezzullo was talking about at the International Summit on Borders.

Friedman's recognition of the "hidden fist" came in an era when new waves of corporations were migrating into the Americas at breakneck speed, facilitated by economic and trade regimes like NAFTA. The wave brought in mining companies like Goldcorp in Zacatecas; African palm and eucalyptus plantations; hydroelectric mega-dams; Walmarts and Home Depots; oil exploration and cross-border pipelines; and subsidized imports from U.S. agribusiness. In Central America, food imports increased by 78 percent. According to trade expert Ben Beachy, "Honduras went from being a net agricultural exporter to the United States in the six straight years before the Central American Free Trade Agreement [implemented in 2005] to being a net agricultural importer from the United States in the six straight years after the deal took effect."[13] The local farmers displaced by this development were supposed to find solace in the many foreign factories also enjoying a borderless world and arriving in Central America. But since CAFTA, in Guatemala, there has been a 40 percent decrease in apparel production, one key sector expected to absorb such workers.

These were factors that Meissner was undoubtedly taking into account for Mexico as she argued for more hardened borders before the U.S. Congress in 1992. After NAFTA, small farmers were so ravaged, as Marco Antonio Velazquez Naverrete of the Mexican Network on Free Trade explained to me in 2008, it was like the aftermath of a war or natural disaster. The New Republic reported, "as cheap American foodstuffs flooded Mexico's markets and as U.S. agribusiness moved in, 1.1 million small farmers—and 1.4 million other Mexicans dependent upon the farm sector—were driven out of work between 1993 and 2005. Wages dropped so precipitously that today the income of a farm laborer is one-third that of what it was before NAFTA."[14] As highly subsidized U.S. corn moved into Mexico through monolith corporate grain movers such as Cargill and Archer Daniel Midland, the number of undocumented Mexicans living in the United States increased from 4.8 million in 1993 to 11.7 million in 2012.[15] Corn imports weren't the only factor driving the exodus: The import of big-box stores killed an estimated 28,000 small and medium-sized businesses.[16] And hotels built in places like the Bahias of Huatulco, where Holiday Inn displaced a whole fishing community, and took all the profits back to their headquarters in the United States. This was "foreign investment." The Zapatistas in southern Mexico saw it coming during their uprising in 1994, when they claimed that "NAFTA was a death sentence to the Indigenous people" on the very day it was implemented. Chiapas, where Campbell and I saw the boy pulled off the bus, which had long been one of the most militarized places in Mexico, had also become a border zone, a prime example of Friedman's "hidden fist."

Chiapas is not only militarized, it is notably rich in resources. Chiapas provides 44.5 percent of Mexico's hydroelectric power and 7.5 percent of its electricity. In 2015, there were 99 mining concessions, there, covering 14 percent of Chiapan territory, with licenses that will last until 2050 and 2060.[17] "Chiapas loses blood through many veins: through oil and gas ducts, electric lines, railways; through bank accounts, trucks, vans, boats and planes; through clandestine paths, gaps, and forest trails," wrote Zapatista subcommander Marcos in his communique "The Southeast in Two Winds: A Storm and a Prophecy," in 1992. "This land continues to pay tribute to the imperialists: petroleum, electricity, cattle, money, coffee, banana, honey, corn, cacao, tobacco, sugar, soy, melon, sorghum, mamey, mango, tamarind, avocado, and Chiapaneco blood all flow as a result of the thousand teeth sunk into the throat of the Mexican Southeast."

Twenty-five years later, anthropologist Rebecca Galemba analyzed the same subject in *Contraband Corridor: Making a Living at the Mexico-Guatemala Border*, a book that examines this border buildup and Mexico's larger plans for regional development, including extraction and Special Economic Zones: "In the context of securitized neoliberalism, a heightened security and military presence in Chiapas creates a climate conducive to securing investment, resource extraction, and road construction that serves mega-developmental projects while silencing and criminalizing opposition and controlling mobility."

Also Chiapas (and Mesoamerica) was a prime example of a place where, as author Dawn Paley argued in her book *Drug War Capitalism*, "the violence and forced displacement resulting from the drug war are experienced most acutely by poor and working people and migrants, often in resource rich or geographically strategic areas."

In a powerful sense, there is little difference between the ultimate goals of counterinsurgency and border militarization; both are sharp examples of the "hidden fist." Galemba expresses the ultimate nugget of truth shown so clearly in Chiapas's recent history: "As neoliberal states rolled back their provision of services and supports for their populations, they have increasingly played the function of "security providers for global capital."[18] Global capitalism's bouncers.

Gustavo Cuevas has all the characteristics of a bouncer for global capitalism. I heard him speak at the Expo Seguridad in Mexico City, after the conversation between Gendarmería commander Benjamin Grajeda and Goldcorp representative Daniel Arvayo. Cuevas, once head of security for President Enrique Peña Nieto's campaign in the early 2010s, was now head of security for Mexico's Electricity Commission, the CFE. When asked about the biggest threats facing Mexico at the time, he did not answer "organized crime" or "drug cartels." Instead, he said one of the biggest problems was the "*tema social*"—social movements. "For a long time," he said, "we have had a 'take over the plant, sit down protest, and don't let anyone enter' culture, 'saying that it's for pollution, saying that it's for whatever.'"

Cuevas was tasked with protecting Mexico's 3,000 electric installations—47 percent run by PEMEX, the semi-privatized national oil company; 17 percent by hydroelectric companies, and 13 percent by his own CFE—against the "problems" of social protests and the demands of *campesinos*.

In February 2014, when a group of small farmers occupied the Adolfo Lopez Mateos hydroelectric dam, Cuevas arrived in a CFE helicopter and immediately began berating and insulting them. Journalist Arnulfo Mora heard Cuevas tell them, "I am warning you if you keep on with this takeover of these installations, I have the ability to immediately ask for the intervention of the Federal Police, and you and your children will be taken, shackled—with your hands tied behind your back, to the capital."[19]

Hearing Benjamin Grajeda and Daniel Arvayo and finally Cuevas talk so openly about the "*tema social*" wasn't a surprise, although officials so often divert attention from social unrest with rhetoric about criminal networks. Through the years I have seen over and over again the Mexican military and security apparatus used to pacify Mexico's vast social movements, which ranged from teachers unions such as the Oaxacan Section 22 to armed uprisings like the Zapatistas in Chiapas. In July 1999, I went to the small town of La Realidad to spend a month as a human rights observer. Every morning at 7:00 a.m. and 10:00 a.m. people from the international community would go out to the dirt road that ran through the community and watch the patrolling army caravan rumble through. I came to La Realidad one person, and left as another. In 2005, I moved to Oaxaca and lived there for the next four years, working with an organization called Witness for Peace that looked closely at U.S. policy impacts in Mexico, especially NAFTA and its connections with displacement and immigration. I remember a 2005 meeting with an indigenous rights organization called Flor y Canto whose main issue at the time was water privatization, particularly the Coca Cola Company's takeover of water sources throughout Oaxaca, not only for the soda but also for their bottled water brand, Ciel. Like the mining companies, this multinational monolith seized the water sources of entire communities. (Although unlike the mining companies, according to Flor y Canto, it often promised to build schools in return.) When I pointed out to Flor y Canto that analysts were saying future wars would be not over oil, but over water, the director Carmen Santiago Alonso immediately corrected me. She told me there wasn't anything "future" about it. The water wars were already on.

Flor y Canto organizers also noted that Oaxaca, a famous tourist destination because of its beauty and its traditions, suffered the same underlying conditions as in Chiapas—76 percent of Oaxaca's people lived in conditions of poverty or extreme poverty. Ten years ago in Chiapas, they said, the result had been an insurrection.

The words were prophetic.

On June 14, 2006, Oaxacan state police violently evicted an occupation of the capital's *centro* staged by the teachers union. By the afternoon, thousands of Oaxacans had organized and driven the police out. The police would not return for six months. I remember walking into the *centro* the evening of June 14, past the barricades of the movement, into an area that looked like the aftermath of a war zone, with piles of rocks and stones covering Oaxaca's beautiful cobblestone streets.

I have seen many marches in Mexico, even two million people streaming into Mexico City in 2006, supporters of Andrés Manuel López Obrador, after dubious election results showed him losing by less than one percentage point to Felipe Calderon of the conservative National Action Party. (In 2018, AMLO, running as the center-left candidate, would win the presidency). But the mega-march that happened in Oaxaca soon after June 14, 2006 and the formation of what would become the APPO (Popular Assembly of the People of Oaxaca) was unlike anything I had seen before. In a driving rain, the marchers proceeded through the city, stopping at the Parque Juarez near Oaxaca's center. Through the downpour, the people kept coming, the young and the old, students and teachers, anarchists and *campesinos*, Oaxacans of all shapes and sizes, marching into the *centro*—every time I thought the human flow was going to end, more people came, unending as the rain. The march was 16 kilometers long. The rain became torrential; the people marched right through it. What I saw on that day was a palpable, unstoppable power. What I saw was what elite interests—the interests represented by Cuevas and Arvayo and Washington, DC—were really worried about: a critical mass of humanity completely fed up with the injustices of the status quo, a mass that had the power to overthrow regimes.

SUBVERTING THE BORDER

At first I didn't notice the family when they drifted by me and Jeff Abbott on one of the inner-tube rafts that crossed the River Suchiate on the Guatemala-Mexican border. We were on another raft and too busy watching the kids in the river swimming around and splashing in the water. We were too busy looking up at the gray official port of entry about a quarter-mile away on the Mexican side of the bridge. We were too busy watching the other rafts not only filled with people but with all kinds of stuff ranging from toilet paper to beer to sodas to boxes of Maruchan, gliding down the river as people had been doing for hundreds of years, long before the international boundary was established. It was an example of how a border crossing operates between two countries when neither the bureaucracy nor the inter-rogations exist.

Then, from where we bobbed on the raft, a soldier caught my atten-tion, patrolling alone along the path on the Mexican side. He stopped and said something to a man who was pedaling one of the large tri-cycles that hauled goods to the shore. We had just heard that day in August 2014 that Mexico was going to send an additional 2,000 sol-diers and 400 police to patrol the border; we were not sure then what that meant. It meant that this was where, as officials have said, the United States border really began.

To reach the soldier, I had to get off the raft quickly, and almost fell into the river. The soldier seemed to be badgering the tricyclist, but he was already walking away when I ran up with an adrenaline-fueled surge of questions. I barely noticed the Guatemalan family—six women and two men—struggling to get off the raft after breaching the border. To the soldier, I yelled a desperate sounding, out-of-breath "*Señor!*" The soldier turned swiftly around, his large automatic weapon following the motion of his body. He wore jungle camouflage and a hat. He looked twenty years old, if that. His face expressed an intense devotion to his job, and at the same time the air of a person who didn't really know what he was doing. Along the path ahead of us came other tricycles stacked with goods. Behind the soldier, below, other rafters awaited *pasajes* (customers) under a shaded tent, briefly safe from the burning sun. Some were playing cards. By the shore, the Guatemalan family was still struggling to get off the raft. Many other people came and went. In the United States, what they were doing would be considered illegal entry and illegal reentry. They would be shackled and brought before a judge. They might receive 30 days in jail, 60 days, 90 days, 180 days, or even 20 years, depending on the charge.

I told the soldier that I was from the press, from the United States, and I just wanted to ask what he was doing, if he was patrolling the border. He said, "yes," though I didn't think he meant it the same way a U.S. Border Patrol agent would. Then he asked, "Are you OK?" "Is everything OK?" His questions came like machine gun fire. His eyes were looking all around me, vigilant, in search of danger. I said, "Yes,

I am OK. I just wanted to know if you were patrolling." When he said yes again, he pointed to more soldiers up the way, walking through the trampled grass, coming right toward us, also, I presumed, patrolling the border. All the men had on camo, carried large guns, and wore helmets. I was meditating upon this convergence of soldiers when the Guatemalan family of six appeared on the path, moving like a force of nature, and they were. They looked at Abbott, who had also wandered up, and yelled, in the most festive of tones, "*Vamos al norte!*" We're going to the north, the United States, can you take us? An older woman looked back at us, cackling, obviously joking, and ignoring the soldier completely. At that moment, as I watched the soldier walk away, that political borderline, which had existed for little more than 100 years, seemed arbitrary, ridiculous.

I thought I'd seen the last of the Guatemalan family. But 30 minutes later, much to my glee, we'd all crammed into a small van together, destination Tapachula. The windows were open, but since we weren't moving yet, only the slightest breeze drifted through the hot van. The woman in front of us, who introduced herself as Sandra, immediately welcomed Abbott and me as part of their family. "At least for this trip to Tapachula." Strong laughter. They were going to the wake of a family member. They were from across the border, Monte Rico, Guatemala. Then Sandra, looking at us dripping with sweat, said, "I see that you came for the cool weather." Her laugh was explosive, and contagious as it swept through the van all the way to the front where the driver and the driver's assistant, who with colorful peso bills wedged between his fingers, appreciated the humor with a smile. The driver and his assistant were the only two Mexicans in the bunch.

Once we were on the road, the humid air swirled blissfully through the van, filling it with a sweet tinge and the slight smell of rain. Up ahead I could see a buildup of clouds that seemed ready to burst. Outside of Ciudad Hidalgo, the landscape became rich, tropical green. We traveled on a two-lane paved road. We came to a place where trucks were pulled off to the side of the road. The driver pulled onto the shoulder and stopped the van. He yelled that there was an immigrant checkpoint up the road. "Do you have all your papers?"

There was a murmured conversation for a moment at the front of the van. During my stay in the region, everybody talked about Mexico ramping up its border patrolling. Everybody talked about the *operativos*. And everybody I spoke with, just about everybody, from the shoe shiners to the hotel proprietors to the *tienda* clerks to the nongovernmental organizations, thought their coming was a result of direct orders from the United States. This statement was often made without evidence, as an unquestioned truth. There was no other way to explain it.

After a murmured conversation, the driver pulled around and headed back on the two-lane paved road toward Ciudad Hidalgo. I figured we were going back to the border, that the family would miss the wake. Then the van took a swift right. We were going back the other way on a bumpy dirt road. Suddenly the purpled clouds were upon us, moving fast over the landscape. We were going parallel to the main road. We were going to evade the checkpoint.

Sandra turned around and gave us a smile.

"We don't have papers!" she exclaimed, and then let out a laugh that was so joyful that her mother, sitting in front of her with a blanket over her shoulders, burst into laughter, too. So did I and so did Abbott and so did everybody. And just then the sky exploded with rain, falling diagonally over the sky.

Off to the side of the road, as we drove into the blowing rain, stood an old *campesino* next to his horse. By his look, he didn't ordinarily see *combis* drive past his land. I wondered how many similar moments like this were happening around the world. It became apparent, even with the billions and billions spent, the investment, the technologies, the drug-sniffing dogs, the smart walls and checkpoints, how easy it was to subvert a border with a little grassroots organizing, the proper coordination, and a joyful spirit.

Part Six

Resistance and Transformation on the U.S.-Middle East Border

Radical change cannot and will not be negotiated by governments; it can only be enforced by the people. By the public. *A public who can link hands across national borders.*

Arundhati Roy

12.

The Unholstered Border

It's not easy to tear down a border wall. Artist Khaled Jarrar is trying anyway. He is hitting the towering thrity-foot concrete wall over and over again with a chisel and a large wooden mallet. Bits and pieces of the wall burst into the air and fall to the ground around him in a brief, powerful blizzard. As Jarrar continues to bang away at one of the most common pieces of nation-state infrastructure of the twenty-first century, his face turns red. He can only do it for so long. What if soldiers or Border Police pass by? The Israeli Defense Forces have shot at Palestinians for much less. Even Jarrar himself doesn't know in that moment that he is going to transform that wall, turn it into a sculpture.

The wall that Jarrar is pounding and carving is in Bir Nabala, East Jerusalem. It is a neighborhood where Palestinian life and commerce once thrived; now it is reduced to a "ghost town." Birds fly back and forth between the industrial park and the abandoned housing, resting from time to time on the concertina wire that tops the towering concrete wall. On the Palestinian side, the birds fly out of the open windows of buildings reminiscent of collapsing empty structures in the ruined towns of the U.S. Rust Belt. What was a three-minute walk to the local school before the wall was constructed has become a journey of three to four hours for those who have the authorization to get through the mega-militarized, time-devouring checkpoint.

On the road en route to Bir Nabala, Jamal Juma of the Palestinian organization Stop the Wall pointed to a pile of rubble off to the side of the road. It was one of the many consequences of border wall construction. Juma said it had been a house, that a man had been building for years and years, to be ready for his children when they returned to Palestine from the United States. The man had used much of his life savings to build it. Then the Israeli bulldozers came and left a pile of crushed concrete.

Juma described the wall construction the way survivors describe hurricanes: an elemental disaster that had left a path of destruction in its wake, demolishing homes, trees, and markets, including one of the main markets where farmers sold their fruits and vegetables. "It had everything," Juma said of that market, even dentists. It was the heart of the region. It was destroyed by bulldozers. It was a disaster," he repeated. The wall destroyed farmland and usurped water sources, including the biggest aquifer in the West Bank. According to Juma, the boundary building was another phase of the Nakba, the catastrophe that began in 1948 with the forced removal of tens of thousands of people for the creation of the state of Israel.

The wall that Jarrar was attempting to destroy with his mallet and chisel was part of this long historic process. At the same time, to Jarrar, this annexation wall represented something far bigger than the Israeli occupation. It had vivid global implications.

"IF YOU ARE GOING TO TAKE OUT YOUR GUN, THEN YOU HAVE TO SHOOT IT."

I saw those global implications at play at a three-day conference in Tel Aviv in June 2017. The man who had just put his hands around the neck of a young activist outside the walls of the convention center was clean-cut: white pressed shirt, khaki pants, a laminated ISDEF name tag dangling on his chest. ISDEF stood for Israeli Defense, Israel's biggest weapons and homeland security convention. On site, 250 exhibitors from different private, primarily Israeli companies hosted 15,000 visitors from around the globe. Like many such conventions, it has grown exponentially, according to Yehiel Gozal, CEO of Yahad-United for Israeli Soldiers, "as world terrorism and the refugee crisis spreads."

I rushed to the scene of the assault, unable to believe it was happening in broad daylight, snapping pictures on the fly, feeling an athletic prowess I was unaware I possessed. By the time I got really close, the man—who I imagined was one of the exhibitors—had released the activist. The activist was taking part in something that rarely happened at these conventions: a small yet boisterous and quite committed protest whose members held up signs at the startled exhibitors and visitors who passed by. A loud, energetic line of drummers banged away, amplifying the protest, making the protesters—who were Israeli and international—seem like thousands. On many occasions exhibitors and other participants quickened their pace, and walked through the armed security who guarded the doors of the convention center that absorbed them. The beating of the drums was like the smash of Jarrar's sledgehammer and chisel against the concrete border wall.

If the assault I'd witnessed was any indication, here, just as at the border, it was "unwise" to challenge the sanctity of the homeland security and weapons industries.

The man with the name tag turned from the Israeli activist and looked directly at me, into the camera. I switched to video. He made a funny face and got so close I could see all the hairs in his well-trimmed mustache. His face reminded me of former Chicago Bears coach Mike Ditka. This guy, I knew, could break.

"Be a man," he said in a deep voice, enunciating every word, "take my picture."

He didn't realize that I was filming. "I am taking your picture," I told him.

"Be a man," he repeated again in a menacing whisper, pausing a little longer—"take my picture."

The drums kept banging away in the background, creating a sense of tension-filled theater. He seemed to think we were engaging in some duel of masculinity.

I was there as part of an international contingent, with people from countries around the world where militaries, homeland security forces, and police were using Israeli technology and weapons. There were people from Colombia, from the favelas of Rio de Janeiro, from Bosnia, New York, Miami, South Korea, and South Africa; there were members of the War Resisters League from the United Kingdom. We were attending a shadow conference, an answer to ISDEF's convention, organized by the Israeli groups Coalition of Women for Peace and Hamushim, where we would discuss in detail the proliferation of Israeli technologies in the world's cities and neighborhoods and at the world's border zones. I was the only journalist there. I'd been invited to discuss the Israeli border control technology exported to the United States.

The ISDEF conference was central to the power of the constellation I call the U.S.-Middle Eastern border. "The con-ops for border breach in that region is not we're going to arrest you," a former CBP agent who now works for a private Israeli company told me, "it's we're going to shoot you." And if you dare challenge the legitimacy of this aggressive border, advertised as the global border of the future, as so many do in different ways, a man like the one I was filming will appear.

"Be a man, take my picture," he said yet again, then abruptly turned and walked away. He joined the small group of ISDEF reps he'd been walking with. Then he stopped, as if something had occurred to him mid-step. He turned around. He walked back to me.

"Let me give you some advice," he said, and then, unintentionally, explained the unholstered borders of the Middle East: "Never pick up a gun if you are not going to use it."

ANGER

Some time after that remarkable experience, I saw Khaled Jarrar again, when he spoke to a class at Prescott College in Arizona and explained his broader reasons for smashing the wall in Bir Nabala. The artist told the students, "By living under occupation, I've come from a place where I've been beaten by soldiers since I was six years old." Some people study social justice, he said. "I have not studied it. I have lived my whole life in social justice."

"I believe in breaking lines of division," he told the class. Divisions are places where "politicians use the fear of the Other."

For Jarrar, at first it was personal. He took up his hammer after his Palestinian uncle began to build the West Bank wall. His uncle was a farmer from Arranah, just outside of Jenin. But Israel's control of the water supply (and how much flowed into the Palestinian occupied territory) and its seizure of land had made it virtually impossible for his uncle to farm. His uncle needed a job, and Colonel Danny Tirza, the wall's architect, was hiring. Jarrar could not believe that his uncle was *building* the wall. It was infuriating. His uncle had joined the immigrant workers—including from the Philippines and Romania—who were the blue-collar boundary builders. It was a solid concrete wall. It was hard labor. They got paid, Jarrar said, maybe $20 to $30 day, where an Israeli construction worker would have earned $70 to $110. They had no benefits, no health insurance, no transportation.

Jarrar had slammed the wall with anger. He said it was a "good anger," a "healthy anger," an anger that he needed to get out of his system, to arrive at a new place where the destruction could lead to transformation. Over and over again, he'd smashed the wall. When he swung the hammer, he looked like an athlete, as if he were participating in an Olympic event. His swings were constant, even graceful. His face went red and sweat streamed down his forehead, as the chips of the world's most complete system of exclusion fell around him like snow. Sometimes he stayed for five minutes. Sometimes twenty minutes. Like a border crossing, as Jarrar showed in his documentary *The Infiltrators*, it depended on the situation. You had to move intelligently, you had to wait and watch, you had to move quickly if needed. Every chunk of concrete that fell to the ground, he put into a drum. On a good day, he accumulated three to four kilograms of broken border wall.

PERFECTED APARTHEID

Although the international contingent had met with many Palestinian groups in Ramallah, in Bethlehem, in Nablus, no Palestinian was able to accompany us to where we stood at that Tel Aviv convention center. This included Jarrar, whose studio was in Bir Nabala. Most did not have the authorized papers or license plates. The man with the ISDEF badge had been strangling an Israeli student (just returned from studying abroad at the University of Michigan), not a Palestinian. In front of the convention center, Terry Crawford-Browne, an ex-banker turned activist with an encyclopedic memory of South African history, compared Israel to apartheid South Africa, with its system of institutionalized racial segregation, which lasted from 1948 to the 1990s. He told me that to enter white South Africa, black people needed a permit signed by their employer, a sort of "work visa," that accompanied a passbook with the holder's picture and address. Police officers, who practiced constant racial profiling, had the power at any time to "demand the production of a passbook." Whoever didn't have a "work visa" from a white employer would become one of the "millions of people" arrested, possibly imprisoned, and then deported back to the *bantustans*, the "homelands" carved out of the 13 percent of South African territory designated for black and mixed-race people. The other 87 percent of the country, including—of course—the most mineral-rich land, was "white South Africa."

The intention of the "grand apartheid scheme" was to make the *bantustans* independent countries with their own capitals, presidents, and parliaments. Stephan Faris, in his essay "Homelands," says "there was no disguising the fact that the division of the country into separate but unequal states was not an alternative to apartheid, but an extension of it."[1] Black people from these countries would provide cheap cross-border labor for the mines, as migrant workers with no rights of citizenship. Once the homelands were separate countries, the apartheid system could carry on without all the horrible public relations. Anti-apartheid activist Steven Biko, who died in police custody in 1977, saw right through this, as did much of the international community, which never recognized the *bantustans* as independent countries. Biko called them "the single greatest fraud ever invented by white politicians."[2]

Although in South Africa the "grand apartheid scheme" failed, the same design implemented at a global level had not. Faris writes:

If I've come to the conclusion that our immigration policies are one of the great moral challenges of our time, it's in part because they very much resemble one of the most clear-cut acts of injustice in recent history: an attempt by South Africa's apartheid regime to preserve racial privileges in the face of worldwide opposition.

Was what we had now even more vicious than the South African system, a sort of unholstered apartheid? I asked Crawford-Browne if between white South Africa and the "homelands" there had been checkpoints guarding the boundary lines. "No checkpoints. We had no apartheid walls. We had no apartheid roads. People could travel, if they could afford it, in search of work in Johannesburg, by train or bus." Still, you had to worry about the police. "You had to have a pass. Now, in comparison to the ID systems here," he said, pointing up at the outside walls of the ISDEF convention where inside it was undoubtedly brimming with biometrics displays, "we didn't have the technology. So it was bad enough, it was humiliating, but it wasn't as vicious as we have it here."

It was worse here in Israel, he kept repeating. This was not meant to privilege one person's pain over another's, but to point out that the fundamental idea behind South African apartheid has not been extinguished. Instead, it has been intensified. Police, militaries, and nation-states now have more ability to stop mobility, to arrest, incarcerate, and segregate. "Technology makes it possible. It's a new level that we just didn't have."

"You might say that Israel has perfected apartheid," Crawford added.

Crawford, of course, wasn't alone in calling Israel an apartheid state. Just a few months before our conversation in 2017, a United Nations report had broken new ground and declared that Israel had established "an apartheid regime that oppresses and dominates the Palestinian people as a whole."[3]

And it was a system—or a series of systems and technologies— not simply confined to this one place in the Middle East but also sold, exported, and deployed around the world in a global industry undreamed of in the days of South African apartheid.

At the end, Crawford looked at me and said, "You think you [the United States] are going to control the Mexican border with a wall?"

But, of course, the United States–Mexico border already had a wall. The enforcement apparatus had a series of checkpoints going deep into a 100-mile border zone. And there was the technology—much of it coming from Israeli companies—already deployed, including the high-tech surveillance towers. There were still huge and important differences between the U.S.-Mexico border and Israel-Palestine. The United States, as one example, was not running bombing campaigns into northern Mexico, nor demolishing houses. However, the systems of border controls and surveillance were strikingly similar. This was a system that operated not only on U.S. territorial borders, but also had been exported throughout the Americas, the Caribbean, the wider Middle East, and Asia. U.S. boundary-building efforts both at home and abroad often involved using and exporting technologies developed in Israel's apartheid "laboratories."

In terms of capacity, of technology, of walls, checkpoints, drones, biometric systems, even prison space, the South African apartheid system was rudimentary compared with not only the United States' or Israel's, but with just about any other border system, developing or developed, around the globe. In terms of hindering or preventing mobility, the apartheid system never really ended. The ability to stop people from crossing lines of division is stronger now than it has ever been.

THE PALESTINIAN PASSPORT

Even before Jarrar began smashing the border wall, the focus of much of his artistic work centered squarely on borders and immigration controls. One of his first exhibitions was called "At the Checkpoint." In 2007, he put up a series of photographs of people passing through and interrogated at checkpoints, along the walkway leading into the actual Hawara checkpoint in the West Bank. The intention was to reveal "the system of oppression, the system of control," in a place where it had been normalized. The intention was to challenge this normalization. Jarrar's art homed in very intentionally, he told me, on what the state declared "untouchable": the wall, the checkpoint, the passport. He wanted to demonstrate without a doubt that not only were these things touchable, but also you could directly alter them, and if you touched them, although you would have to watch out for the attack dogs, you could transform them into something completely different.

For example, Jarrar created a State of Palestine passport stamp. (No such stamp exists, of course.) Front and center it featured a Palestinian sunbird—the national bird of Palestine. The bird had the word "Palestinian" in its official name, Jarrar explained to me with a smile, and there was no way you could remove it or erase it. The name "Palestine" was its own type of untouchable. In different parts of the world, Jarrar had "illegally" stamped 700 real passports. On one occasion, a border guard on the Allenby Bridge, between the West Bank and Jordan, looked at the stamp and said, "I didn't even know that they had one of those."

GLOBAL APARTHEID

In *Clandestine Crossings: Migrants and Coyotes on the Texas-Mexico border*, anthropologist David Spener describes how border guards waved him, an Anglo, light-skinned, middle-class man, through ports of entry in the 1990s without asking him for identification, while dark-skinned, working-class Mexicans were "routinely stopped, questioned, and required to produce passes." Spener remembers thinking, "So this is what apartheid looks like."[4] (This phenomenon is corroborated in a report published by the organization People Helping People in 2015 that shows a clear pattern of profiling at Border Patrol interior checkpoints for people of color.)[5] Spener had in mind the "pass-law system" in South Africa. The same dynamic has become increasingly normal for international boundaries between countries, and "especially vigorous at the boundaries between affluent and poor/light-skinned and dark-skinned regions of the global system," Spener writes.

It wasn't until ten years later that Spener realized there were other scholars who had come to the same conclusion and developed a conceptual framework for understanding world dynamics through these types of border systems. The term *global apartheid* referred to the "reliance on the principle of national sovereignty as a pretext for grossly unequal distribution of wealth, power, and well-being among nation-states in a way that mirrors the operation of the domestic regime of white supremacy in South Africa from 1948 to 1994."[6]

Faris in *Homelands* takes this idea further. "If citizenship is no different than a private club with arcane rules for admission, how can we continue to allow the color of our passport to shape the fate of millions of children?" He quotes the moral philosopher Joseph Carens —a professor at the University of Toronto—who compared the global system of immigration to medieval feudalism, in which "privilege is a birthright and wealth and opportunity are more likely to be inherited than earned. This world is organized into different states with vast inequalities between them."[7]

This cannot work, according to Carens, without closed borders.

"So accustomed are we to this game of geographical roulette that we have been blinded by the fact that it's morally indefensible to divide the people of the Earth into rich and poor," Faris writes, "advantaged and disadvantaged, victims and survivors according to the criterion that is largely arbitrary and completely out of their control." It was the scaffolding of these inequalities that Jarrar sought to destroy with his sledgehammer.

BORDERWORKS

British political scientist Christopher Rumford had a term for what Jarrar was doing: *borderworks*.[8] The late Rumford contended that border building and border eroding were not exclusively in the hands of the nation-state. Borderworks could also be anything that changed the border and its landscape.

Ruben Andersson, the author of *Illegality, Inc.: Clandestine Migration and the Business of Bordering Europe*, writes that this "making and unmaking of borders by citizens" included their shift or erasure.[9] An example of borderworks could be a group—such as Humane Borders—who not only put out water for migrants in the Arizona desert, but also aesthetically changed that border's infrastructure with their large blue water barrels and the high, flapping flags that signaled a humanitarian effort, not surveillance. It could be any organization that treads the terrain of the untouchable in border zones where border patrols and security forces reign supreme. The tension there was caught on video when a U.S. Border Patrol agent was infamously caught kicking and destroying full water jugs under a mesquite tree, which only drew attention to another humanitarian group, No More Deaths, who'd placed them there.

Border infrastructure tends to have an air of indestructibility, yet there are plenty of examples of people and organizations who have contested this permanence by simply creating another presence. Doctors Without Borders has cruised the Mediterranean in search of clandestine, rickety boats en route to Europe. In the small town of Aguada in Puerto Rico residents regularly help undocumented Dominicans; in Veracruz, Mexico, people toss food packets to undocumented people on passing trains headed north. There are the Border Angels in San Diego, California, and Centro de Migrante 72 in Tenosique, Tabasco, Mexico. Added up, these stories of hospitality and altruism—carried out by both groups and individuals—challenge stories of xenophobia that are so often the justification behind the creation and violent enforcement of the dividing lines.

A borderwork may be any act that defies a border. It could be the Guatemalan family from the last chapter simply crossing into Mexico to visit family in a place where people have done so for hundreds—maybe thousands—of years. Or it could be the art of Khaled Jarrar. Such efforts have confronted, challenged, changed, or at the very least created conversations about the pervasive exclusion apparatus that dominate border landscapes, and that is consistently presented by officials, and very often by the media, as desirable, essential, almost sacred, untouchable.

Jarrar is one of many artists. When Ana Teresa Fernandez put on a black cocktail dress and pumps and spray-painted the Tijuana border wall a pale powdery blue at San Diego's Border Field State Park, it was more than an attempt to "erase the border" by making it the color of the sky. It was also, as Jill Holslin put it, meant to explore "women's strength and sensuality in the process of performing labor." Musician Glenn Weyant learned to play the bars on the bollard-style wall on the Arizona-Mexico border like a musical instrument—sometimes using dildos as mallets. Border artist Rigoberto A. Gonzalez told author Stephanie Elizondo-Griest, "My work is about starting a dialogue and maybe starting the healing process. Because it's a holocaust out there."[10] In 2017, the French artist JR installed a gigantic photograph of a smiling toddler known as Kikito on special scaffolding on the Mexican side. From the U.S., the child appeared to be looking over the border with a somewhat mischievous grin, dwarfing the stationed and baffled U.S. Border Patrol agents. On the West Wall in Bethlehem there is an image by the artist Banksy of a young girl frisking a soldier with his hands up, and machine gun by his side.

Jarrar told me, "I understood the needs of my uncle." He was worried about finances, money. He had already been deprived of land and water and now, according to Jarrar, the wall was going to take more. But still his uncle's choice to help build the wall consumed him. There came a point that Jarrar's uncle felt paranoid around his artist nephew: "Who set you on to me?" His uncle began to avoid him. It was then that Jarrar went to the wall and began to tear it down. As one grafitti scrawled on the West Bank concrete wall proclaimed: "The hands that build can also tear down."

The idea of transforming the wall into something else—a soccer ball sculpture—didn't occur to him until later. One day he was talking with some kids in the Qalandiya refugee camp between Ramallah and Jerusalem, and they told him that the wall was going to cut right through the lot where they played soccer. The wall, they said, was going to steal their game. While pulverizing his collected wall chunks at a West Bank cement factory, Jarrar finally decided what he was going to do with the border wall. He was going to give those kids their game back.

13.

The Right to the World on the U.S.-Syria Border

Mohammed thought we might be able to get even closer to the Syrian border at At Turrah, Jordan that day in late September 2016. It was not too far away from where we were: Ramtha, also a small town on the Jordan side. We drove for about twenty minutes through the brown hills until we were on a rumbling dirt road alongside an olive grove. As Mohammed drove (he asked me to use only his first name), he pointed to the end of the road, where a surveillance tower stood peering into Syria. I wondered if it had been constructed by one of the U.S. companies, Raytheon or DRS Technologies, that had contracts with Jordan. Mohammed was driving straight for it.

We were close to where in November 2014 the Jordanian border patrol fired on five Syrians, four of them teenagers, between 14 and 18 years old, and all of them registered with the United Nations High Commission for Refugees. The border patrol accused the kids of entering Jordan without authorization. The kids said they were just riding their motorcycles, just playing. The kids escaped, but one of the bullets punctured a seventeen-year-old's leg. He was bleeding profusely when they arrived at the hospital. Not too long after that, Jordan processed the children for deportation and sent them to Tafas, Syria.[1] Under the tutelage of the United States, Jordan is building a deportation machine.

I'd met Mohammed earlier as we stood on a hill in the U.S.-Syrian borderlands on a windswept day in Ramtha. It seemed like a modern miracle that my colleague Gabriel Schivone and I were there at all. When I was trying to set up the trip, nobody wanted to touch the border, and part of the reason was that the border had been "closed" since 2014.

"You know how things can be about security," one fixer wrote me.

The Jordanian military would not give us permission to see any of the border infrastructure. They insisted that we register with the U.S. Embassy. The border, again, was untouchable; even the mere thought of it was securitized.

I thought at that point that the trip to the border might not happen. Then Samar Salma, a Jordanian-American, courageously agreed to take us here, despite the pervasive discouragement. All this hype and anxiety made what we were doing seem almost "illegal," though all it amounted to was looking out over the white buildings and homes in Ramtha to the edge of the town, where a landscape of brown hills emerged. We thought the hills might be the Syrian border, but who knew for sure?

A group of men, including Mohammed, emerged from a small restaurant and confirmed that we were looking at the Syrian border. Salma spoke to them in Arabic and asked them to help us orient ourselves. Mohammed and the others agreed. What we were seeing was the ominous-sounding "neutral zone." They pointed out a military installation that I could only barely make out, at the top of a small hill parched brown from the drought that had afflicted this region.[2] The men in the parking lot told us that sometimes they could see mortar fire flashing into the night from that very hill.

Now, an hour later, in the car, Mohammed was driving directly at the surveillance tower. I couldn't stop thinking of the meeting I'd had with a retired major-general in Amman the day before. We'd met in a cafe in the Mecca Mall, in an affluent part of the city. The major-general wished to remain anonymous, as did the fixer who'd helped facilitate the meeting—such was life in these parts. The general told me, "We shoot at anything that moves."

The border guard could, he warned me, "100 percent choose to engage, at any moving target."

This was how they closed off the border.

And now we were rumbling past the olive grove, straight toward the unholstered border. The Jordanian border forces had day vision, night vision goggles, the major had said; they had radar. I told Salma, probably too softly, that we didn't need to go all the way to the border. She translated for Mohammed, who kept driving.

The surveillance towers on the border, the major general said, were part of what he called an "integrated system." Matt Oskam, the program manager of the U.S. Logistics and Readiness Center in Jordan, said that this border had the "total package approach," which included a "wide range of sensors, communication towers, and command and control equipment to assist Jordan's Armed Forces in detecting and interdicting smugglers and militants."[3]

This was why I was in Ramtha: I wanted to learn about the $300 million dollars of United States funds that were going into the Jordan Border Security Project, and the contract between Jordan and the U.S.-based Raytheon Corporation. In effect, we were driving into, or else were already in, the folds of a 287-mile enforcement system supplied by Raytheon that ran along 172 miles of the border with Syria and 115 miles of the border with Iraq.[4] According to Raytheon, it was a network of cameras, ground radars, quick reaction team vehicles, and what they called "passive barrier fencing," backed by a series of command and control centers and a Microwave/VHF/HF communications system. The system was designed to "deter threats, detect illicit materials, and interdict weapons" coming from countries caught in the middle of one of the most formidable refugee crises on the planet. As GlobalSecurity.org, an Alexandria, Virginia–based think tank, asserted, "peace in the Middle East" depended on many factors, but one of the most important was "border security."[5]

Important it may have been, but just as important to me was that in a very fundamental way we were driving directly into a human rights violation. The UN Universal Declaration asserts people's right to free mobility, but only when leaving and reentering their own country. Regardless, the construction of such a border regime, in this case by the corporate-U.S. nexus and the Jordanian government, seemed a willful abuse of that right.

"Maybe they'll shoot," Mohammed joked. The closer we came to the border, the more we were all convinced that something would happen if he kept driving.

He stopped momentarily, and relieved I thought we were going to turn back, but he was merely planning out how we would approach it. We lurched forward again, toward where border guards were undoubtedly watching us. It was as if Mohammed, like Jarrar, wanted to test the border, to see what would happen if you came close enough to touch the untouchable.

Earlier Mohammed had talked about how both sides of the border were intimately connected. When I asked him if he had any relatives in Syria, he said everybody did. He said his grandmother was Syrian. The more he talked about the border closure, the more agitated he became. A small businessman himself, he was upset about what the closure did to commerce. "This region," he said, "was artificially separated by the border." It was the same story I'd heard worldwide, in Africa, in Central America, on Hispaniola, and of course where I live, on the U.S.-Mexico border. This border had been imposed by the Sykes-Picot Agreement of 1916, drawn by emissaries of the French and British governments. As geographer Reece Jones notes, "although the Sykes-Picot maps do not match the current borders of Iraq, Syria, and Jordan in the Middle East, the agreement is often used as a stand-in to symbolize the fact that most of the borders were imposed by European powers and are not based on historical, political, or cultural divisions."[6]

Maybe Mohammed thought his name, his residence in Ramtha, his Jordanian citizenship would protect us from the border guards. He wasn't a refugee like the twelve injured Syrians, all with United Nations High Commission on Refugees (UNHCR) certificates, who had been receiving treatment at the Dar al-Karama rehabilitation center in Ramtha in September 2014, right before Jordan shut down its borders. According to Human Rights Watch, police had raided the center and forced it to close. They deported the refugees, six of whom were paralyzed and six wounded. The group included two children. The police deported them all, taking them across the border to a nearby Syrian town, Daraa. A seventeen-year-old whom HRW interviewed said they weren't allowed to contact the UNHCR. He became separated from his mother who was on the other side in Jordan.[7] By 2017, HRW issued another report that explicitly accused Jordan of "summarily" deporting Syrian refugees, including in "collective expulsions of large families."[8]

When Jordan closed the border in September 2014, 5,000 Syrians were immediately stranded. People began heading farther east from Ramitha as Jordan began shutting down its border crossings, including the informal ones, a process that continued into 2015. Syrians trying to get across the border began to pile up, trapped in "neutral zones." The Jordanian border patrol was watching all of this.

"We can see them coming from twenty-five kilometers away," the major general in the Mecca Mall had said of the border crossers, as if explaining the Israeli Defense in Depth–style strategy in layman's terms. "We can drink coffee, smoke cigarettes, and wait for them."

I had heard U.S. Border Patrol agents around Tucson say similar things. In fact, the major-general was familiar with my hometown. He knew Interstate 10, he said. He did not disclose how, but I imagined it had to do with some sort of training. He also knew Route 90, which went to Fort Huachuca, the military base where Customs and Border Protection flew its drones over the U.S.- Mexico border. The northeastern Jordanian borderlands, the major-general said, were "just like" the Arizona desert.

THE RIGHT TO THE WORLD

Satellite images of Jordan showed a rapidly growing encampment in a place called the berm that increased from a few thousand refugees to 75,000 in a single year. In July 2015, according to Amnesty International, there were 363 shelters there, and by the time we arrived in Ramtha in September 2016, only 100 miles away, there were 8,295.[9] Human Rights Watch said that people were living in makeshift tents in "deplorable conditions," that children suffered malnutrition and drinking water was scarce. "The Berm is not a refugee camp," wrote Natalie Thurtle of Medecins Sans Frontieres, "There are no latrines, no intrinsic water, no consistent food or health care."[10] This was perhaps one of the most egregious examples on earth of a violation of the Universal Declaration of Human Rights, but there was hardly a peep in the news.

At the end of 2015, the United Nations High Commission on Refugees reported that the number of forcibly displaced people in the world had topped 65 million, to remind, the most ever recorded. Compared with the 50 million forcibly displaced in 2013, these numbers showed a rapid acceleration. Neither figure included "economic migrants," who are forced to migrate by deprivation and poverty, but not by imminent danger. If you added economic migrants to the total, in 2015, said geographer Joseph Nevins in his essay "The Right to the World,"[11] there would be more people on the move, and crossing borders, than ever before in recorded history.

Jordan's actions formed just another illustration of what Nevins called the "dominant response" coming from the United States, the European Union, national elites, and prosperous countries broadly, a response that "has defaulted to the bounded, exclusionary logic of nation-states via a strengthening of the boundary and immigration policing apparatus." The building of border walls along national peripheries was just one of many examples of this dominant response. One result of it, as Nevins pointed out, was the record number of deaths of people crossing bodies of water like the Mediterranean or the Mona Strait or the South Pacific crammed into unsafe, rickety boats, and people who attempted to walk great distances overland across potentially deadly terrain like the Sahara and Sonoran deserts.

Through the border externalization of the United States, the European Union, and Australia—to "mid-level" and even "poor" countries such as Jordan, Turkey, Egypt, Libya, Morocco, Mexico, Guatemala, Indonesia, and the Dominican Republic, such places have become border zones themselves, the deputized "middle-men", the newest "hires" of the global border regime. These countries can block, monitor, sift, surveil, incarcerate, and deport people and objects before they ever arrive in the countries anthropologist Jeff Halper calls the "core hegemons." These include the United States, members of the European Union, and Australia, places disproportionately white, and "hegemons" because they control in powerful ways the global political systems and economy largely through their leading role in institutions such as the International Monetary Fund, the World Bank, and the United Nations and its Security Council. According to Nevins, the impediments and exclusions instituted by this hegemonic core are, in terms explicitly defined by the Universal Declaration of Human

Rights, violations of human rights. Article 1 of the Universal Declaration, for example, states that "all human beings are born free and equal in dignity and rights ... and should act towards one another in a spirit of brotherhood [sic]."

Border walls and enforcement apparatuses that try to thwart people from crossing political lines of division enforce the antithesis of this freedom and equality, along with other declared universal rights. By not allowing people, such as those at the berm, to cross to a place that would offer them more biophysical and socioeconomic security, in turn stops them from realizing their human rights, and so, Nevins writes, renders them "less than fully human." It is a violation, and so is denying people's right to free mobility, their right to leave and reenter their own country. So is hampering people's quest for a fulfilled and dignified life, or their ability to earn a living wage. National borders, in other words, have become more important than the basic rights of living people, and one's citizenship has become more important than one's humanity. As Nevins puts it, "national sovereignty and the associated regime of territorial policing and exclusion are paramount."

Because of this, Nevins asserts, it is imperative that we recognize a new right—the *right to the world*. There are two big parts to this "right to the world." One is freedom of mobility worldwide, including free movement across international borders. The other is a "just, sustainable share of the planet's resources for all." It is a "right that is both individual and collective, it is one which those fleeing devastation and insecurity of various sorts and knocking on the proverbial doors of spaces of privilege are both demonstrating the need for and already claiming in some ways."[12]

The right to the world would complement the "right to the city," a concept first proposed by French sociologist and philosopher Henri Lefebvre in 1968, which strives toward a dignified life—regardless of citizenship—for people in the face of the vast injustices and inequalities found in the world's cityscapes, where 80 percent of the global population resides. As geographer David Harvey explains, "the right to the city is far more than the individual liberty to access urban resources: It is a right to change ourselves by changing our city ... The freedom to make and remake our cities and ourselves is, I want to argue, one of the most precious yet most neglected of our human rights."[13]

In the past few decades, the right to the city has been used as a response to neoliberal restructuring, and to the fact that those who live in the city are "denied access to it in all sorts of ways," as Nevins points out, "*and increasingly so.*" The United States–based Right to the City Alliance asserts that central to the right to the city is "the right of equal access to housing, employment, and public services regardless of race, ethnicity, and immigration status and without the threat of deportation by landlords, ICE (Immigration and Customs Enforcement) or employers." But although the right to the city stresses inclusion, it does not include the millions of people who are on the move and crossing dangerous borders, or those who might consider doing so in the future—people like Widad, a widowed mother of three. Describing her life in the berm in 2016 to a reporter, she said, "We would wait from 11 a.m. until 6 p.m. and not get food. We lost so much weight, from the second we got to the berm the children were consistently sick and they lost between three and five kilograms each."[14] Once they were stopped at the border, where they were fleeing for their lives (in this case from Da'esh), their assurance to a whole host of universal rights also literally stopped.

If hardened borders were the world's new "intercontinental anti-ballistic missiles" aimed at the poor, persecuted, and environmentally exposed, then the right to the world represented disarmament. Perhaps the time has come to dismantle that arsenal.[15]

THE GREAT WALL OF JORDAN

At the Mecca Mall, the Jordanian major-general told us that he had lived in Washington and knew that the U.S. officials valued their role. Most projects, he said, were covered by the Americans "directly." Perhaps this is why historian Edward Hunt calls the Middle East "another part of the periphery" of U.S. empire. While U.S. officials have "typically approached Latin America as their primary sphere of influence in the world," he says, they "have also extended their imperial ambitions to the Middle East."[16] Greg Grandin, another historian, in his 2006 book *Empire's Workshop*, lucidly illustrates Latin America's role as a proving ground for the U.S. strategies and tactics later seen in the Middle East.

The major concerns for the United States in the region—according to the former senior policy advisor for the U.S. Department of Defense Eric Edelman, while giving testimony on U.S. policy and strategy in the Middle East to the U.S. Senate's Armed Services Committee in December 2017—was much more than terrorism:

> U.S. policymakers have considered access to the region's energy resources vital for U.S. allies in Europe, and ultimately for the United States itself. Moreover, the region's strategic location—linking Europe and Asia—made it particularly important from a geopolitical point of view.[17]

Reporting on the hearing in January 2018, Hunt points out that Edelman cited the Carter Doctrine of 1980, a sort of Monroe Doctrine for the Middle East in which the Persian Gulf was deemed so valuable to U.S. interests that the United States would "militarily intervene in the region to expel outside forces." An example of this was the Persian Gulf War, of course, when the United States expelled Iraq from Kuwait. Edelman rounded out his argument by noting, "the geostrategic and economic factors that made the Middle East so important to our national security in the past are just as potent today." After all, he said, the Middle East contains half of the world's proven oil reserves and accounts for one-third of the world's oil production and exports. Nobody in the hearing disagreed with him, neither his colleagues nor the committee members. With about 80,000 U.S. military forces in the area at numerous bases and offshore sites, Hunt explains, "the U.S. has constructed a kind of informal American empire."

That the Middle East has become a strategic place in the U.S. empire of borders should be no surprise. In Iraq, to remind, U.S. boundary-building efforts began in 2004 with a program, Phantom Linebacker, to train 15,000 border guards.[18] In 2012 Jay Mayfield wrote in CBP's *Frontline* magazine, "for the past six years, U.S. Customs and Border

Protection personnel have been on the ground in Iraq for every twist and turn in the country's rebirth and recovery, and in America's role in that process."[19] Justin Campbell, the historian and former soldier who accompanied me in Guatemala, worked the Iraq-Iran border in 2010 as part of the U.S. occupation doing finger printing and retina scans of people crossing the border.

From Iraq to Israel, the Middle East has become a border zone, and Jordan, as the major-general insisted, was a very strategic piece of the puzzle. In fact, he stated, "If it weren't for us, you'd have to pay Israel $5 billion instead of $3 billion"—a reference to the extraordinarily high flows of U.S. military aid going to Israel.

A U.S. Customs and Border Protection trainer who spent considerable time in Jordan told me a little bit about their program, on the condition of anonymity.

"I really like the Jordanians," he said. "They were very well motivated."

He went (ten times, the last tour in April 2015) "to work with their newly formed border guard." The training was done through a Department of Defense program called the Defense Threat Reduction Agency, or DTRA. DTRA's main functions were threat reduction, threat control, combat support, and technology development. It was with DTRA funding that the Philippines built its Coastal Watch Center.

They held a variety of training courses in Jordan, the CBP trainer said, run by private-sector contractors, "active duty" agents, and "retired" agents, depending on the course. They brought in ICE for "investigations" and CBP for "interdiction" training, in which agents would train future border guards to stop people and goods from crossing borders and border zones. The trainer said he taught border interdiction "with a WMD twist to it." There was also an FBI agent who specialized in biological weapons ("he actually worked on the anthrax case"). There were two retired operatives from Baltimore who were HAZMAT experts, "so they dealt with chemical weapons." There was a military trainer and a retired Border Patrol agent. "And me."

The first week of training concentrated on theory, he said; they looked at "dual-use goods"; biological, chemical, and radiological weapons; and conventional explosives, and then "we'd do a practical outside training where I'd show them how to search a car, truck, bus, passenger car, show them how to do personal searches, show them how to do interviewing techniques to find out who the bad guys were."

Now—as the major-general had also confirmed—the United States had turned the training over to the Jordanians. Jordanian officials went to the United States to get training and came back to impart the knowledge in-country. DTRA had contracted a retired U.S. Border Patrol agent to monitor the operation. But, the trainer stressed, the Jordanians did "a good job." In fact that was the "training model" the United States wanted to carry into the future, in order to institutionalize that knowledge with the partner countries. Teaching the Jordanians how to fish—to steal CBP Air and Marine commander Tony Crowder's words about Mexico.

DTRA also runs a "state-of-the-art facility," the Border Security Maintenance, Sustainment and Security Operations Center, through "an ongoing partnership between the U.S. and the Hashemite Kingdom of Jordan" that includes "equipment upgrades, infrastructure upgrades, and practical exercises."[20] An entire border-building conveyor belt is in place.

In 2015, the United States supplied Jordan with $385 million from Foreign Military Financing, which supported the Jordanian Armed Forces in border policing and "counter-terrorism" efforts, according to a memo by the U.S. Bureau of Political Military Affairs. This paid for more than 26,000 rifles and machine guns, 3 million rounds of small arms ammunition, and 5,000 night-vision devices.[21] Perhaps it paid for the bullet that punctured the 17-year-old's leg when he strayed too close to the border near Ramtha. Also included in the aid package were eight UH-60 Blackhawks, which U.S. Ambassador Alice G. Wells said during a ceremony to receive the helicopters at the Marka Military Airport in Amman would "provide Jordan with another tool for safeguarding its frontiers." Wells also gushed about Jordan's improved border policing, "U.S. funding helped build the Jordan Border Security Program, an integrated border surveillance system … I do not have to tell this group about the sheer number of incursions the Border Guard forces thwart; almost nightly."[22] By 2016, the money from U.S. Foreign Military Financing had doubled to $800 million, then dropped down to just below $700 million in 2017. The current Memorandum of Understanding states that the United States will give Jordan no less than $350 million in such financing each year, to "outline areas of critical security and economic cooperation, while simultaneously helping Jordan mitigate the effects of regional crises, including the strain of refugees from Syria and Iraq on Jordan's budget."[23]

GlobalSecurity.org makes it clear that Jordan plays "a pivotal political and geographic role in the Middle East. Geographically, Jordan acts as a land bridge for passage both east to west and north to south."[24] Jordan, in effect, is not only a U.S.-Syrian border, but also a U.S.-Middle East border.

"US strategic planners will stem the flow of refugees and also wall off the increasingly important American base from the disintegration of Syria and Iraq," journalist and military analyst William Arkin writes in his February 2016 article "The Great Wall of Jordan."[25]

That day in September 2016 on the Jordanian-Syrian borderlands, we were literally driven to the completed first phase of the Jordan Border Security Project, the erection of towers and the beginning of the fence. Arkin noted that Jordan, Raytheon, and the United States were on to phases two and three: the "building of a fully integrated and networked fence," for which U.S. tax payers would shell out approximately $300 million, adding to the coffers of Raytheon Intelligence and DRS Technologies (DRS's slogan a few years ago was "You Draw the Line and We'll Help You Secure It.") and imprisoning people in the worst refugee crisis on earth.

At the Mecca Mall meeting, the Jordanian major general told us that his country had one of the best border security regimes in the Middle East, only behind Saudi Arabia. "We are the most generous country in the world," he said, adding that there were 1.5 million refugees in Jordan. But now we had to get our country in order. We do this, he said, for "our kids. For national security." We do this not only for Jordan, but for the whole region.

Nevertheless, Jordanians were "the losers, because we got 20 percent of the refugees. Ninety percent are trash. They are not the good Syrians on the inside. They are not coming here because of war or because they are looking for a better way of life. They are staying here forever."

I looked at our fixer, who was Syrian, and who'd set up this meeting for us and was ready to translate for the major-general if he switched to Arabic. He had come to Jordan in 2012. He had lost two brothers. They disappeared, he'd told us. But he didn't visibly react to the major-general's words.

The major-general continued, "We pay their expenses: their energy usage, water usage, infrastructure." That was why Jordan needed its border security system. "Without it," he said, speaking as if a border enforcement regime were a basic service, "many suffer."

Back on the Syrian border in At Turrah, there was a collective scream for Mohammed to stop the goddamn car. Finally he hit the brakes; the car skidded on the dirt road, short of the actual international boundary line. I'm sorry, I muttered at him. Probably nothing would have happened. They wouldn't have shot at us, I thought, but they would have stopped us, interrogated us, confiscated my notes and our electronics. And they *could* have shot at us. At this border, artificially drawn 100 years ago, it felt as if they could do anything.

After Mohammed spent the better part of the day with us, we dropped him off in Ramtha, where Samar Salma asked him if he wanted a payment. He said he did not. He said that sort of hospitality to a stranger, free of charge, was part of his religious belief as a Muslim.

HOSPITALITY

Often when I travel abroad I realize that I have a lot to learn when it comes to hospitality. A visit with a different Mohammed was no exception. Schivone and I met him in his apartment in Amman. (Like Mohammed in Ramtha, he requested I refer to him only by his first name.) He was one of the "trash" Syrian refugees, or at least there was a 90 percent chance of it, according to the major-general. After we took off our shoes and sat on the cushions on the floor, Mohammed told me that we were welcome in his house.

He paused, then added that we were not only welcome now, but would always be welcome in his house for the rest of our lives.

For the next few hours he brought Schivone and me coffee, cakes, tea, and cold drinks. He invited us to dinner. He invited us to stay at his house. He invited us to stay a week if we wanted. After we'd spent entire days dissecting the decidedly inhospitable border enforcement situation in Jordan, his hospitality felt not only refreshing but also almost subversive.

In 2012, nine members of Mohammed's family arrived in the Jordanian refugee camp, where they stayed for thirty-nine days. His family had fled Busra—a small beautiful ancient Syrian town that had become a UNESCO heritage site—close to the Jordanian border. Mohammed was a graduate of the University of Damascus and in Busra he had worked as an accountant at the local hospital. I couldn't understand Mohammed since he spoke in Arabic, which our fixer interpreted; but his deadpan delivery needed no interpretation. He clearly had a sense of humor, and it caused our fixer to frequently burst into laughter, sometimes laughter so intense that tears came to his eyes. It was contagious laughter, and made Schivone and me laugh as well, even though we had no idea what Mohammed was actually saying. It was also difficult to know what made so harrowing a subject so funny: how he and his family had fled in the night, avoided the rolling tanks on patrol, and crossed into Jordan before they shut down the border.

Our fixer, laughing, pointed out the thin gray blankets folded and stacked right next to where I sat on the cushion. I touched one. "Those are the blankets we had in the tent," Mohammed said. In the refugee camps, conditions were abysmal. Everything was scarce. Blankets were scarce. Water was scarce. Electricity was scarce. Work permits were scarce, and you could get deported if caught working without one. One night, a "notable person" from Busra arrived in the camp. Mohammed never explained who this was, but I imagined he was an elder or a politician, a person of local importance. Because he was "notable," somebody had to sacrifice something to him, and that, I began to suspect as the story went on, was going to be Mohammed. In other words, those super-thin blankets were key props explaining how Mohammed finally realized he had to get out of that camp.

Normally, Mohammed said, one probably wouldn't complain about being situated next to a bakery, as his family's tent was in the camp. But it made life awful, even before the "notable person" arrived. There were footsteps and commotion early and you could smell the baking bread. Which was great, unless it was 5:00 a.m. and you were trying to sleep. Sometimes there were animated conversations, even political debates, the absolute last thing you wanted to overhear while trying to sleep. It was also winter, and bitterly cold. And the blankets, he said, pointing again to the stack, were light.

When the "notable person" came, Mohammed said, I gave him my blankets, keeping only one. Outside, it was raining. And, of course, with tents there is always a good side and a bad side. On the nights that the "notable person" shared his tent, Mohammed slept on the bad side. One night he woke up drenched. The wind had pried the flap of the tent loose, the drizzle was cold, everything was bitter, bitter cold and then the commotion began in the bakery, people arriving, people talking. Half frozen, sleep-deprived, Mohammed got sick. At this point, he said, the great question beckoned: How do you leave the refugee camp? There were two ways. One, you just fled, stateless, into the night. Or you got a sponsor, a relative who already was living in Jordan. That's what Mohammed and his family did. Since then, he had lived in three apartments in Amman, including the one where we enjoyed his gracious hospitality.

Still, Mohammed said, despite having taken the prudent course, despite possessing all the correct documents, he and his family felt threatened. The possibility of deportation always loomed; you could be arrested and expelled at any moment. It was hard to get work. And hard to get a permit to work. Things had changed since he arrived. Jordan shut down the border. The first time Jordanian authorities catch you without a work permit, he said, they fine you. If they catch you again, "you're gone." If you get into a fight especially a fight with another Syrian, gone. The rent had gone up, he said, from 90 dinars ($126) to 165 dinars ($232). He had a job as an accountant in a water filter shop. The idea of returning to Busra existed, always existed. There were many who passionately wanted to return. But the situation was unsafe, he said. You had to think about your parents, your spouse, your kids. He estimated that of the 35,000 who lived in his part of Busra, 15,000 had left; 10,000 of those refugees were now in Jordan. One third of his hometown fled to Jordan. Then 3,000 had gone back when things seemed peaceful enough. These were the people whose houses still existed.

Then he shifted gears. He said that he was grateful. He didn't share the predicament of Syrians in Busra now, facing a massive, nearby border-building regime in Jordan that struck fear into many people. With compassion, he told us that despite his woes, he knew he didn't have it as bad as people in Aleppo, which had been incinerated by constant bombing that ended right before we met with Mohammed in September 2016. He said at least his family had lived near the Jordanian border, so their escape hadn't involved endless walking, day and night, avoiding checkpoints, on arduous routes, whether through Turkey or across the Aegean Sea to Greece, where most of the media's cameras were focused. Everywhere now the border was being built up. "Maybe I was lucky. I didn't lose my house. I didn't lose my brothers and sisters. Others had their houses destroyed. Others lost everything." And now the border was closed. "My brother," he said, "left Jordan, and now he can't get back." Wounded people were in precarious situations, and the doors had been shut tight. We "are very watched," at the border, Mohammed said. He told us the story of somebody who had gone back to Syria, where the border forces shot him in the leg. He told another story he'd heard—he wasn't sure if it was true—about several Syrians at the border who were lined up and deliberately shot in the knees. "Maybe it was a message to all of us not to cross the border."

"*Shoot at anything that moves,*" the major-general had told us.

And thus, as Nevins notes in "The Right to the World," the very existence of the unwanted, illegalized migrant or refugee—which would include Mohammed or any Syrian refugee—embodies "the contradiction between human rights and nation-statism." The very fact that the nation-state remains the "basic building block of the world order" and that "national citizenship is the principal form of global belonging" is the basis of the contradiction, and has created a world where the idea of state sovereignty trumps human rights. The nation-state not only permits grave violations of those rights, it causes them. Hospitality has become criminalized.

As we were leaving, Mohammed asked again if we wanted to stay at his house. We could stay two nights, the entire week if we wanted. Could he, he asked as we walked to the door, take us out to dinner? Here again was the hospitality I've felt, and received, in so many places—from the retired police commander of FURA in Puerto Rico, from the Maasai in Kenya, from the Sabri Gharib household in Palestine, from a friendly couple in Tel Aviv, and of course from the countless people in Mexico who welcomed me into their houses and let me sleep in their beds year after year after year, even at the border where my country's unwelcoming, towering wall dominated the landscape. And on the U.S. side, hospitality continues to be given by humanitarian groups despite Washington's constant attempts to illegalize their activities. Now volunteers are facing U.S. federal judges and time in prison after leaving water and providing aid in places where undocumented travelers are demonstrably dying of thirst and exposure. No More Deaths volunteer Madeline Huse told Magistrate Judge Bernardo Velasco why she did it in January 2019, "I believe in the sanctity of human life ... I don't want to be walking in 100 degree temperatures, but I feel obligated to be there and do my part." This was before Velasco convicted her of abandoning property and entering a national wildlife refuge in Arizona without a permit."

In the teeth of the antihospitable nation-state and its humiliating borders, the universal human urge to offer hospitality has become subversive.

Yet, challenging the boundaries with hospitality affirms the idea of the right to the world. In making a world where people can freely travel without impediment, kindness toward the stranger, as practiced by Mohammed in Ramtha and Mohammed in Amman, will play a significant part. It reminded me of the line by the Sufi poet Rumi who wrote "Your acts of kindness are iridescent wings of divine love, which linger and continue to uplift others long after your sharing."

KHALED'S LADDER

Khaled Jarrar was on the Mexican side when he climbed the border wall that divided San Ysidro in the United States from Tijuana in Mexico. As soon as he reached the top he saw two U.S. Border Patrol agents, who seemed shocked by the sight of the Palestinian artist's head popping over the wall. One of the agents immediately put his hand on his gun holster. The other pulled out a pair of binoculars.

"Where are you from?" they yelled, according to Jarrar.

"Earth," Jarrar shouted back at them.

Jarrar jumped down to the ground. Within fifteen minutes, a U.S. Border Patrol helicopter buzzed in overhead, spotlighting the scene. Jarrar had come to the border with an international group of artists— from the United Kingdom, Brazil, Italy, Mexico, and the United States. They were part of the Culturunners, a global collaboration of artists and journalists telling stories and creating "art across physical and psychological borders." Jarrar had dislodged a twenty foot metal slat from the border wall earlier that day. He wanted to transform the bar into something new, much as he had when he took a sledge-hammer to the West Bank wall, mixed the chunks with wet cement, and transformed them into a soccer ball, a basketball, and cleats. The sculptures were shown in a London gallery alongside a video of a mother's wrinkled hand moving through the crevice of a wall to touch her daughter's hand on the other side. "How are you mother?" the daughter murmurs. "How are my brother and the kids? I wish I could kiss your hand, mother."

Near San Ysidro, on the Mexican side, there were crosses bearing the names of people who had died trying to enter the United States. Jarrar had the idea of transforming that slat into such a cross. A Mexican federal police car pulled up—called by the Border Patrol. The U.S. agents pressed up against the wall, talking through a small hole to the Mexican agents. It was amazing how quickly law enforcement could coordinate cross-border, and how the simple presence of the artists at the border had merited the call.

At any given moment in the world there may be a thousand challenges to the legitimacy of a border. Civilization relies upon that legitimacy—upon the sanctity of bounded nation-states. Rarely is this organization of the world—of the earth—discussed in terms of the human rights violation it represents, the artificial separation and division of people—of families—and the death and suffering it causes. When Jarrar pounded the cement wall on the West Bank, when he pulled out a piece of the U.S.-Mexico border wall, he was confronting a system of enormous power, a military and economic apparatus that ensured the dominance of the few over the many. But he had another story he wanted to offer: the walls and the bars of the borders could serve a new utilitarian purpose. And that's what he wanted to convey to the Mexican federal police.

The odds were not in his favor when Jarrar showed his art to the police at the border wall. At first, the officers responded with interrogation: "What are you doing? Let us see your passport." They wanted Jarrar to prove he was an artist. Jarrar told them, I am an artist, and as an artist, I work against the wall. He told the Mexican feds that the United States should remove the wall. An agent leaned down and looked at his film *The Infiltrators* on his laptop computer screen and when she saw a scene where several Palestinians were waiting for the right time to jump the West Bank concrete border wall, said, Well, yes that was happening here too. And yes, in Mexico, they didn't like the wall, either. The police let the artists go, but Jarrar decided he needed more time to think about what to do with that piece of the U.S.-Mexico border wall.

Later, on a trip to New Mexico State University in Las Cruces, Jarrar told his artistic colleagues about the idea that had begun to haunt him: He wanted to turn that wall into a ladder. The college approved the project and provided the materials. He wanted to position the ladder right against the wall in Ciudad Juarez, but the Rio Grande was in the way (the wall was built on the U.S. side of the river). Jarrar talked to people in the *colonia* Felipe Angeles, where the artists arrived with the newly minted ladder. The people from the *colonia* said, "Why don't you leave it here as a permanent sculpture"? So the artists arranged the ladder on the Mexican side of the U.S. border wall, about one quarter mile inland. If you stand in front of the ladder, you can see the not only the international boundary in the distance, but also the

Southern Pacific railroad and El Paso's choppy mountains behind it.[26]

Now from Felipe Angeles you can see the transformed border wall as a constant, everyday possibility. In a very utilitarian way, the border can be changed—it does not have to serve the purpose of blockading movement. Indeed, the ladder has a another message: From Bir Nabala to Ciudad Juarez, everybody has the "right to the world."

Part Seven

The U.S.-African Border in the Anthropocene: The Case to Dissolve Borders

I find common cause with border crossers who think that there are some borders worth resisting, particularly those that limit the quality and character of our relationships, care of others and protection of the planet ...

Nancy Wonders

I think that the possibility of recognizing the global-ness of the society we live in ushers in the possibility of expanding affective ties, expanding the definition of who we are, and whom we are with in this world ...

Nandita Sharma

14.

"Shoring up the Frontiers
of Fortress America"

On January 1, 2017, approximately 800 people charged the towering double-steel wall on the periphery of Ceuta, a colonial Spanish enclave on the northern coast of Morocco. Coils of razor wire topped the wall, which was manned by Moroccan and Spanish border guards on both sides. There were virtual guards, too; this was a "smart border," equipped with more than 100 cameras (some with night vision), sensors, and command and control centers where agents of the Spanish Guardia Civil, dressed in forest green, watched the monitors. One agent told a reporter, "There is not one centimeter that is not covered by the cameras."[1] Most of the people scaling the wall were from sub-Saharan Africa. One way to try to get across that fortified divide, like that January day, was to go over together through the razorwire and rubber bullets, into border guards with large clubs who beat people back. And even then, many of them would not make it, and some might even be killed.

It was one of the many twenty-first century battlegrounds between the Global North and Global South that are caught on surveillance monitors but not television cameras. Yet this clash should have been news: It represented not only a world fraught with vast economic inequalities and political turbulence, but also a planet in the throes of ecological devastation. Camila Minerva Rodríguez of Oxfam observed, "The poorest and the most marginalized are five times more likely to be displaced and to remain so for longer time than people in higher-income countries, and [this number] is increasing with climate change."[2]

There is a photograph from Melilla, another heavily fortified Spanish enclave down the coast from Ceuta, that seems to capture it all: A row of young black men from lands to the south—Senegal, Niger, Eritrea—are trapped on top of a wall overlooking the green, sloping hills of a golf course, where white-clad people, unfazed, leisurely swing their clubs.[3] Again, the men on the wall are hyper-monitored, yet invisible.

When I was at the Ceuta border crossing in 2015, I had barely snapped three pictures when a uniformed man opened the door of his inconspicuously parked, unmarked car and yelled, "Hey!" I had to look at him to be sure he was yelling at me. And he was. I looked at the infrastructure of the port of entry; it looked like most major border ports I'd seen. There was very little difference between this and, say, the DeConcini port of entry on the U.S.-Mexico border in Nogales, where individual cars crammed into lanes, creating a zone of collective exhaust, slowly lurch forward toward the CBP agents, trained to be incredulous with each approaching person. I walked through the same waiting, growling cars in Ceuta, where several other men had joined the first and were also yelling, "Hey!" It was as if I'd been caught shoplifting. One of them was a well-built though slightly rotund man in a puffy gray winter coat—even Morocco is chilly in February—and wearing aviation sunglasses. He'd emerged from the customs booth fifty feet away and was walking straight toward me, gaining speed. The uniformed soldier from the first car pointed to a sign depicting a camera with a line through it: No pictures. OK, so that was my violation. I looked back toward the guy in the aviation glasses. He was coming up fast. I turned around and walked quickly back to the taxi, hoping to save my three little photos of the port of entry. Behind me I could hear my pursuer's footsteps.

This border was not passive at all. Like most borders in the twenty-first century, it was aggressive. Like many other countries in North Africa and the Middle East, Morocco has signed multiple agreements on border policing with the European Union. The man in the aviator glasses seemed to be part of the border militarization spillover. In 2006 alone, the EU had given $80 million to Morocco for "border management." Morocco was the first country to sign the European Neighborhood Policy, an agreement promoting a "global approach to migration and mobility."[4] It is now one of thirty-five countries that the E.U. prioritizes for such efforts, with spending that has increased "vastly."[5] In many of these places, the EU's massive border push-out has been done in coordination with, or reinforced by, the United States.

The United States has been working in coordination with the Moroccan government since 2007, through the State Department's Export Control and Border Security Related (EXBS) program. Since the first meeting between the nations the U.S. has put pressure on Morocco to conform to European standards, effectively creating an EU-U.S. border front that bolsters the offshore border enforcement apparatus of both hegemons. In 2007, at the end of that first conference, the U.S. report was positive: there was a "reaffirmation" of the strong bilateral cooperation in "security-related fields." Morocco had presented a "wish-list" that would create the blueprint for customs and border enforcement training in the years to come. After promising to coordinate such trainings, the United States presented the Moroccan delegation with a gift: fifty personal radiation detectors "designed to be worn by customs officials as a first line of defense against radiation hazards."[6] This was how border cooperation began, one where Morocco continues in U.S. good graces, through EXBS, to this day,[7] even though the Moroccan apparatus has since been accused of breaking people's bones in refugee camps to prevent them from crossing the border wall in Ceuta or Melilla.[8]

Perhaps the man on my heels had also been trained by the United States. He caught up with me and signed to me that I needed to erase the three photos I had taken. One photo was of the barbed wire fence. Another was of the cars in line. Boring photos, photos that I might erase anyway. Yet I refused. Maybe because I felt, as geographer Ruben Andersson wrote in his book *Illegality, Inc.*, "the workings of the illegality industry are absurd." My photos in no way compared with the most evocative taken in this area, such as that of the men on the wall above the golf course. Persistent as a pit bull, the man in the aviator glasses tried to get into the taxi with me, much to the chagrin of the astonished driver. I erased the photos.

As we drove back to Tangier, just outside of Ceuta, I saw groups of people camped by the side of the two-lane road, clearly on the move. They'd be facing that heavily fortified Spanish enclave: maybe even that same man with the aviator glasses. But before this they most likely also faced the most significant obstacle to life on earth in this century: the environmental breakdowns caused by accelerated climate change.

CLIMATE CHANGE

It is impossible for me to say why those people on the side of the road outside Ceuta that day were migrating north. To return to journalist Juan Gonzalez, who has written extensively about northward migration in his book *Harvest of Empire*, invariably "the old colonial ties" would impel immigrants to seek the places where the extracted wealth of their lands had gone—"the metropolises of their former colonial powers."

In this context, it is worth remembering the assertion of the 9/11 Commission Report that the "American homeland is the planet." And remembering too the words of former Secretary of State Henry Kissinger, as quoted by Noam Chomsky: "Europe and others should focus on their regional interests, while the United States, which has global interests and responsibilities, will manage the global framework of order, serving as the respected and legitimate law enforcer that the world needs."[9] With that boast, the United States was launched as the "colonial power" superior to all others, the emperor of the empires.

If industrial might were measured in the form of historic greenhouse gas emissions, you could boast the United States has achieved dominion over all other countries in that too. Between 1850 and 2011, according to the World Resources Institute, the United States was the source of 27 percent of the world's carbon dioxide emissions. The second-highest emitter was the European Union, at 25 percent. China comes in a distant third, at 11 percent.[10] Michael Gerrard of Columbia University's Earth Institute wrote that given the forecasts of world disasters if climate trends are not reversed—from the ocean swallowing large parts of places like Bangladesh, the Philippines, and Indonesia to the desertification of huge swaths of African territory, from Sierra Leone to Ethiopia—there will be staggering numbers of human beings on the move. While many will move within their countries, others will cross borders, like the people beside that Ceuta road at the fringes of the European Union. Gerrard writes, "the countries that spewed (or allowed or encouraged their corporations to spew) these chemicals into the air, and especially the countries that grew rich while doing so, should take responsibility for the consequences of their actions."[11] Such responsibility would require each country to take in a number of "climate refugees" equal to the percentage of the world's greenhouse gas emitted by that country. For the United States, this means that if by 2050 climate change worldwide has displaced 100 million people (a low estimate), the U.S. will have to take in and resettle 27 million of them. "None of this would be popular," Gerrard says, "but it would be fair."

Precisely the reverse is happening, of course. The United States and the European Union are militarizing their immediate borders and also sending the same walls, drones, prisons, and surveillance cameras to external borders that extend right up to the places most vulnerable to climate change. The U.S.-Africa border is one of the sharpest examples of this. Sub-Saharan Africa was responsible for 1 percent of carbon emissions from 1850 to 2011, yet it is now one of the regions most vulnerable to climate impacts and one of the poorest places on earth.[12]

Koko Warner, one of the top scholars doing empirical research on connections between climate change and displacement, told me a story about a visit she made to a small town in Senegal where only fifty people remained. Warner said they had been investigating the region generally, and almost without exception people across Mali, Niger, and Senegal spoke of two "great droughts." One had lasted from 1968 to 1974, the other from 1982 to 1984. These droughts, Warner told me, represented "a shift in the entire weather pattern across eastern and western Africa," a shift connected with the global warming caused by an atmosphere increasingly packed with heat-trapping gasses.

On the ground, Warner said, "not a single drop of rain fell in three years." West Africa was once heavily forested, but "now wherever you go it's sparsely forested at best, with heavy desertification." Starved of water, the trees had died. The land was degraded and many people were left absolutely destitute. Warner traveled to that tiny community in Senegal, where she talked with three generations: a grandfather, a middle-aged father, and some young adult men. When the grandfather was young, there'd been no cash economy; the forest had supplied all the sustenance. The middle-aged man was impoverished by the great droughts; he couldn't make ends meet at home. He had to go to the city, get odd jobs, earn a little bit of money to supplement what was left. As for the young men, they "can't make a living here at all anymore." They had to leave, and they wouldn't even have "a chance to come back."

Such places in the world are not only becoming more difficult places to live, they are becoming uninhabitable. It's a fate that's been forecast for large swaths of territory through the African continent.

Displacement driven by climate change is already happening. According to the Internal Displacement Monitoring Centre, between 2008 and 2015 approximately 22.5 million people per year have migrated directly as a result of climate-related hazards.[13] That number doesn't even include those, like the family in Senegal, who can no longer make a living because of slower-moving catastrophes such as drought.

In 2017, the IDMC estimated that drought conditions had displaced 892,000 people in Somalia. Other massive environmental displacements in the same year included almost 2 million people in Cuba after Hurricane Irma, more than 1.5 million in China after floods in Hunan, and more than 1.3 million in India after wide-ranging monsoon floods wreaked havoc on eight states.[14] Projected estimates of the number of people who will be displaced in the future vary widely, ranging from 25 million to 1 billion by 2050, but the most common estimate is 200 million, based on a study by the Institute for Environment and Human Security of the United Nations University.[15] But although the exact numbers are debated, Warner writes in her report "In Search of Shelter: Mapping the Effects of Climate Change on Human Migration and Displacement," it is certain that future migration caused by climate change will be "staggering" and "surpass any historic antecedent."[16]

Sociologist Christian Parenti calls what is happening in the twenty-first century the "catastrophic convergence" of political, economic, and increasing ecological crises that are displacing people already and are ultimately symptoms of a world that is no longer sustainable.[17] This unsustainable world is held up by the scaffolding of nation-states and glued together by the iron fist of the armies and militarized security.

If current trends remain the same, tomorrow's climate-displaced will not be welcomed by the countries historically most responsible for the emissions that changed the climate. Rather, they will be block-aded, arrested, imprisoned, and expelled, often with unfathomable cruelty, in a process as predictable as heat waves and droughts. As the climate pressure increases, exacerbating poverty, something will have to give.

DEMILITARIZING THE BORDER, TOWARD A NEW WORLD

"A radical No Borders politics acknowledges that it is part of rev-olutionary change," write sociologists Nandita Sharma, Bridget Anderson, and Cynthia Wright in their essay "Why No Borders?"[18] "If successful, it will have a very profound effect on all of our lives." They argue that a movement to eliminate borders must be part of a powerful global reshaping of "economies and societies in a way that is not compatible with capitalism, nationalism, or the mode of state-controlled belonging that is citizenship."

When I spoke to Sharma she outlined the post–World War II reor-ganization of the world, the transition from a world of imperial states and colonial territories to a world divided by countries. A blurry shift, it created at once "a world of nation-states, each and every one of them with their immigration controls." What has emerged from it is a global lockdown.

After the Second World War, national identity was reinforced. Capitalism expanded. Borders opened and closed—no accident and no contradiction. This was the creation, upon a colonial foundation, of a world of access, of inclusion and exclusion. Borders, according to Sharma, have become one of the key structures by which the global economy is regulated and organized. On one side of the artificial and imposed political lines, labor is cheaper, natural resources are easier to exploit, and environmental regulations are either lax or ignored. This world upholds the precepts of free-market capitalism, in which all impediments to profit are removed, including a living wage and regulations for a healthy planet. Meanwhile it creates impediments of another kind, entrapping, restricting, and incarcerating the victims of inequality, while pitting people who might otherwise be allies against each other.

In "Why No Borders?" Sharma et al. argue for a movement toward common land, toward a dissolution of borders, and, ultimately, toward a shared resources—including basic natural resources such as air, habitable earth, and water—without exclusionary boundaries around them. They envision a world like England before the rise of land privatization in the seventeenth century. And as climate change will radically rearrange everything, including the geography of the globe, a turn toward the system of commons may be one of the most practical solutions for the oncoming impacts of the Anthropocene, the new geologic era characterized by human activity as a dominant force impacting the climate and the environment.

Far from stopping people (the 244 million that the United Nations calculates are living outside of their countries of origin is up 41 percent from the year 2000), border and homeland security has created a global classification system that divides the rich from the poor, the powerful from the marginalized, the disproportionately white populations from those that are predominantly people of color. In an interview, Sharma told Fiona Jeffries, "I believe we really do live in a global society today, and one of the ways in which hierarchies are maintained is through migration controls. And they not only attempt to thwart the unauthorized, but also create a new category of "illegal" migrants—in other words, they produce "illegality."[19] Fear—of arrest, of incarceration, of violence or even death—creates new categories of "hard workers," "good wives," "good parents," and "good children," to be distinguished from the bad, "illegal" people.

Criminologist Nancy Wonders, in her essay "Transforming Borders from Below," says, "The subjective power of bordering is profound. It shapes who we think we are and our understanding of our individual and collective power. The borders of subjectivity shape and constrain our sense of possibilities, and therefore, quite literally, our life chances."

Immigration controls undermine the ability of migrants to imagine a future in which they belong—in which, as Nevins suggests in the "Right to the World," the "rights to move or stay are understood as a necessary part of a contemporary system of *common rights*."[20]

Northern Arizona University political scientist Luis Fernandez, in an interview with geographer Jenna Loyd in the book *Beyond Walls and Cages*, defines it as the right "to live, love, and work, wherever you please."[21] This includes, Fernandez says, freedom of movement "so I can live here or there, I can live on this side of the border or that side of the border, and the government should not be involved in that." The decriminalization of movement means the decriminalization of work and the decriminalization of love. And I would add to that list of rights the right to organize wherever and with whomever you please, even and especially across borders.

On organizing, scholar-activist Harsha Walia writes, "In order to rid ourselves of border imperialism along with the barriers we erect within ourselves against one another, our movements have to supplant the colonial and bordered logic of the state itself." Walia notes that almost a century ago, the anarchist Gustav Landauer asserted, "The State is a condition, a certain relationship between human beings, a mode of behavior; we destroy it by contracting other relationships."[22] It seems to me that Landauer's recipe could be used right now in the Anthropocene: What is required of humanity today is immense and powerful creativity, which requires making new relationships that offer new possibilities, and borders inhibit the ability to do that.

KENYA BORDER PATROL

The taxi turned into the Nairobi neighborhood Eastleigh, far from any of Kenya's international borders. Eastleigh is predominantly inhabited by Somalis. As we entered the main street leading into the neighborhood, a woman in the green uniform of the Administrative Police—the agency in Kenya tasked with immigration and border policing—waved us down, and then motioned for the driver to pull off to the side of the road. In discussions of border policing in this young nation-state (Kenya got its independence from Great Britain in 1963), often the first location brought up is the eastern border with Somalia. Kenyan officials have talked about building a wall along the 440-mile divide, and they have sought Israeli counterterrorism expertise for its construction.

Officials complain about Somalia's faltering government and the presence of Al Shabaab, a group recognized as a terrorist organization by the U.S. government, but one of the most significant dynamics behind Somali upheavals has been massive droughts. This checkpoint epitomized the situation: Droughts and superstorms leave people in one country homeless or without means of living at home; they move, hoping for respite in another country; their arrival at the border is met with blockades, surveillance, and armed guards; and those who manage to cross find that the border operates not only around but within that entire country. It's something they must cross not once but every day. In this sense, Kenya is no different from anywhere else. Unauthorized Somali refugees, like the Maasai during British colonial rule, need a movement pass to get through the substantial checkpoint infrastructure *within* Kenya, from Garissa County in the Somali borderlands all the way—350 miles—to Nairobi.

And once they reached the capital? We were in Nairobi when the taxi driver pulled off to the side of the road. Just as there are borders around and within countries, there are borders around and within cities. Geographer Stephen Graham describes them in his book *Cities Under Siege*. As he says, borders have become "ubiquitous."

The border we had crossed when the Kenyan "homeland security" police motioned us to stop divided the Eastleigh from Muthaiga, the neighborhood we'd just left, wealthy, highly securitized, described by the city guide *Wanted in Africa* as "Nairobi's long-established Beverly Hills." Along the road, international embassies hid behind bunkers and armed security. As we drove, I spotted guards wearing the insignia of G4S, the Fortune 500 U.K. company that thrived on border enforcement contracts, including contracts with CBP to provide armored transportation for undocumented people arrested in the

U.S. borderlands. Passing the heavily guarded embassies, I wondered if it had been a mistake to suggest to the Custom and Border Protection attaché Kevin Martinson that we meet in the hotel where I was staying in central Nairobi. As a U.S. Embassy employee, he was obviously used to something else, if this drive through Muthaiga was any indication. Martinson had abruptly canceled the meeting, which had taken months to arrange, after I mentioned the Khweza Bed and Breakfast on Ngara Road. His email stated, with no elaboration, that he simply had to cancel. I wrote back asking for a telephone interview, but he never replied. A journalism student once asked me if I had ever felt animosity from people in other countries because I was from the United States. I'd thought for a moment, then answered that people in other countries usually didn't give me trouble—in fact, they often generously shared sensitive stories with me. It was the United States government, and officials connected with it that gave me trouble. From the International Narcotic and Law Enforcement Bureau to CBP, there was a metaphorical wall around information and U.S. policies and practices, and I ran into it everywhere. In Kenya, not just CBP but also staff at the Export and Border Security Related Program (EXBS) and the United States Agency for International Development (USAID)—which was also involved in developing the Kenyan border policing apparatus—only gave me the most rudimentary answers after multiple attempts at communication over several months.

As I close this book, I would like to underscore the U.S. government's dismissive treatment of journalists making straightforward inquiries about the United States' foreign mission operations. In Africa, I found the "border wall" around such information especially high and well fortified. Perhaps this can be understood in the context of what journalist Nick Turse calls "sweeping and expansive" U.S. military operations on the continent. A map of the U.S. "pivot to Africa" from 2012 to 2013, Turse says, shows an upsurge in military outposts, security cooperation, and deployments across Africa that looks like a "field of mushrooms." An investigation by *TomDispatch* found U.S. operations in forty-nine of Africa's fifty-four countries. The reason? According to Turse, U.S. African Command (AFRICOM) claimed that its core mission "of assisting African states and regional organizations to strengthen their defense capabilities better enables Africans to address their security threats and reduces threats to U.S. interests."[23]

U.S. Army Africa, too, said it was "helping" different African nations "secure their own borders as well as their own regions." Major Albert Conley III told Mindy Anderson, of U.S. Army Africa Public Affairs, that his outfit is helping "Africa solve African problems" and, "as a secondary effect," securing whatever "American interests" are in that region or country. "If Africans are solving African problems," Major Conley said, "that means the U.S. government won't need to use the United States Army to solve African problems."[24]

Central to U.S. African Command strategy is its doctrine on climate security. In February 2016, AFRICOM representatives participated in a Washington, DC, panel titled "Climate Change, Disasters, and Security: Unconventional Approaches to Building Stability." AFRICOM reported that since many places lack the resources for disaster prevention and preparedness, "climate-related natural disasters can act as a threat multiplier, undermining the stability of nations and regions while exacerbating insecurity."[25] African Command has worked "to strengthen responses to climate change through a jointly developed training course" encouraging a "whole of government approach"— that is, the homeland security approach, the fusion of military, intelligence, and law enforcement.

The difficulty I had interacting as a journalist with the U.S. government became in itself a reportable event, a story that seemed even more pertinent as we drove past the gigantic, fortress-like U.S. Embassy complex in Muthaiga. The double image of dominance and inaccessibility, expressed in a land so distant from its own, could only be that of an imperial power. As we drove by, I looked up and saw a man in combat gear on top of one of the buildings of the complex, most likely a sniper. Instead of the CBP attaché, we got to see a sniper. Later I Googled Kevin Martinson, and brought up a group picture of CBP agents deployed to Iraq in 2011. He and the other agents were smiling and holding machine guns, as if they were a military operation. But, as the accompanying article explained, they were here to "create a more secure and prosperous nation."[26]

When we entered the Somali Eastleigh neighborhood, the scene changed radically. Fifteen minutes after seeing the imposing embassy, we were suddenly at a line of division it helped create. The Kenyan Administrative Police, with its training and equipment from the United States, had constructed a border in the middle of Nairobi. Maybe crossing that border, like seeing the sniper, would be just as educational as learning about Martinson's work at CBP. The administrative police agent came to the window and talked to our driver in Swahili. The driver handed her an identification card. A call to prayer from a nearby mosque floated in through the window. The scene behind the agent almost did look like another country that was not Kenya. Men dressed in long shirts and robes pushed wooden carts stacked sky-high with shirts or furniture or bananas through a bustling crowd of pedestrians that overflowed both sides of the road. Many of the women wore a hijab. Only a mile away, wealthy foreigners hunkered down behind walls, fences, bunkers, private security forces.

According to a U.S. Embassy dispatch titled "Security Sector Assistance in Kenya, Part II: Land Border Security Training," it was in 2003 that at the request of the Kenya Ministry of Defense "the United States began to assist in the development of military units capable of responding to cross-border security challenges." The dispatch noted, "due to the threat of spillover effects from fighting in Somalia, the Government of Kenya views border control as one of its top national security priorities." It certainly felt that way on the fringes of Eastleigh as the agent meticulously eyed our passports. In coordination with AFRICOM and other Defense Department entities, the dispatch said, the "land-based force" had been formed of both "conventional army infantry battalions" and "an elite Kenya Army Special Operations Force/Ranger Strike Force." The United States had sent Kenya Humvees, personal protective and navigational equipment, handheld radios, small arms, and ammunition. The dispatch noted further, "the KSOF [Kenya Special Operations Force] is central to Kenya's national defense strategy and can directly support our [Washington's] peace and security goals in the region."[27]

In February 2009, personnel from the U.S. Border Patrol conducted a weeklong assessment of Kenya's proposed new border patrol program. At this point Kenya did not have a dedicated border guard. But the Kenyan government, according to a U.S. Embassy cable, had a "vision" to create new "dedicated border patrol units."[28] They would be jointly staffed by the Administrative Police—whose agent at East-leigh, after examining our passports, finally waved us through—and, remarkably, the Kenyan Wildlife Service. To complete the new border guard, Washington told the Administrative Police, they would have to add 3,000 to 4,000 new agents. The border unit would need special-ized training, and more equipment. And so between 2007 and 2009, Washington sent Kenya $53 million in Border Security Assistance.[29] And the money was spent to create the Rural Border Patrol Unit, in a country where more than half of the people live below the poverty line.[30] The unit's motto was "Secure border for all." Its stated goal was "to be the leading Rural Border Patrol Security provider to all people in Kenya." And when its camouflaged, heavily armed units—they even had tanks—initiated an operation, residents of the town of Migori were so terrified of an imminent crackdown, they closed their shops and ran to hide in their houses.[31] But it was just the new global border patrol, freshly constructed by the United States of America.

INFINITE POSSIBILITIES, ENDLESS OPPORTUNITIES

I thought about Ruben Andersson's remark about the absurdity of the "illegality industry" again while in the office of Kenyan Police Commandant Peter M. Maanzia, whose name was prominently carved into a wooden plaque that extended a good length along his desk. When we entered, the commandant was looking down at a piece of paper the receptionist had just brought in. Luckily, we were there to interview him, not because we had been arrested at the Eastleigh checkpoint. The whole illegality industry really did seem absurd—not only Maanzia, but the whole apparatus of exclusion, from global sea to shining sea, that he seemed to represent: its bureaucracy, its logic, its profiteering, its authoritarianism, its stonewalling. The insignia on the lapels of Maanzia's camo uniform showed that he was from Kenya, but he could have been from so many different places: Guatemala,

Israel, the United States. When he finally looked up, he indicated that he could say nothing.

The baffling pause that followed, the vacuum of silence, showed the uncertain security apparatus in its perfect form. When I explained that the reason we were sitting before him—speaking over a commercial blaring from the TV behind me—was to learn about the border police, he repeated that he could not talk. Then he said that the "border police" was "just a name." They were deployed in many different places. So I asked, thinking of the Administrative Police checkpoint, were they deployed in Nairobi? But now he was engrossed with the television. I thought, though, that what he had said before ignoring my second question was extremely interesting. He had implied that the border was ubiquitous. And "just a name," everywhere and nowhere at once, a true security force. Maanzia looked down once more at the paper in front of him. A picture of President Uhuru Kenyatta hovered behind him, looking as if he were about to offer a comment.

"Who are you?" asked Maanzia when he finally looked up. "Where are you from?" Did we have permission to do research? Had we registered with the U.S. Embassy? The Embassy "could filter between the good and the bad," he said.

He continued, "I mean, you look nice, but you may have other intentions." You might want to use this information. "You might want to sell this information," he said.

It was as if we weren't in the middle of Nairobi, but at yet another border crossing. Maanzia had strong facial features. He was bald and had intense eyes, eagle eyes. His questions sounded as if he'd learned them from a training manual, completely disassociated from the warmth and hospitality I had felt since arriving in Kenya.

The receptionist walked in. There was another sheet of paper. Maanzia abruptly stopped talking. As I watched him staring down at it, I remembered what a trusted advisor in Kenya had told me—if you get too close to the security apparatus, they will interrogate you.

Behind us was a large green map of the new railroad that ran from the Kenyan port city of Mombasa to Nairobi, positioned so Maanzia could see it from where he sat. After all, he was a commandant of the Railroad Police. It was why I was there: I wanted to learn how the border police and the railroad police intersected, how it all became a security apparatus for the global economic system. Indeed, this railroad was just the beginning of a series of capital-intensive projects. Another one, in the north of Kenya, the Lamu Port, South Sudan, Ethiopia Transport corridor, or LAPPSET, was ten times the size of this railroad, we were told, and East Africa's "largest and most ambitious infrastructure project." Still in its beginning phases, it was a huge transportation corridor that would go to and from the port on Kenya's Lamu Island. The project would cross borders into South Sudan and Ethiopia. There would be a highway. There would be a railroad. There would be a fiber-optic line. There would be three international airports. There would be hydroelectric dams. And to seal the deal, there would be oil pipelines coming from Turkana, through the drought-stricken borderlands of Somalia. "A seamless connected Africa," the LAPPSET website advertised. "Infinite possibilities. Endless opportunities."[32]

Finally, Maanzia began to talk. He talked about working on the Kenyan border. He talked about working on the Ugandan border, the Ethiopian border. He'd worked in the Maasai Mara, along the border with Tanzania. He knew about borders. He'd worked for the dreaded General Service Unit, Kenya's anti-riot police, which had been implicated in killings and disappearances of people. He'd worked for the Wildlife Agency, now part of the border units. Behind him was a glass cabinet displaying large blue binders, each etched with the title LAW OF KENYA. The weighty rule of law hung there, almost over his head, as if its weight could crash the cabinet and tumble to the floor. He kept repeating that the police were there "for the protection of all the people and their property." Then he picked up his phone. He looked at it for a second. Then he looked at me and asked, "Are you married?" I told him yes. "Well," he said, "you could marry again and have a wife here too!" He laughed. Americans, the implication was, divorced a lot and had many wives.

Just like that, Maanzia kept turning the conversation around. He went from promoting Kenyan wives to questioning just how we'd arrived at his office. He wanted to know how we'd funded our trip, how much it cost. His questions came suddenly, like a burst of gunfire.

We were caught between an interview and an interrogation. I wondered again, did he learn this double-edged method, this staggered interrogation, this double rendition of good cop/bad cop, from any of the multiple trainings he had received from the United States, from the U.K., from Israel? In the United States he had trained in Texas and in Chicago, he said. In Israel the courses had been more specialized. "In Israel everyone cares about security," Maanzia exclaimed. "The children care about security. The grandmothers care about security."

The global security apparatus created by this U.S.- Israeli synergy had arrived in Kenya and its borderlands. That was the main message I got from Maanzia, and it put me on edge. I feared he might arrest me for doing research without permission, even after I left the building.

The multinational lockdown was sharply evident near where the oil pipelines met climate change in the rain-scarce Kenya-Somalia borderlands. Here, journalist Margot Kiser reported, British, Israeli, and Jordanian contractors, spies, and commandos joined the "undeclared if not unmentioned U.S.-backed war."[33] Kiser's focus was the Kenyan Boni National Reserve in the borderlands, just north of the port city of Lamu. Lamu was a place where U.S. troops were part of a 1,500-strong combined joint task force. "With the Somali border about 100 kilometers north of Lamu, U.S. officials were eager to accept Kenya's invitation to bolster their sea and land defenses," according to GlobalSecurity.org. The U.S. military regularly marched through Lamu's narrow streets "in a show of force."[34]

Kiser described the national reserve to the north as a "fairy-tale paradise" with "elephantine baobab trees" and "hydra-headed doum palms." The Green Berets rumbled through its resplendent ecosystem in armored cars, in an effort to "shore up the frontiers of Fortress America."[35] Who knew the United States went so far, so wide, so vast, so everywhere?

In 2011, an estimated 300,000 Somalis crossed the international border into Kenya, Ethiopia, Djibouti, and Yemen.[36] The main cause of the exodus was not the "failed state" of the Somalian government, as the security narratives go, but a super-drought that threatened the livelihoods of 9.5 million people throughout southern Somalia,

Kenya, and Ethiopia, the same area covered by the LAPPSET corridor and the planned oil drilling and transportation project.[37]

Although Al Shabaab and a faltering government might also have been relevant, there were much bigger and powerful issues at play, issues that were literally world-shaking. An addicted global economy sucking up oil, an atmosphere packed with heat-trapping gasses, and a scrambled weather system menaced a world where fixed, hardened borders made no sense at all for the preservation of life on earth. In fact, borders worked against survival in the crises of the living planet. Yet the empires of the borders were still anchored in the colonial lines of division that dominated the political worldview, as the Spanish fortifications in Ceuta and Melilla in Morocco displayed so clearly. While Nandita Sharma and her colleagues make a compelling argument for a practical political project to eliminate borders, projections of future climate catastrophes have brought assessments that forecast the precise opposite: a world jam-packed with militarized border zones and sharp lines of division. In the face of this, Sharma et al. call for the creation of a twenty-first century global commons, a world where national identities and their implicit divisions melt away, and new possibilities for relationships arise:

> Many taking a No Borders political position, therefore, move from challenging national forms of belonging to trying to activate new subjectivities, ones that correspond with the global level at which human society is actually organized, in order to arm a conception of freedom based on the collective political action of *equals*. A No Borders politics, thus, redefines equality by positing it as a relationship among co-members of a global society and not one among national citizens.[38]

Environmental writer and activist George Monbiot, in his book *Out of the Wreckage: A New Politics for an Age of Crisis*, makes such a collective movement toward the commons not only seem doable, but also pragmatic:

> A commons consists not only of a resource over which a community has shared and equal rights, such as land, fresh water, minerals, knowledge,

culture, scientific research or software. It also describes the community of people organizing themselves to manage and protect the resource, and the rules, systems and negotiations required to sustain it.

As I traveled to Maasailand—where southern Kenya borders the Serengeti Plain in Tanzania—I could see the return to the commons as not a distant dream, but rather as one of the most practical things human civilization could do in the Anthropocene.

15.

Negotiating Borders
on a Warming Planet

When I first visited Maasailand, I traveled in a small, ten-seater plane, despite my dislike for planes. I was struck by the stunning views as we lifted over Nairobi. On the outskirts of Kenya's capital, I saw the corrugated roofing of Africa's largest urban slum, Kibera, said to contain as many as 1 million people. Urban historian Mike Davis notes in his 2006 book *Planet of the Slums* that satellite reconnaissance shows more than half of Nairobi's population densely concentrated into 18 percent of the city space.[1] Now from the plane I could see that urban inequality for myself; and even more dramatically when, just minutes later, we flew over a sort of fantastical subdivision with gigantic houses that could each encompass five or six of the houses in Kibera. Attached to the houses I saw square blue pools and green, manicured lawns. This sort of spectacular inequality was a glimpse into the heart of an unsustainable planet, where the top 1 percent have more money than the entire bottom half of humanity. It was what this world of borders was really about.

On the plane, in front of me, the two pilots were conversing as we flew through the clouds toward a landing strip on the Maasai Mara. The only other people on the plane were a white British couple dressed in khaki safari gear. A brownish green plain appeared below, extending miles and miles into the horizon. We had reached the Tanzanian-Kenyan borderlands. I was further from home than I had ever been in my life, yet I knew that the U.S. Border Patrol had arrived even here. CBP had provided training for fifteen law-enforcement departments from Kenya, Tanzania, and Uganda—including the Kenya Police Service and the General Service Unit, the Kenya Administration Police Service, the Kenya Wildlife Service, the Tanzania Police, the

Tanzania National Parks Agency, the Tanzania Wildlife Department, the Uganda National Police, the Uganda Customs Police, the Uganda Wildlife Service, and the Uganda Anti-Terrorism Unit. According to the U.S. Embassy in Nairobi, CBP trained 330 law-enforcement personnel in the area "to better secure the region's borders," an example of its dedication to "advance peace and security and promote opportunity and development in the region." [2]

Traveling to the Maasai Mara that day, I marveled at the vastness of the U.S. border. It was in the train yard in Arriaga, Chiapas where Gerardo, en route to Miami, showed me the photo of his son; in Occupied Palestine, where the Sabri Gharib family lived in an enclave of wall; on the stormy island of Puerto Rico, where fast boats cruised the Mona Strait in search of rickety *yolas* filled with Dominicans or Haitians; in the ever-flooding Manila harbor; at the Vancouver airport; on the Guatemalan-Honduran divide; in the halls of Mexico's Expo Seguridad; and on the border between Jordan and Syria.

Using funds from DHS, the State Department, the International Bureau on Narcotics Enforcement, the Export Control and Border Security Program, and the Department of Defense, the United States is pouring billions into its international border operations in the form of training programs and resource transfers. Attachés, advisors, and trainers are spread throughout the world. For every place I describe in this book, there are many other countries and locales with similar CBP advisory and training programs, receiving resources and learning how to blockade people from crossing borderlines. It is all powered by an immense global surveillance industry, one that takes places like Palestine-Israel and the U.S.-Mexico border as the profitable model that every country *just needs to have.*

The last place I visited for this book was this beautiful area in southern Kenya.

From the plane, I saw a herd of animals (gazelles, maybe?) on a mountaintop burst into a run in graceful unison. Their vivid synchronicity made it seem an illusion, as if I were momentarily dreaming. I saw a lone elephant that appeared to be washing itself in a pool. I saw an ostrich. I saw wildebeests streaming in packs. Later, I would be taken with their long gray beards and stately faces that regarded their surroundings with a sort of beautiful wisdom. Soon up to 3 million wildebeests would be migrating from the Serengeti Plain to the Maasai Mara, from Tanzania to Kenya, completely disregarding the European-designed political boundary that had cut Maasailand into two separate countries.

Once we landed, it took just fifteen minutes to travel on to the Maasai Mara and see a lion, with a full mane, panting. Soon there were also giraffes craning their necks, their large nostrils sniffing the air. Seeing these animals up close and so vivid brought a new awareness. I had barely arrived, and Maasailand already seemed a place where things not only could be but also were imagined quite differently. It was a place where peoples, animals, and the living world coexisted and had always coexisted in a world of flexible, negotiated, and moveable borders—well before English colonialism brought with it private enclosures surrounded by hardened lines of division.

The Maasai knew a lot about borders. They had learned about them not only from the straight line drawn during the 1884 Berlin Conference that divided them in half, when Europe created what was to become the Kenya-Tanzania divide, but also from the lines of division that surrounded the first Maasai reservations, which were modeled on apartheid South Africa's "homelands" and the U.S. Native American reservation system. These lines corralled the Maasai into two separate reservations, northern and southern. Then the British discovered that the northern reservation had water and was good for agriculture, and deported the northern Maasai en masse, relocating them to the more arid southern reserve, the savannah that connected with the Serengeti Plain. The British in effect were carving up the commons, much as they had in the seventeenth century in their own country before the Midlands Revolt.

For the Maasai, their "commons" was a place where the collective was given more importance than the individual. It was a place where the community raised children. It was a place where, as Maasai elder Meitamei Olol-Dapash told me, private ownership was not the custom because it was simply inefficient.

"I am against lines of division," Austin Parsaloi told me at the

Maasai Education, Research and Conservation Institute (MERC). It was June 2017. Parsaloi was working in the campaign of Olol-Dapash, which was in full swing, with the August elections coming quickly. Parsaloi had just said that he didn't celebrate Kenyan independence. In 1963 when Kenya was declared free and a nation-state, the land in the highlands, in the areas of the headwaters, was not given back to the Maasai. That was a "historic injustice," said Parsaloi. In Kenya, and especially in Maasailand, colonization was still powerfully present, raw and pulsating through everyday life. The formal transition from colony to the nation-state hadn't really fooled anybody.

"I'm against lines of division because when land is subdivided, it means there is ownership of the land. It means the owner can do whatever they want to the land. They can fence the land. I like conservation, so I don't like fencing," said Parsaloi. "Land subdivision is not the Maasai lifestyle."

"So the Maasai lifestyle is that you have more communal land?" I asked.

Borders, he answered, are the key reason why the current world is ill-prepared for climate breakdowns. "For example, if you are in one place and it is not raining, then you simply move your cows to another place," he said. "Right now there is a big problem of drought. And there's no place you can go for green pasture. So you need to stay there. There. There. *There. There,*" he repeated, insisting on the point that you can't move, that you have to stay *there* and endure whatever is *there* "your entire life."

As the climate alters, seasons get scrambled, and people need more flexibility, more freedom of movement to be able to adapt and adjust. This means not only people affected by the droughts in sub-Saharan Africa but also the hundreds of millions of people on the shores of the rising seas everywhere. The bounding of private property not only keeps people out, it also hems people in, in places that cannot sustain life. In some areas, stronger foundations for climate resilience can be laid: large sea walls; drought-resistant seeds for dying soils, perhaps. However, in many cases the simple ability to move from one place to another—made much easier by common lands—will be the inevitable answer.

We live in an age when the earth's geography and geology are going to be altered in ways that will make our current maps antiquated and downright inaccurate. Places where people live now will be wiped off the map. The shapes of others will change. Free, flexible, unpoliced movement will be paramount. Right now, projections estimate millions if not billions of people on the move. Will those future refugees be slashed with razor wire, like the black men atop the wall in Melilla, watching the people leisurely golf, below?

Fixed borders are prison walls. They are a geographical straitjacket.

Austin Parsaloi spoke of a simple solution: Breaking the lines of today's borders will break the divisive ideas and institutions imposed by the colonial mindset. This includes private property. The idea that individuals should be stationary, confined to one place, will be replaced by a spirit of collectivity, a way of living in this world that inspires new strategies, and new negotiations—new ways of making relationships, including borders, with other peoples and with the natural world.

"When there's a drought in Laikipia," Parsaloi said, "there's no drought here. And when there's a drought here, there's no drought in Laikipia. So this rotational grazing makes sense. To me, these boundaries, that this is Kenya and that is Tanzania makes no sense. I don't like that. I need to be free. I just need to go free."

According to Nandita Sharma et al., the idea of the commons is based on one fundamental right: "the right to not be excluded."

THE GENIUS OF MOVEABLE BORDERS

In *Learning to Die in the Anthropocene: Reflections On the End of a Civilization*, author Roy Scranton argues that climate devastation has pushed human civilization past the point of no return. He believes we should begin to simply mourn, because it is dying and there's not much we can do about it. At the beginning of the book, he describes his experience as a soldier entering an eviscerated Baghdad in 2003—after the U.S. campaign of "shock and awe." It was like moving into a future of "hell and ruin." A mere two and a half years later, when Scranton witnessed the aftermath of Hurricane Katrina while stationed in Fort Still, Oklahoma, he wrote, "The grim future I'd seen in Baghdad had come home: not terrorism, not WMDs, but the machinery of civilization breaking down, unable to recuperate from shocks to its system."[3]

I have thought much about Scranton's compelling analysis. Many others have warned that "forced migrations and economic collapse might make the planet ungovernable, threatening the fabric of civilization," as the renowned climate scientist James Hansen has said.[4] But what exactly is this civilization? Is it the same civilization that was, effectively, the source of the historical injustice committed against the Maasai and indigenous people around the globe? The civilization, built on the foundations of colonialism, that is still constructing global inequality and has also left a crushing carbon footprint? A civilization that currently relies on a scaffolding of borders to enforce a suicidal status quo?

Perhaps that civilization is what needs to die.

As Scranton writes, "learning to die as an individual means letting go of our predispositions and fear. Learning to die as a civilization means letting go of this particular way of life and its ideas of identity, freedom, success, and progress."[5]

This civilization is based on a system of exclusion, based on a wage structure that pays a pittance to most workers while a few hoard billions. This civilization is taking a wrecking ball to the planet, poisoning the water, poisoning the land, and poisoning the sky. As philosopher and cultural ecologist David Abram writes in his book *Becoming Animal*, "Even as we discern the imminent danger to ourselves, we seem unable to locate any exit from the hall of mirrors, so thoroughly transfixed have we become by our own reflections."[6]

Perhaps today's vastly unsustainable civilization is indeed what needs to die, so another can have the space to be born.

Borders are not only ways of dividing nations, cities, and land, they also are ways of dividing people, corralling people, organizing people, producing compliance in people, extracting profit from people. The new era of people moving in situations of massive droughts or rising seas may be the final straw that breaks the back of the global system of border regimes. A world where the worst polluters and exploiters are rewarded with lavish profits and the rest of us are slowly but surely walled in.

The Maasai offer an alternative to our current dysfunctional, destructive national borders. The Maasai model would not eliminate borders, but it would change them from colonially imposed lines of division to borders newly negotiated between peoples who stand on equal ground. The borders would be not fixed, but moveable, able to change with changing times and circumstances. Borders negotiated not only between different peoples but also between people and the animals, between people and the natural world.

Mary Poole, a resident historian from Prescott College, pointed at the tall grass around the Maasai Educational Research Center and said that was a border negotiated with the snakes. The snakes, she said, knew they had the tall grass.

"There is such a genius to moveable borders," Poole said. "Borders being built in all kinds of ways other than cement. Like there's borders with all of us right now," she said, referring to all of us who were standing together. "And there are borders between us and the snakes that are in the grass over there."

"If you're not negotiating," she said, "then you're colonizing land rather than living on the land."

There are endless instances of this kind of border negotiation. For example, the negotiations with the elephants at the MERC center. When humans were physically present at the center and using the land, the elephants respected the boundary—demarcated by a fence —and did not enter. When people were not there, as happened during parts of the year, the elephants would barge through, knock over the fences, occupy the land, and eat the trees. The people at the MERC center, though distressed at the loss of their beautiful trees, also understood that this was a fundamental part of the negotiation. Borders were changeable and unfixed, meant different things in different contexts, and were negotiated on equal grounds, even with animals. Another example: One elephant kept coming into the camp. On the first night, the staff in the camp chased it out. It returned the next night. This time the staff went around to talk to the surrounding community, because everyone in the community was networked into what was happening in the natural world and with the animals. Through a sharing of information, the staff learned that the elephant had a newborn. She also had a "teenage" offspring. The three of them were on their own. An elephant couldn't move with a newborn; it was just too dangerous. So the elephants had set up camp by the fence. They came in to eat at night. So the humans negotiated the border with the elephants and the border was moved. The staff permitted them into the camp, but kept them away from the tents. There were "millions of examples," Poole said, of this sort of negotiation.

"There is nothing more core to Maasai culture than respect for other living beings on our shared land, and for us to lose that quality would be to lose our culture," Meitamei Olol-Dapash stressed. He also recognized this to be the reality of many indigenous peoples around the globe. Borders were a result of slashing up and stamping out these sorts of traditions.

The Maasai's resilience in droughts, as Parsaloi noted above, is based on negotiations between peoples and lands on equal terms. Since droughts are "increasing over time," these terms are becoming urgent.

One such border negotiation involved a "deep drought reserve" where underground streams created by runoff from Mount Kilimanjaro emptied into a swamp. Olol-Dapash described the place as one of "glorious, crystal water and grasses tall enough to hide a full-grown hippo." People agreed not to graze the area unless no other grasses could be found. But they would go there during the worst droughts, camp nearby, and allow their cattle to eat the grass until the rains came. It was a Maasai drought safety net. But it was also an example of shared-use land, shared not only by different peoples but also by wildlife in their migrations. After the colonial and independence governments carved up the land and created boundaries, using British guns and bayonets to force the Maasai onto reserves, this "glorious" place of crystal water became inaccessible, roped off into a national park for the exclusive use of the wildlife and big-game hunters. Now the park's boundary is easy to see. "It is the line where the brown-red dust meets vibrant green of the swamp grasses," Olol-Dapash said. He writes, "Maasailand is being privatized and sold at staggering rates over the last 50 years. As fences spring up on communally used grazing land, the entire economy of Maasailand is threatened."[7]

Multiuse, shared spaces based on negotiations have been replaced by imposed bounded exclusion zones, privatized spaces, and private property. These are the spaces that police agent Peter Maanzia in Nairobi said it was his department's mission to protect.

The truth obscured by all of this is that the Maasai people—like most indigenous people across the world—already know what to do, especially as climate changes scramble weather and increase drought. They simply need the freedom to roam on their aboriginal land, unhampered by hardened boundaries, including the international border with Tanzania. The borders are obstructions to their flourishing, organizing, and survival. "Borderlines," Olol-Dapash told me, "are very disempowering because [a border] disrupts the community's unity. It disrupts culture. It disrupts the political coordination of things. It disrupts the economic sustainability of the Maasai people."

"African countries were made without the knowledge of the African people, without their consultation … These were peoples to be colonized, to be ruled, to be controlled, and Africa took itself to be used as a continent to provide resources for the development of Europe."

The lines of division carried the poison of historic injustice. Olol-Dapash said, echoing the sentiments of Austin Parsaloi, "I think Kenya as a nation-state is 100 percent illegitimate." Dissolve the nation-state, or at least its foundational power structures, and the fixed lines and borders that today's police swear to protect will, perhaps, begin to dissolve as well.

DELIGHT OF KINSHIP

Back at the MERC center, I ask Poole what a more sustainable world of moveable, negotiated borders might entail.

"What if we had political realities that were more emergent from local places?" The change would start with the most basic and the most practical: Not only would people be more accountable for their watersheds, but they would also learn to deal with each other on equal grounds of "fair negotiation, diplomacy—the art of figuring out how to talk in another language."

We would also need to relearn how to live and work in a community. Poole uses the United States as an example. People there have lived for so long "in privatization that when people try to [set up] community households it takes ten to twenty years because nobody knows how to do it. All you know how to do," Poole said, "is declare that it's my yogurt." And then there's the job wheel on the refrigerator: "It's your turn to wash the bathroom. Because that's the law."

And then, Poole says, "you learn that it's not all about counting beans. It's about relationships. There's an art and a skill to a communal use of land, and some communities have forgotten that. And I think that we [in the United States] are so far away from that in the pendulum of our cultural experience that it seems impossible. But it's not."

The good news is that there is a powerful counterforce to the privatized, individualized, fixed-border worldview. Besides the Maasai there are many peoples who understand the intricacies of their region, biosphere, soil or sea. There are the small farmers in Guatemala and Mexico, the fisher folk in the Philippines and Puerto Rico, the Palestinian communities on the West Bank, and the communities that crisscross the Jordan-Syria border. On the other side of profits, guns, militaries, police, and borders, on the other side of the securocratic wars, in each different place around the world there are people, peoples, groups, and among them many leaders who will be able to lead humanity away from our current situation. Many of those natural leaders are, like the Maasai, indigenous people that know the land, and view the land and its connection with environment as sacred.

Father Greg Boyle, known for his work with gang members in Los Angeles, talks about crossing boundaries and connecting with people as the "delight of kinship." An exclusionary border can stunt this delight and growth. It can stunt the compassion, admiration, even awe we should be able to feel toward another person, other peoples, other places. Remembering Maasailand, as I stood and talked with Austin Parsaloi, hearing the soft June winds blow through, knowing the landscape around was teeming with life, and listening to him describe a world unencumbered by lines of division, I was struck by that awe.

16.

Conclusion

The Future:
The Airport and the Ceiba in Copan

We operate daily within the confines of myriad lines—class, creed, sexuality, gender—that mainly serve to suppress our quality of life. Spend enough time straddling one, and you can't help but wonder what bliss might follow if we all just embraced the spaces in between.

Stephanie Elizondo Griest

And this is what I learned: the world's otherness is antidote to confusion, that standing within this otherness—the beauty and mystery of the world, out in the fields or deep inside books—can re-dignify the worst-strung heart.

Mary Oliver

Colonel Ramón Macoto had a cell phone pressed to his ear as we rumbled down the road towards the archeological site of the Copán Ruinas in Honduras, near the Guatemalan border. The Maya Chorti task force, the new Honduran border police unit, had only been around for two months. This patrol worked in tandem with the Guatemalan force, the Chorti, with whom I began this book.

On his phone, Macoto was catching news that the Maya Chorti had stopped and detained eighteen people at one of the checkpoints that the patrol had set up on one of the roads leading to the Guatemalan border. A soldier, dressed like Macoto in green camo, drove the silver truck. In the back sat several more soldiers with assault rifles between their legs. Jeff Abbott was also there, snapping photographs as we cruised through the emerald green hills. I heard Macoto say "*Mi coronel*" into the phone. I heard him say "*ilegales*." There were Dominicans. There were Ecuadorians. Flores, of the Honduran National Police, sat at my side.

He wore the dark navy uniform of the police. He was also a commander of the Maya Chorti; the force was a fusion of the military and police. He told me, "Every day. Every single day this happens." He seemed exasperated. "Everybody wants to go to the United States."

Two hours before, Abbott and I had met Macoto and Flores at the Copán Ruinas airport. This airport did not appear to be open to the public. Public transportation, of course, did not arrive there; the van dropped us off on the side of the road. From there we followed the vague directions of the driver, who said the airport was over there, somewhere, near the clear cut. The sun beat down on that broiling June morning in 2015, and as always in this part of Honduras I caught the subtle, sweet smell of burning copal, a type of tree resin used as incense and to help light fires for cooking and warmth. We were close to the Copán archeological site, a major Mayan city from the fifth to ninth century, in one of southeasternmost areas of what historians consider Mayan territory. Copán was dominated by ceiba trees, which could grow as high as 230 feet: thick, branchless trunks that spread at the top into a wide, shade-giving canopy of branches, connecting the underworld with the sky.

As we walked down the long, clear-cut two-lane road toward the airport, hoping we were going the right way, a single soldier appeared in the distance. He was, at first, a silhouette. It looked, for a minute, as if we were walking into a still from a dystopian movie. When the soldier reached us he told us that we were almost there. We found out quickly that he was one of many camouflaged, heavily armed troops doing perimeter surveillance around the airport, which turned out to be the size of a house in a U.S. suburban subdivision. Although officially inaugurated a few months before, the airport building was cavernous and empty. It looked as if it saw very little use.

"Copán means the scientific city of the Mayan culture," the Honduran president Juan Orlando Hernandez had said at the inauguration earlier that year in March. "This for us is something extraordinary, and in that sense this airport is going to bring in a great amount of profit, not only from national but international tourism."[1]

Macoto and Flores sat on benches in the center of the airport. Our voices echoed in the empty room. Except for the benches, the only thing installed was a biometric system: a scanner for fingerprints and cameras for facial recognition. The technology bore the red logo of the 3M company, famous for Scotch tape. Now part of the growing big-brother tech market, 3M was logging annual sales of $30 billion—a sum equivalent to the GDP of Honduras.[2] Next to the biometric installation was a large glossy placard with the reassuring image of a white woman with a gleaming smile, welcoming passengers to this new world of surveillance, explaining that it was for everyone's safety. She was the "Border Force Officer of the Future"— the title of a panel I attended at the International Border Summit in Washington, DC, in June 2018, where one official quipped that "the face that God gave you the day you were born will be your passport." Here was a world without passports, where tourists would be ushered in and out of countries in a "happy flow" biometric suite. Here was a world where facial recognition smoothly delivered you and even your suitcase to your hotel room. But it was also a world where you were in trouble if you didn't get through the digital algorithms and the virtual gatekeepers. At the airport, I kept glimpsing the soldiers patrolling outside through the glass doors, as if we were under threat. Rather than an airport, the place seemed like a black site, a miniature de facto military base, a place instructors at the School of the Americas might suggest as an ideal location for an interrogation.

Colonel Macoto thanked us profusely for coming to Honduras to see the changes that were happening. He told us that he'd wanted to meet in the airport so we could see his country's "future."

This was the future: The flights would eventually arrive from Tegucigalpa, the Honduran capital, and Tikal, in Guatemala, connecting the Mundo Maya.

The future was also the Maya Chorti: its mobile patrols, its border reconnaissance, its checkpoints, its search for human intelligence.

Macoto described the border force as dynamic, ever changing, ever evolving. The Maya Chorti patrolled the four departments along the Guatemala border and often coordinated with the Guatemalan Chorti. The Honduran Maya Chorti was part of a bigger force known as FUSINA, the *Fuerza Nacional de Seguridad Interinstitucional*, basically an alliance of the national police, military police, and armed forces to fight the wars with no end: the drug wars, the arms trafficking wars, the war on people crossing borders—including Hondurans leaving Honduras. Flores told us about an operation centered around "single mothers," designed to "support" an economic development program run by the "First Lady's Commission" with patrols by the military and police. The patrols, Flores explained, were "for mothers who were with their children, that's why we call it Salvemos un Angel, Let's Save an Angel, the angel was a child."

"So they don't migrate," Macoto added, to clarify that the Honduran forces were stopping Honduran children and mothers from leaving their own country.

This was also the future: confinement and enclosures, big brother, tourism and free-trade capitalism, and the empty airport seemed like a good place to contemplate that.

And the future was also that rumbling military truck on the two-lane highway. Macoto still had his flip-top phone pressed against the side of his head when dozens of bony brown and white cattle suddenly took over the road. The soldier driving the silver truck slammed on the brakes. Above us the cloud formations were swirling, some showing dark bellies filled with impending rain. Nobody in the truck said a word as the cows came right up to the vehicle—giving a good view of their large, tender eyes and floppy ears—and then walked around us like water flowing around a barrier. Cowboys rode up and tried to corral them. Macoto took this moment to look back to tell us about the "*ilegales.*"

Flores, the police commander, looked concerned at Macoto's report. For much of the meeting back at the "airport," Flores hadn't said much, and at times had had a slight scowl on his face. When he did start to talk, toward the end, his voice was friendly. It was also slightly effeminate, which would have been unusual among the hypermasculine patrols of the United States and much of the rest of the world. Now, as we sat together in the back of the truck, I asked him if they'd seen many sad cases. He said "yes." Just today there'd been one, a family—two parents and a child—from Ecuador. Later, the agents would return to the town of Entrada where the Maya Chorti were holding the group of eighteen migrants in custody. They would question them. "Especially," Flores told me, "that family." Since there were children involved, they might be traffickers. Then, "they will be deported," added Macoto, who appeared to be already coordinating the possible expulsion of this group right before my eyes. His words sounded like those of U.S. Border Patrol agents I've been talking to for more than fifteen years. For a second, I forgot that I was in Honduras. I thought that I was on the U.S. "border." And I was.

"One day," writes Reece Jones in *Violent Borders*, "denying equal protection based on birthplace may well seem just as anachronistic and wrong as denying civil rights based on skin color, gender, or sexual orientation." By allowing free movement of people, opening borders would address global wealth inequality. So would global rules for working conditions, including a global minimum wage, global standards for working conditions, and global safety nets for the poor: "These basic regulations would prevent corporations from playing different countries against each other to get the lowest wages possible."

Jones also writes that to address climate change, "we must rethink the idea that states have the exclusive right to make environmental decisions in their territories."[3] This is the right to the world, a vision based on free mobility and equal access to resources.

As we drove, I looked out the window at the rolling hills and remembered traveling through this same region fifteen years earlier. I was on a rattletrap bus coming up from the Guatemalan border to the Honduran capital of Tegucigalpa, when the driver stopped to take a five-minute break. Getting off to stretch, I met a man standing outside the bus who told me that he had tried to go to the United States once. But he was unsuccessful. His story ended with a U.S. Border Patrol agent tackling him, pushing him into sharp cactus thorns that scraped and punctured his flesh.

Just as the bus driver called to us to get back on the idling bus, this man asked me, "Why am I not allowed to travel there, but you can travel here?"

This question has haunted me for fifteen years. As I could see in any airport, some people are allowed and encouraged to travel. Those of us who fill international airports and can enter so many countries without visas, are from the very places—the United States, the European Union—that are erecting massive global border regimes restricting the movement of others. The U.S. border was the truck where I sat, it was Macoto on the phone, it was the eighteen people from the Dominican Republic and Ecuador incarcerated by the Maya Chorti, including a family with a small child, who would probably be deported, probably traumatically, with no reporters to capture the banality and inhumanity of their plight.

Maybe that was why I felt a burden lift when Macoto and Flores dropped me off at Copán Ruinas. No place could have been more different from the barren airport with its biometric systems, surrounded by Honduran border unit soldiers with assault rifles, than this ancient site of the original Maya Chorti.

Instead of going directly to the ruins, I wandered off on an empty trail, past where lumps on the ground showed where the people of ancient Copán used to live. The sky darkened with clouds, and I kept going, passing under the immense ceiba trees. I felt the urge to take a picture with my phone, but the trees would never fit in one. No matter how many times I tried to capture them, the photo was inadequate. So I gave up. I looked at the branchless smooth trunks, which seemed to represent the present moment.

The roots below, sunk into the *inframundo*.

And the branches extending into a canopy touching the sky, the future.

It seemed to me, as it seemed to the ancient Maya, that the ceiba was the World Tree, the central axis, a place of immense history and power.

As I walked back, I heard thunderclaps in the distance. Now there was almost nobody there. Just the empty archeological site and a slow, steady breeze, slightly cool, that presaged the coming rain. This was the Mundo Maya that Central America's colonial borders had bisected and divided. Regardless of how one feels about archeological sites, the fact that their cities existed is proof that there have been, and are, other ways to live and love in the world.

It also shows that ideas of civilization flourish and decline, and that sometimes things that seem inevitable, indestructible, fade away.

That barren airport, guarded by the soldiers with assault rifles, was only one vision of the "future." And to my eye, that place was a ruin, too, an archeological ruin to be. The cool rain, falling into the emptiness of Copán, seemed to tell me that something new could be imagined.

Acknowledgements

I started writing this book before I even knew I was writing it. Perhaps the writing started in August of 2012 after a trip to Puerto Rico and the Dominican Republic when I saw that the U.S. Border Patrol could get as close as 30 miles from the Hispaniola Island and still be in U.S. territory. Or perhaps it was even before then, in early 2010 when I wrote a piece for NACLA at the encouragement of editor Fred Rosen about how the U.S. border arrived to the Haiti coast in the aftermath of the January earthquake. Whichever the case, this book has been in progress for many years, meaning I have many, many people to thank and I am going to inevitably forget somebody.

There are so many who breathed life into this project. I remember, for example, arriving to the Verso offices out-of-breath in late 2014. This was when I first verbally pitched this book project to editor Andrew Hsiao. Since that moment, Andy became the key person responsible for shepherding *Empire of Borders* into existence, and then bringing it to life. Andy, if it were not for you, this book would not exist. Thank you.

I typed the first written proposal on a tablet with a cheap barely-functioning keyboard extension in a hotel room in Chiapas, Mexico, a place that would faithfully show up in the pages of this book.

For a book about borders, and thus a systemic policy of inhospitality, the hospitality I received in the places I visited like Chiapas, Guatemala, Honduras, Puerto Rico, the Philippines, Palestine, Israel, Jordan, and Kenya is worth underscoring multiple times. In Chiapas, much gratitude to the offices of Voces Mesoamericanas in San Cristóbal de las Casas and Miguel Ángel Paz and Enrique Vidal, to the Casa del Migrante "Hogar de la Misericordia" in Arriaga and Carlos Bartolo Solis, and to the Centro de Derechos Humanos Fray Matias in

Tapachula and Diego Lorente, Salva La Cruz, and Gerardo Espinoza. Thanks to my longtime friend Miguel Pickard and his compelling analysis around U.S. policy issues. Alas, in general, I have a deep love for Mexico, a place where I not only lived for extensive periods, but also a place that galvanized my own transformations.

A constant companion for my research trips in Central America was journalist and photographer Jeff Abbott, whose deep knowledge of Guatemala illuminated the pages in this book, as did the meetings across the beautiful country with people in the Scalabrini shelters in Tecun Uman and Guatemala City, and activists in Sayaxche, Peten. Many thanks too to Gladys Tzul for helping to coordinate meetings, your valuable time and insight was appreciated.

One person who deserves a special shout out is my good friend and colleague the exceptional researcher Miriel Manning. Miri helped set up meetings and slog through the endless bureaucracies for trips to Guatemala, Kenya, and Washington D.C. It is clear that this book has been enlightened in special ways because of Miri's relentless curiosity and analytic brilliance. I met Miri through my work with Prescott College, an institution whose students and professors have long supported my work—especially Zoe Hammer and Paul Burkhardt. Both Zoe and Miri read the initial proposal drafts for this book, as did other students from the Prescott's Social Justice and Community Organizing Masters Program such as Allissa Stutte and Ashleigh Hass. Also Prescott College allowed me to stay at the Maasai Education, Research, and Conservation Institute in the southern Kenyan borderlands with Tanzania. Endless gratitude goes to Metamei Olol Dapash and Mary Poole who helped me understand borders in a new, insightful way, and to Austin Parsaloi and John Ole Tira for their stories, analysis, and guidance. Also thanks to Kate Cabot, Zoe Caras, and Savannah Gibson.

Melinda St. Louis of Public Citizen and Ben Beachy, the trade expert of the Sierra Club, both dear old friends, spent time explaining what was going on with trade agreements. Other dear, old friends like Anna Fink, Alberto Fernandez, Amy Morris, and Mark Shmueli helped out with a bed at night while on these research trips in the DC area.

Special thanks goes to Justin Campbell, who sat down with me for a series of interviews about his former life as a soldier working on borders around the world. He also proved to be a great travel companion, accompanying me for more than 1000 miles on a bus trip from Guatemala City to Tucson.

I owe much to writer and author, the persistent, prolific, and thorough Gabriel Schivone, who travelled with me to Israel, Palestine, and Jordan in September 2016, when we were funded by the generous Sparkplug Foundation. And heartfelt thanks to Mohyeddin Abdulaziz and Sarah Roberts of the Tucson-based Arizona Palestine Solidarity Alliance for their constant support and encouragement. And also gratitude to journalist Dan Cohen. Not only for his hospitality while we were in Ramallah, but also his courageous journalism over many years in Gaza, the West Bank, and Israel that only deepened my understanding of the situation.

Thanks to Sahar Vardi, Shahaf Weisbein and Hamushim, Who Profits, Jamal Juma and Stop the Wall, and to the Sabri Gharib family. Khaled Jarrar, your work is some of the most inspirational art I have ever come across. I hope that that shines through loud and clear in this book.

There are many people who I'd like to thank here, but have to keep their names quiet, for various reasons. These are people who come from every place I visited in this book, but this reality was particularly acute in Jordan. That said, I can't thank enough Sam McNeil and Samar Salma for helping me to get oriented and connecting me with people in Amman and the Syria-Jordan borderlands.

For Puerto Rico, thanks to Kelly Fay Rodriguez, José La Luz, Braulio Torres, Jose "Lole" Rodríguez Báez, Wilfredo Ramírez, and Natasha Lycia Ora Bannan. Much gratitude for all your help, connections, and hospitality on the beautiful *Isla de Encanto*. And I have to thank Stephanie Quintana for keeping Puerto Rico, and the Border Patrol's presence there, always at the forefront of my mind.

For the Philippines, Tita Agnes Apeles: thank you for the numerous ways you helped me during that trip in 2015, including connecting me with extended family. And journalist Alex Devoid for your hard work setting up interviews and accompanying me on that intense visit.

There are many people who read through the drafts of this book, even in the earliest stages. Writer and journalist John Washington, I thank you so much for your willingness to slog through my very first drafts and offer insightful feedback (and accountability). Marjorie King, thanks for being such a reliable reader and your excellent edits. Many thanks to Katie Sharar, Julia Lindberg, and Lauren Dasse for looking over drafts carefully, and responding with insight and feedback.

And many thanks to the great geographer Reece Jones for giving the manuscript a thorough reading. Your insight and feedback really made a difference, and your scholarship foundational to my work.

Audrea Lim, the manuscript would not be what it is without your ideas, feedback, and editing. Honestly, I don't think I could have asked for a more insightful editor, it was such a pleasure to work with you. And, really, many thanks to Verso Books and the many wonderful people who ushered this book into life including Duncan Ranslem, Ben Mabie, Emily Janakiram, Anne Rumberger, and Cian McCourt. Jane Halsey's keen eye and excellent line edits really gave the book its final flourish.

And here I will list the many people and organizations I owe gratitude for myriad reasons:

Randy Mayer, the Good Shepherd United Church of Christ Church, and the Green Valley Samaritans, Tucson Samaritans, Norma Price, Mary Goethals, and the late Kathryn Ferguson (among many others). The Earlham Border Studies program has placed so many exceptional interns with me: Nora Collins, Millicent Frankel, and Jesse Herrera, I appreciate so much all your hard work. And gratitude to Tom Engelhardt and Nick Turse from TomDispatch, not only because TomDispatch has been a longstanding home for my writing, but also because it is a venue where cutting edge analysis about the expanding national security state is always at hand.

NACLA has been somewhat of an institutional home for so long and published earlier versions of some of this research. I only can offer appreciation for a publication that has long supported my work, especially Laura Weiss.

So much gratitude to Guadalupe Castillo, Joseph Nevins, Alison

Mountz, Jenna Loyd, Greg Grandin, Nandita Sharma, Rebecca Galemba, Eduardo Garcia, Juanita Sundberg, Greg Ruggiero, Chris Carosi, Elaine Katzenberger, Sara Elizabeth Williams, Erik Morrison, Sanho Tree and Chuck Collins from the Institute for Policy Studies, Alexis Stroumbelis and Laura Jean Embry-Lowry of the Committee in Solidarity with the People of El Salvador, James Jordan and Nasim Chatha of the Alliance for Global Justice, the great Ankur Singh, Alexander Yanish, Maureen Meyer and Adam Isaacson of the Washington Office on Latin America, Emma Buckout, Danielle Burgi-Palomino, and Lisa Haugaard from the Latin America Working Group, Faith Mugo, Victor Nyamori, Larry Gatti and Keith Zabik of Tucson Community Acupuncture, Chrysta Faye, Michelle Marks, Dora Rodriguez, Laurie Melrood, Blake Gentry, The Park Center for Independent Media, Patricia Rodriguez, Jeff Cohen, Geoff Boyce, Sarah Launius, Jill Williams, Melissa Del Bosque, Brad Jones, Bill Remmel, Stephanie Elizondo-Griest, David Cates, Brother David Buer, Kat Rodriguez, Dan Abbott, Ben Ehrenreich , John "Lory" Ghertner, Tim Shenk, Isabel Garcia, Margo Cowan, John Fife, Timothy Dunn, Josiah Heyman, José Luis Benavides, James Loucky, Gabriela Galup, Tshilo Galup, Randy Serraglio, Louise Misztal, Aaron Bobrow-Strain, Molly Molloy, Zaira Emiliana Livier, Sam Husseini, In These Times, Antigone Books, Nancy Wonders, Robert Neustadt, People Helping People, Amy Juan, Josh Garcia, Nellie Jo David, David Garcia, Radio Dispatch: John Knefel and Molly Knefel, Unauthorized Disclosure: Kevin Gosztola and Rania Khalek, Sara Meza, César Cuauhtémoc Garcia Hernández, Élisabeth Vallet, Kenneth Madsen, Sharon Hostetler, Witness for Peace, BorderLinks, Voices from the Border in Patagonia, No More Deaths, SOA Watch, Humane Borders, Joel Smith, Riley Merline, the Transnational Institute, *Tucson Weekly*, Ernesto Portillo Jr., EDUCA, Flor y Canto, Sam Chambers, Sierra Club Borderlands, Dawn Paley, Luis Solano, Tom and Kemper Brightman, Reina (may you rest in peace, I miss you), the Florence Immigration and Refugee Rights Project, and the Kino Border Initiative.

One of my best readers over the years has been my Mom. But that isn't a surprise, she's the one who has instilled in me a love of books from an early age. Thank you Mom and Dad for everything. I love you dearly. As do I my brother Mark, who has taught me so much about life and transformation. He is my idol.

And thanks to Peggy and Dennis, Tom and Shannon, Wes, Kim, and little Miles! I have been so touched by your support over the years and so happy to call you all family.

On November 15, 2018, my beloved Sofia was born, right when I was about to delve into the final edit of this book. My dear one, I thank you for gracing me with your presence as I put in my final thoughts. And my beloved Memito, you've been at my side for many consultations while I was writing this book (thanks for your wisdom, though you are only three). Why I write to begin with is because of you two and your generation. You have breathed life and love into these pages more than you ever know, and I can only hope that the pages live up to it. And Lauren I will never forget watching you birth Sofia with an inspiring strength that I can only begin to imagine. I know this book covers many hard issues but moments like when Sofia emerged from the water, give me that surge of hope, and thus energy, to continue to walk towards and work for a new and better world. Lauren, for you I only have love and gratitude. Thank you for making my heart truly sing.

Notes

Introduction

1   Passport Index, "Global Passport Power Rank 2018," passportindex.org.

2   Jane Guskin and David L. Wilson, *The Politics of Immigration: Questions and Answers*, Monthly Review Press, 2017.

3   Christine Negroni, "How Much of the World's Population Has Flown in an Airplane?" *Air & Space Smithsonian*, January 6, 2016, airspacemag.com.

4   Aviva Chomsky, *Undocumented: How Immigration Became Illegal*, Beacon Press, 2014.

5   Todd Miller, *Storming the Wall: Climate Change, Migration, and Homeland Security*, City Lights Books, 2017.

6   World Food Programme, "Guatemala declares 'state of calamity,'" September 9, 2009, wfp.org.

7   U.S. Customs and Border Protection, "Border Patrol Tactical Unit (BORTAC), February 2014, cbp.gov.

8   Nick Jacobellis, "BORTAC: The US Border Sentinels," *Tactical-Life*, November 3, 2014, tactical-life.com.

9   "U.S., Iraq reinforcing porous borders, prevent crossings," *USA Today*, August 14, 2004, usatoday30.usatoday.com.

10 Edward P. Hunt, "The Politics of Empire: The United States and the Global Structure of Imperialism in the Early Twenty-First Century," College of William and Mary, Fall 2016, scholarworks.wm.edu.

11 Alan Bersin, "Lines and Flows: The Beginning and End of Borders," *Brooklyn Journal of International Law*, 37:2, 2012, brooklynworks.brooklaw.edu.

12 "What to Do? A Global Strategy," *The 9/11 Commission Report*, W.W. Norton, 2004.

13 Immigration and Naturalization Service Archive 1975–2002, Department of Justice, justice.gov.

14 National Immigration Forum, Omnibus Appropriations for Fiscal Year (FY) 2018: Department of Homeland Security (DHS), immigrationforum.org.

15 Christopher Woody, "Trump's Homeland Security pick is seen as the best man for the job, but they may not always get along," *Business Insider*, January 11, 2017, businessinsider.com.

16   Michael Flynn, "Dónde Está La Frontera?" *Bulletin of the Atomic Scientists*, 58:2, July/August 2002.

17   Nancy Wonders, "Transforming Borders from Below."

18   Nancy Hiemstra, "The U.S. and Ecuador: Is Intervention on the Table?", *NACLA*, January 27, 2013.

19   Seth Freed Wessler, "The Coast Guard's 'Floating Guantánamos,'" *The New York Times*, November 20, 2017.

20   "Eight people flee U.S. border patrol to seek asylum in Canada," Reuters, February 17, 2017, reuters.com.

21   "Woman who died trying to cross border was trying to get to daughter in Toronto," *The Star*, June 1, 2017, thestar.com.

22   *United States Homeland Security Laws and Regulations Handbook*, Vol. 1: *Terrorism and Homeland Security Laws*.

23   "CBP Attaches: Extending the Zone of Security," *Customs and Border Protection Today*, May 2004.

24   "Today's Realities in Homeland Security," The White House: President George W. Bush, 2007, georgewbush-whitehouse.archives.gov.

25   "Remarks by Secretary Michael Chertoff to the Johns Hopkins University Paul H. Nitze School of Advanced International Studies," May 3, 2007, hsdl.org.

1. Twenty-First Century Battlefields

1   Jeff Halper, *War Against the People*, Pluto Press, 2015.

2   "Exclusive Look: Hannity Tours the Texas Border With Gov. Perry," *Fox News Insider*, July 10, 2014, insider.foxnews.com.

3   Melissa del Bosque, "Over the Wall," *Texas Observer*, June 27, 2017, texasobserver.org.

4   "244 million international migrants living abroad worldwide, new UN statistics reveal," United Nations blog, January 2016, un.org.

5   "International Migration in Numbers," International Organization for Migration, egypt.iom.

6   "Record 65 million people displaced in 2016: UN," *Al Jazeera*, June 19, 2017, aljazeera.com.

7   Joseph Nevins, "The Right to the World," *Antipode*, 49:5, 2017, academia.edu, published online March 7, 2017.

8   The U.S. Department of Homeland Security, The 2014 Quadrennial Homeland Security Review, dhs.gov.

9   Baher Kamal, "Climate Migrants Might Reach One Billion by 2050," Inter Press Service, August 21, 2017, ipsnews.net.

10   Koko Warner et al., *In Search of Shelter: Mapping the Effects of Climate Change on Human Migration and Displacement*, CARE, CIESEN, UNHCR, United Nations University, May 2009, ciesin.columbia.edu.

11   Norwegian Refugee Council, "Disaster and climate change," nrc.no.

12   International Organization for Migration, *Fatal Journeys*, Vol. 2, June 14, 2016.

13   Julio Manuel L. Guzman, "Suman mas de 70 mil migrantes desaparecidos en Mexico: activistas," *El Universal*, November 25, 2016, eluniversal.com.

14   Marta Sanchez Soler, "El Holocausto Migrante," *Movimiento Migrante Meso-americano*, July 27, 2017, movimientomigrantemesoamericano.org.

15   Centro de Derechos Humanos Fray Matias, "Comunicado de Prensa," January 20, 2016, cdhfraymatias.org.

16   Raul Zibechi, "The Militarization of the World's Urban Peripheries," *Upside Down World*, February 13, 2008, upsidedownworld.org.

17   George S. Rigakos and Mark Neocleous, *Anti-Security*, Red Quill Books, 2011.

18   Ibid.

19   Stephen Graham, *Cities Under Siege: The New Military Urbanism*, Verso, 2011.

20   U.S. Embassy & Consulates in Mexico, "Embassy Statement," July 8, 2014, mx.usembassy.gov.

21   Todd Miller, "Mexico: The US Border Patrol's newest hire," *Al Jazeera America*, October 4, 2014, america.aljazeera.com.

2. The U.S. "Border Set" on the Guatemala-Honduras Divide

1   David Vine, "Where in the World Is the U.S. Military?" *Politico*, July/August 2015, politico.com.

2   Arundhati Roy, *The End of Imagination*, Haymarket Books, 2016.

3   Juan Gonzalez, *Harvest of Empire: A History of Latinos in America*, Penguin, 2011.

4   Anna Pha, "Out of their own mouths: 'Maintaining imperial order,'" *The Guardian*, June 25, 2003, cpa.org.

5   Harsha Walia, *Undoing Border Imperialism*, AK Press, 2013.

6   "US Instructors train Ukraine's special force unit 'Sokil,'" *Censor.Net*, October 15, 2015, en.censor.net.

7   "EXBS and Native American Trackers Train Polish Border Guard," June 2014, state.gov.

8   Kim Hjelmgaard, "From 7 to 77: There's been an explosion in building border walls since World War II," *USA Today*, May 24, 2018, usatoday.com.

9   "U.S. Customs and Border Protection Strategic Plan, Vision and Strategy 2020," cbp.gov.

10   The U.S. Department of State, "Congressional Budget Justification Department of State, Foreign Operations, and Related Programs 2019," state.gov.

11   Sherman Hinson, "On the front lines: International and Law Enforcement Affairs," U.S. Department of State, May 1997, 1997–2001, state.gov.

12   Ronald Vitiello, "The Unaccompanied Children Crisis: Does the Administration Have a Plan to Stop the Border Surge and Adequately Monitor the Children?" U.S. Senate Committee on the Judiciary, February 23, 2016, judiciary.senate.gov.

13 The U.S. Department of State, "Congressional Budget Justification Department of State, Foreign Operations, and Related Programs 2019."

14 Central America Regional Security Initiative, Bureau of International Narcotics and Law Enforcement Affairs, January 20, 2017.

15 Adam Isacson and Sarah Kinosian, "Which Central American Military and Police Units Get the Most U.S. Aid?" *WOLA*, April 15, 2016. wola.org.

16 Ibid.

17 Lesley Gill, "Soldiering the Empire," *NACLA Report on the Americas*, September 25, 2007.

18 "What is the School of Assassins?" SOA Watch Info, soaw.org.

19 Martin Andersen, "Craig Deare's 'ethical and moral flaws' make him unfit for NSC job. He should follow Flynn out the door," *Miami Herald*, February 15, 2017, miamiherald.com.

20 Julia Harte, "Flagship military university hired foreign officers linked to human rights abuses in Latin America," The Center for Public Integrity, March 11, 2015, publicintegrity.org.

21 Wonders, Nancy A., "Transforming Borders From Below," in Leanne Weber, ed., *Rethinking Border Control for a Globalising World: A Preferred Future*, Routledge, 2015, 190–198.

22 *Guatemala Memory of Silence: Report of the Commission for Historical Clarification, Conclusions and Recommendations*, CEH, aaas.org.

23 Greg Grandin and Elizabeth Oglesby, "Washington Trained Guatemala's Mass Murderers—and the Border Patrol Played a Role," *The Nation*, January 30, 2019, thenation.com.

24 Ibid.

25 *Guatemala Memory of Silence*.

26 Tracy A. Bailey, "Ranger graduates from Kaibil School," 75th Ranger Regiment Public Affairs, *USASOC News Service*, December 18, 2012, web.archive.org.

27 U.S. Army Staff Sgt. Osvaldo Equite, "Guatemalan Kaibiles, U.S. Special Forces Promote Security through Partnership," *Diálogo*, February 19, 2015, dialogo-americas.com.

28 "Guatemalan National Civil Police Fact Sheet, Guatemala Human Rights Commission," ghrc-usa.org.

3. "Selling a Security State"

1 Neve Gordon, "Working Paper III: The Political Economy of Israel's Homeland Security/Surveillance Industry," *The New Transparency*, sscqueens.org.

2 Armed, Autonomous Ford Trucks to Patrol Gaza's Besieged Border, IMEMC News & Agencies, September 8, 2016, imemc.org.

3 Israeli intelligence veterans' letter to Netanyahu and military chiefs—in full, *The Guardian*, September 12, 2014, theguardian.com.

4 "The Global Surveillance Industry," *Privacy International*, July 2016, privacy international.org.

5   Alex Kane, "How Israel Became a Hub for Surveillance Technology," *The Intercept*, October 17, 2016, theintercept.com.

6   Amir Rapaport, "The World is Switching from Defense to HLS," *Israel Defense*, June 11, 2014, israeldefense.co.il.

7   "Homeland Security and Emergency Management Market worth 742.06 Billion USD by 2023," MarketsandMarkets, May 2018, marketsandmarkets.com.

8   Eyal Weizman, *Hollow Land: Israel's Architecture of Occupation*, Verso Books, 2007.

9   Todd Miller, "War on the Border," *The New York Times*, August 17, 2013, nytimes.com.

10   "Beit Ijza Village Profile," Applied Research Institute—Jerusalem, 2012.

11   Neve Gordon, "Working Paper III."

12   "iHLS Security Accelerator is Looking for Next Generation Startups!" i-hls.com, April 3, 2018, i-hls.com.

13   Anna Ahronheim, "Israeli Military Exports Rise to $6.5 billion," *The Jerusalem Post*, March 30, 2017, jpost.com.

14   Yaniv Kubovich, "Israel's Arms Exports Spike, Hitting record $9 Billion," *Ha'aretz*, May 2, 2018, haaretz.com.

15   Ora Coren and Gili Cohen, "Record Europe Sales Push Israeli Defense Exports to $6.5 Billion in 2016," *Ha'aretz*, May 29, 2017, haaretz.com.

16   "Collaboration Agreement Signed Between iHLS and South Korea–GT Korea," i-hls.com, November 23, 2016, i-hls.com.

17   "Jimmy Carter: Israel's 'Apartheid' Policies Worse Than South Africa's," *Ha'aretz*, December 11, 2006.

18   Sarah Westwood, "Trump: Border Wall will provide '99.9 percent stoppage,'" *Washington Examiner*, January 26, 2017, washingtonexaminer.com.

19   Marcy Newman, "Will Palestinians hit Hillary's glass ceiling?" *The Electronic Intifada*, December 2, 2008, electronicintifada.net.

20   Michel Foucault, *Discipline & Punish: The Birth of the Prison*, Vintage Books 1995.

21   Weizman, *Hollow Land*.

22   Jeff Halper, *War Against the People: Israel, the Palestinians, and Global Pacification*, Pluto Press, 2015.

4. Securing Inequality on the U.S.-Mexico Border

1   Stephen Graham, *Cities Under Siege: The New Military Urbanism*, Verso Books, 2010.

2   Jeremy M. Sharp, "U.S. Foreign Aid to Israel," Congressional Research Service, April 10, 2018, fas.org.

3   Gabriel Schivone, "How Israel's War Industry Profits from Violent U.S. Immigration Reform," *The Electronic Intifada*, April 8, 2014, electronicintifada.net.

4   Elbit Systems of America Peregrine Video, The Cirlot Agency, YouTube, April 24, 2012.

5   Kobi Yeshayahou, "Elbit Systems revenue exceeds $1b in Q4," *Globes Israel's Business Arena*, March 20, 2018. globes.co.il.

6   Shawn Musgrave, "The US Spent $360 Million on Border Drones Thanks to This Flimsy Report," Motherboard, January 12, 2015, motherboard.vice.com.

7   Maricopa County Sheriff's Office, "NiceVision Case Study," nice.com.

8   "Golan Group teaches Krav Maga to federal agents," Homeland Security News Wire, May 3, 2007, homelandsecuritynewswire.com.

9   The Law Enforcement Exchange Program (LEEP), "Empowering Law Enforcement Protecting America," docplayer.net.

10 John Ferziger, "Israeli Company That Fenced in Gaza Angles to Help Build Trump's Mexico Wall," Bloomberg, January 29, 2017, bloomberg.com.

11 Callum Paton, "Trump Wall: Israeli Company to Make Prototype for His Mexico Border Wall," *Newsweek*, September 14, 2017, newsweek.com.

12 Jimmy Johnson, "A Palestine Mexico Border," *NACLA*, June 29, 2012, nacla.org.

13 David Habfinger, Isabel Kershner, and Declan Walsh, "Israel Kills Dozens at Gaza Border as U.S. Embassy Opens in Jerusalem," *The New York Times*, May 14, 2018, nytimes.com.

14 Chuck Collins, "Is inequality in America irreversible?", Polity Press, 2018.

15 Jason Hickel, "Global inequality may be worse than we think," *The Guardian*, April 8, 2016, theguardian.com.

16 Graham, *Cities Under Siege*.

17 Vera Pavlakovich-Kochi and Gary D. Thompson, "Bi-National Business Linkages Associated with Fresh Produce and Production-Sharing," The University of Arizona College of Agriculture & Life Sciences, June 2013, ebr.eller. arizona.edu.

18 "An Economy for the 99%," OXFAM, January 16, 2017, oxfamamerica.org.

5. Maps of Empires

1   James Anderson & Liam O'Dowd, "Borders, Border Regions and Territoriality: Contradictory Meanings, Changing Significance," *Regional Studies*, 33:7.

2   Reece Jones, *Violent Borders: Refugees and the Right to Move*, Verso, 2016.

3   Jones, *Violent Borders*.

4   James Torpey, *The Invention of the Passport: Surveillance, Citizenship and the State*, Cambridge University Press, 1999.

5   Branko Milanovic, "Income Inequality and Citizenship: Quantifying the Link," *VoxEU.org*, May 6, 2015, voxeu.org.

6   Anderson and O'Dowd, "Borders, Border Regions and Territoriality: Contradictory Meanings, Changing Significance."

7   Jones, *Violent Borders*.

8   Ian G. R. Shaw, *Predator Empire: Drone Warfare and Full Spectrum Dominance*, University of Minnesota Press, 2016.

9   Jones, *Violent Borders*.

10 Ibid.

6. The Caribbean Frontier

1 "U.S.-Caribbean Border: Open Road for Drug Traffickers and Terrorists," June 21, 2012. democrats-homeland.house.gov.

2 Rafael Bernal, "Poll: Nearly half in US unaware that Puerto Ricans are citizens," *The Hill*, September 26, 2017, thehill.com.

3 Jenna M. Loyd and Alison Mountz, *Boats, Borders, and Bases: Race, the Cold War, and the Rise of Migration Detention in the United States*, University of California Press, 2018.

4 Peter Schwartz and Doug Randall, "An Abrupt Climate Change Scenario and Its Implications for United States National Security," October 2003.

5 Juan Gonzalez, *Harvest of Empire: A History of Latinos in America*, Penguin, 2011.

6 Greg Grandin, *The End of the Myth: From the Frontier to the Border Wall in the Mind of America*, Metropolitan Books, 2019.

7 Ethan Nadelmann, *Cops Across Borders: The Internationalization of U.S. Law Enforcement*, Penn State University Press, 1993.

8 2014 interview with author.

9 Dee Brown, *Bury My Heart at Wounded Knee: An Indian History of the American West*, Bantam Books, 1971.

10 Michelle Garcia, "The Border and the American Imagination," *The Baffler*, July 2, 2018, thebaffler.com.

11 Tom Nichols, Twitter, July 4, 2018, twitter.com/RadioFreeTom.

12 Timothy Bancroft-Hinchey, "John Kerry, Secretary of State: 'Latin America is our back yard,'" April 23, 2013, pravdareport.com.

13 Howard Zinn and Rebecca Stefoff, "A Young People's History of the United States."

14 Gonzalez, *Harvest of Empire*.

15 Brooks Adams, *The New Empire*, MacMillan Co., 1902.

16 Loyd and Mountz, *Boats, Borders, and Bases*.

17 U.S. Customs and Border Protection, "Ramey Sector Aguadilla Puerto Rico," cbp.gov.

18 Alison Mountz and Nancy Hiemstra, "Spatial Strategies for Rebordering Human Migration at Sea," *A Companion to Border Studies*, Blackwell Publishing, 2012.

19 Loyd and Mountz, *Boats, Borders, and Bases*.

20 Adam Goodman, "The Human Costs of Outsourcing Deportation," *Humanity*, 8:3, Winter 2017.

21 "U.S.-Caribbean Border: Open Road for Drug Traffickers and Terrorists," June 21, 2012, democrats-homeland.house.gov.

22 Luis Barrios and David C. Brotherton, "Dominicans' dance with want," *Le Monde Diplomatique*, February 15, 2012, mondediplo.com.

23 "McCaul Hearing Exposes America's Unprotected 'Third' Border," June 21, 2012, mccaul.house.gov.

7. The Philippines and the Periphery of Empire

1   Reece Jones, *Violent Borders: Refugees and the Right to Move*, Verso, 2016.

2   Howard Zinn, *A People's History of the United States*, Harper & Row, 1980.

3   Henry Cabot Lodge, "The Business World vs. the Politicians," 1895, wps. ablongman.com.

4   Zinn, *A People's History of the United States*.

5   Ibid.

6   Ibid.

7   General James Rusling, "Interview with President William McKinley," *Christian Advocate*, January 22, 1903, ksassessments.org.

8   Senator Alfred J. Beveridge, "Our Philippine Policy," Congressional Record, Senate, January 9, 1900.

9   Zinn, *A People's History of the United States*.

10 Bryan Bender, "Chief of U.S. Pacific forces calls climate biggest worry," *The Boston Globe*, March 9, 2013, bostonglobe.com.

11 Vera Bergengruen, "Trump May Doubt Climate Change, Pentagon Sees It as 'Threat Multiplier,'" McClatchy DC Bureau, June 1, 2017, mcclatchydc.com.

12 "U.S. Ambassador Helps Open National Coast Watch Center to Enhance Philippine Maritime Domain Awareness," U.S. Embassy of the Philippines, April 30, 2015, ph.usembassy.gov.

13 "Border Security and Critical Infrastructure Protection," *Mission: A World of Innovation*, Raytheon, May 2016.

14 Walden Bello, "A 'Second Front' in the Philippines," *The Nation*, February 28, 2002.

15 Alfred W. McCoy, *Policing America's Empire: The United States, the Philippines, and the Rise of the Surveillance State*, Univ. of Wisconsin Press, 2009.

16 Alfred McCoy, *Policing the Imperial Periphery: The Philippine-American War and the Origins of U.S. Global Surveillance, Surveillance and Society*, 13:1, 2015.

17 Ibid.

18 Ibid.

19 Ibid.

20 Mark Rockwell, "CBP looks to consolidate data," *FCW*, May 16, 2017, fcw. com.

21 Matt Apuzzo and Michael S. Schmidt, "U.S. to Continue Racial, Ethnic Profiling in Border Policy," *The New York Times*, December 5, 2014, nytimes.com.

22 "Report by the Policy Planning Staff," PPS/23, U.S. Department of State, *General; The United Nations (in two parts) Part 2, vol. 1 of Foreign Relations of the United States*, 1948.

23 Edward P. Hunt, "The Politics Of Empire: The United States and the Global Structure Of Imperialism in the Early Twenty-First Century," Dissertations, Theses, and Masters Projects, paper 1477068418, 2016, doi.org.

24 George Kennan, "The Current Situation," Central Intelligence Agency Conference, October 14, 1949, George Kennan Papers, Public Policy Papers,

Department of Rare Books and Special Collections, Princeton University Library.

25   R.D. McKenzie, "The Concept of Dominance and World-Organization," *American Journal of Sociology*, 33:1, July 1927.

8. "We've Got Big Brothers and Sisters All Over the Place"

1   Ed Ou, "I'm a Journalist and I was Stopped From Covering Standing Rock," *Time*, December 5, 2016, time.com.

2   Susan Holliday, "Cleared for Landing," *Frontline*, 7:2, December 2015, cbp. gov.

3   Ibid.

4   Rob Salerno, "What non-Americans can do to protect their privacy at the border," *Xtra*, February 20, 2017, dailyxtra.com.

5   Cynthia McFadden, E.D. Cauchi, William M. Arkin, and Kevin Monahan, "American Citizens: U.S. Border Agents Can Search Your Cellphone," *NBC News*, March 13, 2017, nbcnews.com.

6   Alex Johnson, "Judge sharply questions warrantless electronic searches at U.S. border," *NBC News*, May 10, 2018, nbcnews.com.

7   Ibid.

8   Olivia Becker, "Donald Trump's 'extreme vetting' plan for immigration has a long history in the US," *VICE News*, August 16, 2016.

9   Dara Lind, "Donald Trump proposes 'total and complete shutdown of Muslims entering the United States,'" *Vox*, December 7, 2015, vox.com.

10   Donald J. Trump, @realDonaldTrump, Twitter, twitter.com.

11   Bryan Logan, "'Tears are running down the cheeks of the Statue of Liberty': Lawmakers unload on Trump's moves to limit refugee programs," *Business Insider*, January 27, 2017, businessinsider.com.

12   Ibid.

13   National Immigration Forum, "Omnibus Appropriations for Fiscal Year 2018: Department of Homeland Security," immigrationforum.org.

14   Gordon Rayner, David Chazan, Henry Samuel, and David Barret, "Paris attacks: Seven hours and 5,000 bullets—the full story of the Saint-Denis shootout," *The Telegraph*, November 18, 2015.

15   James Bamford, "Shady Companies with Ties to Israel Wiretap the U.S. for the NSA," *Wired*, April 3, 2012, wired.com.

16   "Verint Spending by Prime Award," USA Spending, usaspending.gov..

17   Verint Systems, Verint Reports Third Quarter Results," December 6, 2018, verint.com.

18   Bob Brewin, "State Department to provide Mexican Security agency with surveillance apparatus," *Nextgov*, April 30, 2012, nextgov.com.

19   "Our Company," Verint, verint.com.

20   Alan Bersin, "Lines and Flows: The Beginning and End of Borders," *Brooklyn Journal of International Law*, 37:2, 2012.

21   Department of Homeland Security, "Fact Sheet: U.S. Customs and Border Protection National Targeting Center," September 7, 2004.

22   Kurt Stout, "National Targeting Center to Consolidate," *Colliers International Government Solutions*, February 11, 2014, capitolmarkets.com.

23   CBP, "National Targeting Center," YouTube.

24   Wikileaks, EXBS Turkey Advisors Monthly Report-(November 2008), December 24, 2008, wikileaks.org.

25   Daniel Victor, "What are your rights if border agents want to search your phone?" *The New York Times*, February 14, 2017, nytimes.com.

26   Becker, "Donald Trump's 'extreme vetting' plan for immigration has a long history in the US."

27   Deloitte, "Deloitte ranked as the No. 1 global consulting organization for the 5th consecutive year," deloitte.com.

28   Deloitte, "DHS EAGLE II: Information technology program support services," deloitte.com.

29   Kevin Granville, "Facebook and Cambridge Analytica: What You Need to Know as Fallout Widens," *The New York Times*, March 19, 2018, nytimes.com.

30   Customs and Border Protection, "Preclearance Locations," cbp.gov.

31   Department of Homeland Security, "DHS Announces 11 New Airports Selected For Possible Preclearance Expansion Following Second Open Season," November 4, 2016, dhs.gov.

32   Department of Homeland Security, "Written testimony of CBP Acting Deputy Commissioner Kevin McAleenan for a House Committee on Foreign Affairs, Subcommittee on Terrorism, Non Proliferation, and Trade hearing titled "The Abu Dhabi Pre-Clearance Facility: Implications for U.S. Businesses and National Security," dhs.gov.

33   Camila Domonoske, "TSA's 'Quiet Skies' Program Tracks Observes Travelers In The Air," NPR, July 30, 2018, npr.org.

34   Adam Liptak and Michael D. Shear, "Trump's Travel Ban Is Upheld by Supreme Court," *The New York Times*, June 26, 2018, nytimes.com.

35   Tim Cushing, "Border Patrol Stops Journalist From Heading to Dakota Pipeline Protests, Searches All of His Electronic Devices," *techdirt*, December 1, 2016, techdirt.com.

36   Ed Ou, "I'm a Journalist and I was Stopped From Covering Standing Rock."

9. The Global Caste System

1   Paul Adepoju and Kieron Monks, "Africans wary of U.S. travel after series of border denials," CNN, April 19, 2017, cnn.com.

2   Lucky, "Etihad's Abu Dhabi Pre-Clearance is Still a Disaster," *One Mile At a Time*, September 7, 2014, onemileatatime.boardingarea.com.

3   "Automated Border Control Market: Opportunities, Sales Revenue, Emerging Trends, Competitive Landscape, Top Key Players Study by Forecast to 2025," Data Bridge Market Research, digitaljournal.com.

4   Aruba HappyFlow, arubahappyflow.com.

5   From the Border Security Expo, San Antonio, April 2017.

6   Cynthia McFadden, E.D. Cauchi, William M. Arkin, and Kevin Monahan, "American Citizens: U.S. Border Agents Can Search Your Cellphone," NBC News, March 13, 2017, nbc.com.

7   Alex Kane, "Even Muslim-American Citizens Have Been Caught in the Net of Trump's Travel Ban," *The Nation,* March 23, 2017, thenation.com.

8   Ibid.

9   "INA: Act 212- General Classes of Aliens Ineligible to Receive Visas and Ineligible for Admission; Waivers of Inadmissibility," uscis.gov.

10   "Can I visit the U.S. while pregnant and what are the risks involved?" cbp.gov.

11   Adepoju and Monks, "Africans wary of U.S. travel after series of border denials."

12   Ron Nixon, "Why It's Already Difficult to Gain Entry Into the U.S.," *The New York Times,* January 30, 2017, nytimes.com.

13   Jane Guskin and David L. Wilson, "The Politics of Immigration: Questions and Answers," Monthly Review Press, 2017.

14   U.S. Embassy & Consulate in Morocco, "Refusal Under Section 214 (b)," ma.usembassy.gov.

15   Ibid.

16   Alan Yuhas, "New visa rules could also cause problems for Americans visiting Europe," *The Guardian,* January 21, 2016, the guardian.com.

17   Michael Pezzullo, "Keynote address at the International Summit on Borders (Washington, DC)," Australian Government of Home Affairs, June 19, 2018. homeaffairs.gov.

18   Ginger Thompson, "Listen to Children Who've Just Been Separated From Their Parents at the Border," *ProPublica,* June 18, 2018, propublica.org.

19   Seth Freed Wessler, Shattered Families: The Perilous Intersection of Immigration Enforcement and the Child Welfare System, Applied Research Center, November 2011, asph.sc.edu.

20   Daniel Howden, "Looking Past Outrage and Violence to See the Border," *Refugees Deeply,* July 16, 2018, newsdeeply.com.

21   Douglas Massey, *Categorically Unequal: The American Stratification System,* The Russell Sage Foundation, 2007.

10. Armoring NAFTA

1   Liezel Hill, "Goldcorp 'weeks' from big milestone at Penasquito," *Mining Weekly,* July 30, 2010.

2   James Rodriguez, "Project of Mass Destruction: Goldcorp's Penasquito Mine in Mexico," August 30, 2010, upsidedownworld.org.

3   Alfredo Valadez Rodriguez, "Mineros de Zacatecas protestan por bajos salarios," May 22, 2010, jornada.com.mx.

4   "Movilizacion Social Doblega al Monstruo de Goldcorp," *Periodico Expresion Zacatecas*, October 7, 2016, periodicoexpresionzac.wordpress.com.

5   Allison Martell, Frank Jack Daniel, Noe Torres, "Exclusive: Goldcorp struggles with leak at Mexican mine," Reuters, August 24, 2016, reuters.com.

6   Rodriguez, "Mineros de Zacatecas protestan."

7   David Bacon, "Unlikely allies: Mexican miners and farmers unite over toxic spill," *Al Jazeera America*, April 15, 2015, america.aljazeera.com.

8   "Canadian Mining Company Dumps Toxic Waste into Mexican River," *Telesur*, June 20, 2015, telesurtv.net.

9   Secretaría de Economía, Dirección General de Desarrollo Minero, "Diagnóstico de Empresas Mineras con Capital Extranjero en la Industria Minero Metalúrgica del País," gob.mx.

10 Andrew Smolsky, "Privatizing Mexico," *Jacobin*, October 9, 2014, jacobinmag.com.

11 Bill Moyers, "Trading Democracy," PBS, February 1, 2002, billmoyers.com.

12 "Table of Foreign Investor-State Cases and Claims under NAFTA and Other U.S. 'Trade' Deals," *Public Citizen*, February 2018, citizen.org.

13 Ethan Lou, "TransCanada's $15 billion U.S. Keystone XL NAFTA suit suspended," Reuters, February 28, 2017, reuters.com.

14 Sierra Club, "Trump's NAFTA Deal Threatens Our Air, Water, and Climate," sierraclub.org.

15 Laura Carlsen, "Armoring NAFTA: The Battleground for Mexico's Future," NACLA, August 27, 2008, nacla.org.

16 Brianna Lee, "Mexico's Economy: Rising Poverty, Inequality Undermine Peña Nieto's Economic Agenda," International Business Times, September 3, 2015, ibttimes.com.

17 Arturo Ángel, "México invierte más de 2 billones de pesos en seguridad, pero los delitos se quedan sin sentencia," *Animal Politico*, February 26, 2015, animalpolitico.com.

18 Xanath Lastiri, "154 mil millones a seguridad en 2016, tres veces más que en 2006; ?y para qué?: analistas," Sin Embargo, September 28, 2015, sinembargo.mx.

19 Shaw, *Predator Empire*.

11. "A Return on Our Investments"

1   Congressional Research Service, "Mexico: Evolution of the Merida Initiative, 2007–2019," July 23, 2018.

2   Adam Goodman, "The Human Costs of Outsourcing Deportation," *Humanity*, 8:3, Winter 2017, 527–9.

3   Adam Isacson, Maureen Meyer, and Hannah Smith, *Mexico's Southern Border: Security, Central American Migration, and U.S. Policy*, WOLA, June 2017, wola.org.

4   Ibid.

5   "Statement of General Lori J. Robinson, United States Air Force Commander,

United States Northern Command and North American Defense Command," Senate Armed Services Committee, April 6, 2017, northcom.mil.

6   Clare Ribando Seelke and Kristin M. Finklea, "U.S.-Mexico Security Cooperation: The Mérida Initiative and Beyond," Congressional Research Service, July 22, 2011.

7   Clare Ribando Seelke and Kristin Finklea, "U.S.-Mexico Security Cooperation: The Mérida Initiative and Beyond," Congressional Research Service, June 29, 2017.

8   Thomas L. Friedman, "A Manifesto for the Fast World," *The New York Times*, March 28, 1999, nytimes.com.

9   "Global Partnerships for Global Security," cbp.gov, September 28, 2016, cbp.gov.

10   Ibid.

11   John Washington, "Global Capitalism's Bouncers," *Jacobin*, October 9, 2014, jacobinmag.com.

12   Alan Bersin, "Lines and Flows: The Beginning and End of Borders," *Brooklyn Journal of International Law*, Vol. 37.2, 2012.

13   Ben Beachy, "CAFTA and the Forced Migration Crisis," Eyes on Trade: A Public Citizen Blog on Globalization and Trade, September 26, 2014.

14   John B. Judis, "Trade Secrets," *The New Republic*, April 9, 2008, newrepublic. com.

15   Jeffrey S. Passel, D'Vera Cohn, and Ana Gonzalez-Barrera, "Population Decline of Unauthorized Immigrants Stalls, May Have Reversed," Pew Research Center: Hispanic Trends Project, September 23, 2013, pewhispanic.org.

16   Jose María Imaz, "NAFTA Damages Small Businesses," *El Barzón* (Mexico City), January 1997.

17   Rebecca Galemba, *Contraband Corridor: Making a Living at the Mexico-Guatemala Border*, Stanford University Press, December 2017.

18   Ibid.

19   Arnulfo Mora, "Amagan con desalojar a campesinos de Infiernillo," *Quadratin*, February 15, 2014, quadratin.com.mx.

12. The Unholstered Border

1   Stephan Faris, "Homelands: an orphan named Patience and an argument for open global migration," *Deca*, July 2014.

2   Ibid.

3   Ben White, "UN report: Israel has established an 'apartheid regime,'" Al Jazeera, March 17, 2017, aljazeera.com.

4   David Spener, *Clandestine Crossings: Migrants and Coyotes on the Texas-Mexico Border*, University of Cornell Press, 2009.

5   Check Point Monitoring Report, "People Helping People in the Border Zone," October 26, 2014, phparivaca.org.

6   Spener, *Clandestine Crossings*.

7   Faris, "Homelands."
8   *Citizens and borderwork in contemporary Europe*, Christopher Rumford, ed., Routledge, 2009.
9   Ruben Andersson, *Illegality, Inc.: Clandestine Migration and the Business of Bordering Europe*, University of California Press, 2014.
10 Stephanie Elizondo Griest, *All the Agents and Saints: Dispatches from the U.S. Borderlands*, Univ. of North Carolina Press, 2017.

13. The Right to the World on the U.S.-Syria Border

1   "Jordan: Vulnerable Refugees Forcibly Returned to Syria," Human Rights Watch, November 23, 2014, hrw.org.
2   Brian Kahn, "Syria's Drought Has Likely Been Its Worst in 900 Years," Climate Central, March 1, 2016, climatecentral.org.
3   Matt Oskam, "The Syrian Refugee Crisis and the Jordan Border Security ..." CECOM, September 23, 2013.
4   Raytheon, "Border Security and Critical Infrastructure Protection," May 2016.
5   GlobalSecurity.Org, "Jordan Border Security."
6   Reece Jones, *Violent Borders: Refugees and the Right to Move*, Verso, 2016.
7   Human Rights Watch, "Jordan: Vulnerable Refugees."
8   "Jordan: Syrian Refugees Being Summarily Deported," Human Rights Watch, October 2, 2017, hrw.org.
9   "Syria-Jordan border: 75,000 trapped in desert no man's land in dire conditions," Amnesty International, September 15, 2016, amnesty.org.
10 Natalie Thurtle, "People in the Berm are stuck between life and death," Medecins Sans Frontieres, August 11, 2016, msf.org.
11 Joseph Nevins, "The Right to the World," *Antipode*, 9:5, November 2017.
12 Ibid.
13 David Harvey, "The right to the city," *International Journal of Urban and Regional Research*, 27:4, December 2003.
14 Sara Elizabeth Williams, "'I Thought I Was Going to Die': Syrian Refugees on Giving Birth in the Desert," *Vice*, May 31, 2016, broadly.vice.com.
15 Paul Currion, "The Walls That Exist in Our Minds," *News Deeply*, June 27, 2016, newsdeeply.com.
16 Edward Hunt, "The Politics of Empire: The United States and the Global Structure of Imperialism in the Early Twenty-First Century," *Dissertations, Theses, and Masters Projects*, 2016.
17 Edward Hunt, "A Rare Glimpse into the Inner Workings of the American Empire in the Middle East," *Foreign Policy in Focus*, January 19, 2018, fpif.org.
18 "U.S., Iraq reinforcing porous borders, prevent crossings," *USA Today*, August 14, 2004, usatoday30.usatoday.com.
19 Jay Mayfield, "A Powerful Presence," *Frontline*, Vol. 5, no. 1.

20   "Jordan Border Operations Center," Defense Threat Reduction Agency, dtra.mil.

21   Khetam Malkawi, "Jordan receives eight Blackhawks from US," *The Jordan Times*, March 4, 2015, jordantimes.com.

22   Ibid.

23   "U.S. Security Cooperation With Jordan," Bureau of Political-Military Affairs, U.S. Department of State, March 23, 2018, state.gov.

24   "Jordan Border Security," GlobalSecurity.org, October 6, 2015, global security.org.

25   William Arkin, "The Great Wall of Jordan: How the US Wants to Keep the Islamic State Out," *Vice*, February 24, 2016, news.vice.com.

26   Carolina Miranda, "Palestinian artist Khaled Jarrar turns a piece of the U.S.-Mexico border wall into sculpture," *Los Angeles Times*, April 6, 2016, latimes.com.

14. "Shoring up the Frontiers of Fortress America"

1   "Storming Spain's Razor-Wire Fence: Europe or Die (Episode 1)," *Vice News*, January 26, 2015, youtube.com.

2   "Bonn: Participants at UN conference examine human mobility in an era of climate change," *UN News*, November 8, 2017, news.un.org.

3   Ashifa Kassam, "African migrants look down on white-clad golfers in viral photo," *The Guardian*, October 23, 2014, theguardian.com.

4   Obinna Anyadike, "Morocco: The Forgotten Frontline of the Migrant Crisis," *IRIN*, July 29, 2015, newirin.irinnews.org.

5   Mark Akkerman, "Expanding the Fortress: The policies, the profiteers and the people shaped by EU's border externalisation programmes," Transnational Institute, May 2018.

6   "EXBS: Morocco Seeks Enhanced Border Enforcement," Public Library of U.S. Diplomacy, July 18, 2007.

7   The Export Control and Related Border Security (EXBS) Program, The United States Department of State, state.gov.

8   "Abused and Expelled: Ill-Treatment of Sub-Saharan African Migrants in Morocco," Human Rights Watch, February 2014.

9   Noam Chomsky, "Noam Chomsky on the crises of immigration," Links international journals of socialist renewal, November 15, 2016, links.org.au.

10   Mengpin Ge, Johannes Friedrich, Thomas Damassa, "6 Graphs Explain the World's Top 10 Emitters," World Resources Institute, November 25, 2014, wri.org.

11   Michael Gerrard, "America is the worst polluter in the world. We should let climate change refugees resettle here," *The Washington Post*, June 25, 2015, washingtonpost.com.

12   Ge, et al., "6 Graphs."

13   "Seizing the Momentum: Displacement on the Global Climate Change

Agenda," Internal Displacement Monitoring Centre, November 2016, internal-displacement.org.

14   Global Internal Displacement Database, "2017 Internal Displacement Figures by Country," Internal Displacement Monitoring Centre, internal-displacement.org.

15   Baher Kamal, "Climate Migrants Might Reach One Billion by 2050," Inter Press Service, August 21, 2017, ipsnews.net.

16   Koko Warner et al., "In Search of Shelter: Mapping the Effects of Climate Change on Human Migration and Displacement," United Nations University Institute for Environment and Human Security, et al., CIESIN, UNHCR, CARE, May 2009, ciesin.columbia.edu.

17   Christian Parenti, *Tropic of Chaos: Climate Change and the New Geography of Violence*, Nation Books, 2012.

18   Nandita Sharma, Bridget Anderson, Cynthia Wright, "Why No Borders?" *Refuge*, 26:2, 2009.

19   Fiona Jeffries, *Nothing to Lose But Our Fear*, Zed Books, 2015.

20   Nevins, *Right to the World*.

21   Jenna M. Loyd, Matt Mitchelson, Andrew Burridge, *Beyond Walls and Cages: Prisons, Borders, and Global Crisis*, University of Georgia Press, 2012.

22   Harsha Walia, *Undoing Border Imperialism*, AK Press, 2013.

23   Nick Turse, *Tomorrow's Battlefield: U.S. Proxy Wars and Secret Ops in Africa*, Haymarket Books, 2015.

24   Mindy Anderson, "U.S. Army Africa training helps African Nations secure their own borders," Army.mil, February 3, 2014, army.mil.

25   "AFRICOM Participates in DC Panel on Climate Change and Security," Africom.mil, February 2016, africom.mil.

26   "Following Training in Texas, CBP Team Deploys to Advise, Train Iraqi Officials," CBP.gov, September 16, 2011, cbp.gov.

27   "Security Sector Assistance in Kenya, Part II: Land Border Security Training," Public Library of US Diplomacy, January 5, 2010, wikileaks.org.

28   "Cablegate: Kenya Police Overview, Part Two: U.S. Assistance," Scoop WikiLeaks, June 11, 2009.

29   "Ambassador's Letter to GOK on Expanding US Support to Kenya's Border Management Capacities," Public Library of US Diplomacy, WikiLeaks, December 15, 2009, wikileaks.org.

30   "Rural Border Patrol Unit," Administration Police, administrationpolice.go.ke.

31   Elisha Otieno, "Panic as border patrol unit mistaken for GSU," *Daily Nation*, August 23, 2011, nation.co.ke.

32   "What is the LAPPSET Corridor Program?" LAPPSET, lapsset.go.ke.

33   Margot Kiser, "Big Game: U.S. Soldier's Secret Hunt for Jihadists in a Kenyan Forest," *Daily Beast*, February 8, 2017, thedailybeast.com.

34   "American Military Bases in Africa," GlobalSecurity.org, globalsecurity.org.

35   Kiser, "Big Game."

36   "UN: Somali famine is over, but action still needed," *The Journal*, February 6, 2012, thejournal.ie.

37   Ibid.
38   Sharma, et al., "Why No Borders?"

15. Negotiating Borders on a Warming Planet

1   Mike Davis, *Planet of Slums*, Verso, 2006.
2   "U.S. Department of Homeland Security, Customs and Border Protection Donates Books to Kenya Wildlife Services Training Academy," U.S. Embassy in Kenya, January 1, 2014, ke.usembassy.gov.
3   Roy Scranton, *Learning to Die in the Anthropocene: Reflections on the End of a Civilization*, City Lights, 2015.
4   Eric Holthaus, "Earth's Most Famous Climate Scientist Issues Bombshell Sea Level Warning," *Slate*, July 20, 2015, slate.com.
5   Ibid.
6   David Abram, *Becoming Animal: An Earthly Cosmology*, Vintage, 2011.
7   Meitamei Olol-Dapash, *London is Burning: The Life of a Maasai Activist*. (This manuscript is a work in progress. I was offered a preview of it by the author.)

Conclusion. The Future: The Airport and the Ceiba in Copan

1   "Presidente de Honduras inaugura aerodromo en Copán," *La Prensa*, March 10, 2015, laprensa.hn.
2   "Annual Financials for 3M Co," MarketWatch, marketwatch.com.
3   Reece Jones, *Violent Borders*.

Index